Java™ 2 Database Programming For Dummies®

Extracting Data from a ResultSet

The DownRow() function creates a series of String objects and two long data type variables that are assigned values returned in the ResultSet. The getString() methods extract data from the column of the ResultSet that is referenced as a parameter to the getString() method. The number 1 refers to the first column of the ResultSet, the number 2 refers to the second column, and so on. The getLong() method extracts numeric values from a column of the ResultSet. Values assigned to String objects and long variables are concatenated, assigned to the printrow String object, and displayed onscreen.

```java
private void DownRow ( ResultSet
DisplayResults )
    throws SQLException

{

    String FirstName= new String();
    String LastName= new String();
    long Sales;
    long Profit;
    String printrow;

    FirstName = DisplayResults.
    getString ( 1 ) ;
    LastName = DisplayResults.
    getString ( 2 ) ;
    Sales = DisplayResults.
    getLong ( 7 ) ;
    Profit = DisplayResults.
    getLong ( 8 ) ;
    printrow = FirstName + " " +
            LastName + " " +
            Sales + " " +
            Profit;
    System.out.println(printrow);

}
```

Create Table

The following code segment creates the address table, which has a CustomerNumber column, CustomerStreet column, CustomerCity column, and CustomerZip column — all having 30 characters:

```java
try {
    String query = "Create Table
    address ( CustomerNumber
    CHAR(30), CustomerStreet
    CHAR(30), CustomerCity
    CHAR(30), CustomerZip
    CHAR(30))";
    DataRequest = Database.
    createStatement();
    DataRequest.executeQuery
    (query );
    DataRequest.close();
    Database.close();

}
```

Insert Rows into a Table

The following code segment inserts a new row into the customername table. The FirstName column receives the value Bob. The LastName column receives the value Jones. The CustomerNumber column receives the value 2, and the StartDate column receives the value 10/11/2001.

```java
try {
    String query = "INSERT INTO
    customername (FirstName,
    LastName,CustomerNumber,
    StartDate ) VALUES ( 'Bob',
    'Jones',2,'10/11/2001') ";
    DataRequest = Database.
    createStatement();
    DataRequest.executeQuery

}
```

For Dummies: Bestselling Book Series for Beginners

Java™ 2 Database Programming For Dummies®

Cheat Sheet

Updating a Table

The following code segment places the string
5 Main Street into the Street column of the
customers table, where the FirstName column
of the customers table has the value Bob.

```
try {
    String query = "UPDATE
    customers " +
        "SET Street = '5 Main
        Street' " +
        "WHERE FirstName =
        'Bob'";
    DataRequest = Database.
    createStatement();
    Results = DataRequest.
    executeQuery (query );
    DataRequest.close();
}
```

Create Index

The following code segment creates a unique
index called custnum. It uses values in the
CustomerNumber column of the customername
table as the key value for the index:

```
try {
    String query = "CREATE
    UNIQUE INDEX custnum " +
        "ON customername
        (CustomerNumber) ";
    DataRequest = Database.
    createStatement();
    DataRequest.executeQuery
    (query );
    DataRequest.close();
    Database.close();
}
```

Selecting Data from a Table

The following code segment selects values
from the FirstName column and the LastName
column of the customers table in rows where
the LastName has the value Jones:

```
try {
    String query = "SELECT
    FirstName, LastName " +
        "FROM customers " +
        "WHERE LastName =
        'Jones' ";
    DataRequest = Database.
    createStatement();
    Results = DataRequest.
    executeQuery (query);
    DisplayResults (Results);
    DataRequest.close();
}
```

Drop Table

The following code segment drops the address
table from the database:

```
try {
    String query = "Drop Table
    address ";
    DataRequest = Database.
    createStatement();
    DataRequest.executeQuery
    (query );
    DataRequest.close();
    Database.close();
}
```

Hungry Minds™

For Dummies: Bestselling Book Series for Beginners

Java™ 2 Database Programming

FOR

DUMMIES®

Java™ 2 Database Programming

FOR

DUMMIES®

by Jim Keogh

Hungry Minds™

Best-Selling Books • Digital Downloads • e-Books • Answer Networks • e-Newsletters • Branded Web Sites • e-Learning

New York, NY ◆ Cleveland, OH ◆ Indianapolis, IN

Java™ 2 Database Programming For Dummies®

Published by
Hungry Minds, Inc.
909 Third Avenue
New York, NY 10022
www.hungryminds.com
www.dummies.com

Library of Congress Control Number: 2001089324

ISBN: 0-7645-0881-4

Printed in the United States of America

10 9 8 7 6 5 4 3 2 1

1B/RY/QZ/QR/IN

Distributed in the United States by Hungry Minds, Inc.

Distributed by CDG Books Canada Inc. for Canada; by Transworld Publishers Limited in the United Kingdom; by IDG Norge Books for Norway; by IDG Sweden Books for Sweden; by IDG Books Australia Publishing Corporation Pty. Ltd. for Australia and New Zealand; by TransQuest Publishers Pte Ltd. for Singapore, Malaysia, Thailand, Indonesia, and Hong Kong; by Gotop Information Inc. for Taiwan; by ICG Muse, Inc. for Japan; by Intersoft for South Africa; by Eyrolles for France; by International Thomson Publishing for Germany, Austria and Switzerland; by Distribuidora Cuspide for Argentina; by LR International for Brazil; by Galileo Libros for Chile; by Ediciones ZETA S.C.R. Ltda. for Peru; by WS Computer Publishing Corporation, Inc., for the Philippines; by Contemporanea de Ediciones for Venezuela; by Express Computer Distributors for the Caribbean and West Indies; by Micronesia Media Distributor, Inc. for Micronesia; by Chips Computadoras S.A. de C.V. for Mexico; by Editorial Norma de Panama S.A. for Panama; by American Bookshops for Finland.

For general information on Hungry Minds' products and services please contact our Customer Care Department within the U.S. at 800-762-2974, outside the U.S. at 317-572-3993 or fax 317-572-4002.

For sales inquiries and reseller information, including discounts, premium and bulk quantity sales, and foreign-language translations, please contact our Customer Care Department at 800-434-3422, fax 317-572-4002, or write to Hungry Minds, Inc., Attn: Customer Care Department, 10475 Crosspoint Boulevard, Indianapolis, IN 46256.

For information on licensing foreign or domestic rights, please contact our Sub-Rights Customer Care Department at 212-884-5000.

For information on using Hungry Minds' products and services in the classroom or for ordering examination copies, please contact our Educational Sales Department at 800-434-2086 or fax 317-572-4005.

For press review copies, author interviews, or other publicity information, please contact our Public Relations Department at 317-572-3168 or fax 317-572-4168.

For authorization to photocopy items for corporate, personal, or educational use, please contact Copyright Clearance Center, 222 Rosewood Drive, Danvers, MA 01923, or fax 978-750-4470.

Hungry Minds™ is a trademark of Hungry Minds, Inc.

About the Author

Jim Keogh is on the faculty of Columbia University and is the former chair of the Electronic Commerce Track at Columbia University. He has developed systems for major Wall Street firms and is the author of more than 54 books on computers and computing programming, including the popular *Linux Programming For Dummies* and *UNIX Programming For Dummies*. He was one of the first to introduce PC programming internationally in his Programmer's Notebook column in *Popular Electronics* magazine, four years after Apple Computer was born in a garage. Keogh is also a former contributing editor to *Popular Electronics* magazine and associate editor for *Personal Computing* magazine.

Dedication

This book is dedicated to Anne, Sandra, and Joanne. Without their help this book wouldn't have been possible.

Publisher's Acknowledgments

We're proud of this book; please send us your comments through our Hungry Minds Online Registration Form located at www.dummies.com.

Some of the people who helped bring this book to market include the following:

Acquisitions, Editorial, and Media Development

Project Editor: Colleen Williams Esterline

Acquisitions Editor: Steven Hayes

Technical Editor: Brian Bernier

Editorial Manager: Constance Carlisle

Media Development Specialist: Carmen Krikorian

Media Development Coordinator: Marisa Pearman

Media Development Manager: Laura Carpenter

Media Development Supervisor: Richard Graves

Editorial Assistant: Jean Rogers

Production

Project Coordinator: Regina Snyder

Layout and Graphics: Amy Adrian, Barry Offringa, Jacque Schneider, Julie Trippetti, Brian Torwelle, Jeremey Unger, Erin Zeltner

Proofreaders: Linda Quigley, TECHBOOKS Production Services

Indexer: TECHBOOKS Production Services

General and Administrative

Hungry Minds, Inc.: John Kilcullen, CEO; Bill Barry, President and COO; John Ball, Executive VP, Operations & Administration; John Harris, Executive VP and CFO

Hungry Minds Technology Publishing Group: Richard Swadley, Senior Vice President and Publisher; Mary Bednarek, Vice President and Publisher, Networking; Walter R. Bruce III, Vice President and Publisher; Joseph Wikert, Vice President and Publisher, Web Development Group; Mary C. Corder, Editorial Director, Dummies Technology; Andy Cummings, Publishing Director, Dummies Technology; Barry Pruett, Publishing Director, Visual/Graphic Design

Hungry Minds Manufacturing: Ivor Parker, Vice President, Manufacturing

Hungry Minds Marketing: John Helmus, Assistant Vice President, Director of Marketing

Hungry Minds Production for Branded Press: Debbie Stailey, Production Director

Hungry Minds Sales: Michael Violano, Vice President, International Sales and Sub Rights

◆

The publisher would like to give special thanks to Patrick J. McGovern, without whom this book would not have been possible.

◆

Contents at a Glance

Cartoons at a Glance

By Rich Tennant

page 7

"Your database is beyond repair, but before I tell you our backup recommendation, let me ask you a question. How many index cards do you think will fit on the walls of your computer room?"

page 145

"Sometimes I feel behind the times. I asked my 11 year old to build a database for my business, and he said he would, only after he finishes the one he's building for his baseball card collection."

page 273

"I STARTED DESIGNING DATABASE SOFTWARE SYSTEMS AFTER SEEING HOW EASY IT WAS TO DESIGN OFFICE FURNITURE."

page 107

"Look, I've searched the database for 'reanimated babe cadavers' three times and nothing came up."

page 333

Cartoon Information:
Fax: 978-546-7747
E-Mail: richtennant@the5thwave.com
World Wide Web: www.the5thwave.com

Table of Contents

Introduction

*W*elcome to the world of Java database programming. Just the thought of programming a computer to access data is enough to make most people give up immediately; it sounds too complicated. Clear your mind of that myth — it ain't that difficult!

Can you write a grocery list or directions to your house? Of course you can! And you can also write a Java database program (seriously!).

This book is not like the other computer books you may have attempted to read. I scrapped most of the confusing technical jargon. In its place, I have put some honest-to-goodness common-sense English words that tell you how to make a computer do what you want it to do.

The pages of this book are filled with simple explanations for things you may have believed required an engineering degree to understand. I provide plenty of examples for you to copy and try out on your computer.

Writing instructions to tell a computer to access data doesn't have to be difficult. After you find out how to perform a few simple tricks, Java database programming really is a great deal of fun.

About This Book

Pretend that this book is a private tutor who comes to your home to make sure that you understand how to write a database program in Java. Programming an application or applet to access a database isn't difficult, but sometimes it requires that you provide many small details to tell your computer how to do something.

Here are a few samples of the subjects I discuss in *Java 2 Database Programming For Dummies:*

- Planning a Java database program
- Developing a database, tables, and indexes
- Inserting, retrieving, updating, and deleting information in a database

You may think that understanding how to program a Java database application or an applet requires you to take technical courses in abstract mathematics at your local college. You're wrong. The purpose of this book is to walk you through all the steps you need to know in order to write a Java database program.

How to Use This Book

In this book, you read the procedures for designing and creating a database, and then you can begin to write the Java code that tells the computer how to access the database to store or retrieve data.

All the code in this book is set in monospace type, like this:

```
Type VariableName
```

You should type, character for character, anything that appears this way. I'll tell you when you need to make substitutions, such as using a real variable name in place of VariableName. Java does care whether you use uppercase, lowercase, or a mixture of uppercase and lowercase letters, so look closely at any code that you see.

Because of the length of the margins in this book, some long lines of code may wrap to the next line. On your computer, however, these wrapped lines display as a single line of code; be sure not to insert a hard return when you see one of them onscreen.

You'll find tests sprinkled throughout this book. Don't get too concerned — just use them to test your knowledge (no grades are given). You'll know immediately how you're doing because only one answer is correct; the other answers are outrageously wrong.

Foolish Assumptions

Here are some things you should be sure to know how to do before you read this book:

✔ Program a basic Java application and an applet

✔ Compile a Java application or an applet source file into a working program

✔ Read

But seriously, remember that this is a Java programming book. You probably already know what a bug is, what a command line is, and so on. I don't think you are someone who has never even touched a computer. I bet you may have read *Java For Dummies* or maybe even *JavaScript For Dummies* (both from Hungry Minds, Inc.). You may even be a programmer who wants to learn Java database programming.

However, even if you have no previous knowledge, you should still be able to follow along. You don't have to know how a computer works, and you don't have to have a high SAT score. A little common sense is the only requirement to understand what's in this book.

Of course, you also need a computer that has the Java Development Kit — or a Java development environment. You'll also need access to database management software (DBMS), such as Microsoft Access, Oracle, or Sybase.

I wrote this book using the Java Development Kit downloaded from the Sun Microsystems Web site (www.sun.com) because it's free. I also use Microsoft Access as the DBMS for examples in this book since it came with the copy of Microsoft Office I purchased.

But even if you are using another DBMS, don't despair. Commands I use in the book will work with most database management software. I'll let you know when it doesn't and suggest how to work around the problem.

If you qualify and have the guts to continue, get ready for an interesting and fun adventure into the creation of Java database programs for your computer.

How This Book Is Organized

This book has five parts, and each part consists of several chapters. If you've had no Java database programming experience, a lot of the material in this book will make more sense to you if you read the chapters in order. But if you have a little previous knowledge and can figure some things out, feel free to just pick up this book and start anywhere.

Here's a breakdown of the parts and what you can read about in them:

Part I: Getting Down to Database Basics

Part I is a brief introduction to all the major features of designing a professional database. This part of the book is the place to begin to help relieve your fears about building a database application or an applet from scratch.

Part II: Java Database Connection

To find out how to write a Java program that connects to a database, read Part II. It helps you understand how to use the Java programming language to give your computer instructions on how to open access to a database.

Part III: Database Interactions 101

Part III tells you how to instruct your computer to interact with the database so your Java program can do something special without asking for additional directions. Your instructions, in effect, let your computer become self-reliant.

Part IV: Picking and Choosing Data

Just the thought of browsing a large database is enough to make any sane person run far, far away. Part IV shows you how to request just the information you need to get your job done by writing a query into your Java program.

Part V: The Part of Tens

Part V contains several chapters of miscellaneous information that you may find useful and interesting, including tips about Java you can use with your programs.

Icons Used in This Book

This icon denotes technical details that are informative (and sometimes interesting) but not necessary for programming. Skip these paragraphs if you want.

The Tip icon flags useful or helpful information that makes programming even less complicated.

The Remember icon indicates important information — don't pass up these gentle reminders.

This icon alerts you to something you shouldn't do. Proceed cautiously when you encounter this icon.

The On the Web icon tells you that you'll find more information on our Web site at www.dummies.com/extras/Java2DataProg. These include downloadable code and a few bonus chapters thrown in for good measure.

Where to Go from Here

Now it's time to launch your exploration into the world of Java database programming. Grab a comfortable chair, sit back, and get ready to have some fun. Begin with Part I, "Getting Down to Database Basics," if you're new to databases. You'll find all the information you need to design your own database to work with Java. Jump over to Part II, "Java Database Connection," and begin Java database programming if you don't need to brush up on database basics.

Part I
Getting Down to Database Basics

The 5th Wave   **By Rich Tennant**

PROGENITORS TO THE JAVA PROGRAMMING LANGUAGE

Lava | Developed in Hawaii, objects would suddenly erupt into a hot flowing stream of information.

Guava | Objects "grew" on computer's tree structure which users could convert to a data jam to be spread across the Web.

Jabba "The Hut" | Named after the developer, objects tended to get lost in cyber-space.

Fava | Objects were referred to as "beans", but would repeat themselves when over used.

In this part . . .

You'll learn how to design a database with your specific needs in mind. By planning your database before hammering out the code to make your database dreams come true, you'll save yourself — and your co-workers — a lot of headaches. This part reveals the basics of database design. Tables, indexes, primary and secondary keys — yep, they're all in here.

Chapter 1

Everything Is Relative in a Relational Database

In This Chapter

▶ Understanding how information is stored and how you can retrieve it

▶ Introducing tables, rows, and columns

▶ Getting your data organized

▶ Understanding the advantages of a relational database

▶ Following a database model

*R*ather than using a notebook and pencil, you'd be better off storing product prices or other important information in an electronic filing cabinet called a *computerized database*. Whether you use a handheld, laptop, or desktop computer or a computer connected to the Internet, you're sure to find a computerized database available for filing information.

A computerized database is a better manager of information because it

✔ Stores information in an orderly way

✔ Relates some information to other information

✔ Protects data (called data integrity)

✔ Uses a smart way to find information quickly

Not to mention that a computerized database becomes a necessity when you need to manage a lot of information at the same time. However, you don't need to be a computer engineer to understand how a computerized database manages your information. Just read this chapter and you'll see the secrets of how it stores and organizes information.

Keeping Track of Things the Database Way

Whenever I want to include a person in my address book, I basically ask the person for his name, address, and telephone number. This is the way most of us identify the information we need to contact our friends and relatives. Yet this isn't exactly the way a computerized database would collect this same information.

A computerized database stores *data* rather than information. Data is the smallest piece of information that has meaning for us. If you were to ask someone for his name, he would respond with his first and last name. The name is information that can be further broken down into smaller parts — the person's first name and last name. We can reduce those parts into even smaller pieces, such as each letter of the person's first name, but a letter by itself would be meaningless to us. A first name, however, is meaningful. Therefore, a person's first name and last name each are the smallest pieces of information that hold meaning for us; we call this data.

The same holds true for an address, which is comprised of a street, city, state, postal code, and country. As you write down the address given to you by your friend into your address book, you are writing data without realizing it.

A computerized database stores information as data such as street, city, and the other components of an address rather than as simply "the address." Storing data that comprises an address is relatively simple. However, defining data — called data modeling — can get very complicated. I show you how to simplify data modeling in this book.

You and I think in terms of blocks of information, so we need to change the way we think — to think the same way a computerized database looks at information — to be able to use pieces of data. In this way, we can better understand and use computerized databases.

It's more than just a storage place

You probably have heard your work colleagues talk about "the database" whenever they need to produce a sales report or present other kinds of business information. The database they refer to is what I've been calling a computerized database. Actually, a computerized database is more than just a storage place for data. It's a set of sophisticated programs and files used to manage data.

The technical name for a computerized database is a *database management system (DBMS)*. A DBMS consists of a set of programs that organizes data and lets you

- ✔ Save data
- ✔ Retrieve data
- ✔ Update data
- ✔ Manipulate data
- ✔ Delete data

You can probably find a DBMS for practically every computer that exists. Microsoft Access is a DBMS commonly used on personal computers. Networked computers, including those used to run Web sites, use DBMSs such as Microsoft's SQL Server, Oracle, or Sybase. And DB2 is probably the most notable DBMS for mainframe computers.

Many DBMSs can be used on more than one kind of computer. For example, the Oracle DBMS is designed for networked computers, but it also has a version that works on personal computers.

A DBMS has a language of its own

A DBMS can answer any question you have regarding data stored in its database. Of course, the DBMS database must already store the data you're requesting; otherwise, it won't know what you are talking about. If, for example, you want to look up your friend Bob's telephone number, you'd better hope you entered it into the system or you won't be able to retrieve it.

You also must ask your question of the DBMS in the proper way. Don't yell your request at the DBMS because you'll find this is like yelling at a wall. The DBMS will simply ignore you. Even speaking in a low, polite voice and peppering your request with "pretty please" won't get the DBMS's attention.

The only way to have the DBMS answer your question is to use the only language it understands, *Structured Query Language (SQL)*. SQL is similar to English, Spanish, or any other language you speak in that there are sentences called *statements* that are formed using words called *keywords*.

Your job is to use the right words in the right order to construct statements that the DBMS understands. However, leaving out a word or misplacing a word in the statement is likely to baffle the DBMS — and, as a result, you probably won't get the data you requested.

This is similar to asking, "Street Aunt Get Mary's address." What? You and I probably can figure out what is being asked, but the DBMS isn't as smart as us. Therefore, you need to ask the question properly, such as "Get Aunt Mary's street address." Of course you need to use SQL rather than English to phrase your question. Part II covers SQL in detail.

Down and Dirty Inside a Database

You can think of a database as an electronic filing cabinet and you wouldn't be mistaken, but a database is more than that. Let's sneak a peek at the database and see how the DBMS organizes data that you place into this electronic filing cabinet.

A filing cabinet typically contains several drawers, each identified by a label on the front of the drawer. If you were to open a drawer, you would find that it's divided into compartments called file folders. Within each folder are papers containing information.

The DBMS is like a filing cabinet, and each drawer is like a database. This means that a DBMS can have many databases. File folders within the filing cabinet drawers are similar to tables within a database. A table is the place where you can find information, such as Bob's telephone number, stored. A database can have more than one table, just as a file drawer can have more than one folder.

All of the information stored within the tables of a database relate to each other in some way. For example, you may have one database that contains information about your friends. One table in that database might contain your friends' telephone numbers. Another table in that same database could store your friends' addresses, such as home addresses and business addresses.

Tables: Placing information in one spot

A *table* is where you store all the nitty-gritty pieces of information (in other words, data). This is where the computer would place your aunt's first name, last name, street, city, state, and Zip Code. You might find this concept a little difficult to visualize, but a table is very easy to understand if you think of it as a spreadsheet.

A *spreadsheet,* such as Microsoft Excel's spreadsheet, has columns across the top and rows going down the side. The place where columns and row intersect is called a cell. A table has similar features to a spreadsheet:

- Columns are called *columns* or *fields* and are used to store similar types of data, such as first names.
- Rows are called *records* and contain rows or records that are related to each other, such as your aunt's first name, last name, street, city, state, and Zip Code.
- A unique name identifies each column, which is very similar to the name you assign to a column of a spreadsheet. However, the name of each column must be unique to the table. This means you can't have two columns in the table called "First Name."

A table doesn't have a cell; at least database programmers don't call the intersection of a column and row a cell. I think of the intersection of a column and row as the place where data is stored, such as a person's first name.

When you use a DBMS to create a table, you might find that the DBMS uses different terminology to refer to fields and records. Likewise, SQL, which is the language used to request information from a DBMS, calls a field a column and a record a row. Regardless of what name is used, the concept is the same.

Rows and columns: Setting up a simple table

Seeing is believing, so let me show you what a table looks like. Figure 1-1 contains a table used to store addresses. My Address table is kind of skimpy because I have only two friends, but I can easily insert the name and address of any new friend I meet in a row at the end of the table.

Figure 1-1:
Columns go down and rows go across a table. You place data in the area where a column and row meet.

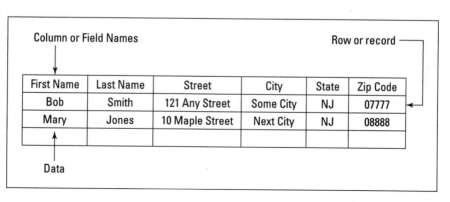

First Name	Last Name	Street	City	State	Zip Code
Bob	Smith	121 Any Street	Some City	NJ	07777
Mary	Jones	10 Maple Street	Next City	NJ	08888

As you can see, the table has one empty row. The number of rows you can have in a table is limited only by the space that you have available on the hard disk. Your database administrator, who is the technician in your company's Information Technology department responsible for administrating the database, may limit your space as well.

The first row of the table contains names that identify the contents in each column. The first column is where I place my friend's first name, so it only makes sense to call the column First Name. Likewise, the second column is where I place my friend's last name, and I call the second column Last Name. I'm sure you can figure out how I came up with the rest of the column names.

All but the first row contain data related to one of my friends. You'll notice that the second row has all the information about my friend Bob's address. The third row has my friend Mary's address. The fourth row is empty. This is where I'll place the address of my next new friend.

Keeping the Data Orderly

A table is a perfect way to organize data because rows and columns define where to store and find data. If I wanted to find a person's last name, I'd look down the Last Name column until I found the name that I was looking for. Then I could look across the row to find other information, such as where my friend lives.

Many times the data in one or more columns of a row uniquely identifies the row. A unique identifier helps you find the person you're looking for (see Chapter 4).

Organizing data into columns and rows to form a table makes data easy for us to read, but a table is a figment of the computer display. Tables don't exist on the hard disk as they appear onscreen. Data isn't stored as neatly when it's saved to a disk. A disk doesn't save the table with rows and columns; it contains only a series of data.

Data on a disk looks like a long string of characters with one row running smack into the end of another row in the order that the DBMS entered the data into the database.

This is even confusing for the DBMS because there isn't any indication where the columns and the first row begin and end. You have two options to make the columns and rows clear:

- ✔ **Insert delimiters:** A *delimiter* is a fancy word for marker, which is any character that is inserted into the data to indicate where columns and rows begin and end. The *comma-delimited format* — where commas separate columns and double quotations enclose alphanumeric characters — is frequently used for this purpose. These are any characters or numbers that aren't used in calculations. Numbers used in calculations aren't enclosed in double quotations. See the next section for more about comma-delimited format.

- ✔ **Fix the length of each column:** A *fixed-length column* requires that all columns contain the same number of characters. Spaces fill the column if the length of the data is less than the fixed length of the column. Data longer than the fixed length of the column is truncated, so characters that don't fit are chopped off — ouch!

The DBMS worries whether to use delimiters or fixed length to distinguish between columns and rows. A DBMS might use its own way to make this distinction. It calls this a *proprietary method,* and the manufacturer of the DBMS keeps it top secret.

Come 'ma delimited . . . Come on

You must enter your data in the right order so that it appears in the correct columns. Imagine your columns appearing in this order: First Name, Last Name, Street, City, and Zip Code. If the order of the delimited data was Last Name, First Name, Street, City, and Zip Code, the last name data would appear in the First Name column and vice versa — something you don't want to happen.

Don't be concerned of where you need to place commas in the data; the DBMS takes care of that for you.

Here is an example of a comma-delimited file:

```
"Bob","Smith","121 AnyStreet","Some
     City","NJ","07777",\n"Mary","Jones","10 Maple
     Street","Next City","NJ","08888"
```

I placed double quotations around each piece of data to tell the DBMS that these are alphanumeric data. Even the numbers in the street address and Zip Code are alphanumeric data because the numbers aren't used in calculations.

Test your newfound knowledge

1. What is a table?

a. A place where you eat lunch

b. A place where data is organized into columns and rows

c. Part of a data file

d. A new DBMS application

2. What are columns?

a. The horizontal place in a table where you place related data

b. The vertical place in a table where you place like data

c. A place in a file where you place a new line character

d. The place where you get the inside dope on what's going on in Washington

Answers: (1) b. (2) b.

You might be wondering how the DBMS knows when to start a new row. A slash and the letter *n* characters are called the new-line characters, and they tell the DBMS to begin a new line. When a DBMS sees a new-line character, it knows to go to the first column of the next row and continue placing data in columns using commas to identify when to move to the next column.

The fixed is in . . . it's fixed length

A column in a fixed-length file has a set number of characters that you can stuff into that column. Blank spaces are used to fill up the column if there aren't enough characters to fill out the column.

So, for example, if your column can hold 20 characters and the data in your column takes up only 3 of those characters, 17 blank spaces would be added to the end of the data. The next column would then begin after the 20 characters.

The DBMS knows the maximum number of characters that fit into each column because you tell it so when you create your table (see Chapter 2). And the DBMS knows when the first row ends and the second row begins by adding together the maximum number of characters that fit into all the columns of one row.

Building a Good Relationship with a Relational Database

Columns and rows, which neatly organize data on the computer screen, are really a long string of characters when the data is stored in a file on a hard disk.

Imagine how many rows and columns are in a table that holds the personnel records of your employer. If you work for a large company, you might have enough data in the personnel record's table to wrap around the earth several times!

Actually, the personnel records of your employer utilize more than one table because one table just can't store that much data. In fact, most databases have more than one table. The person who designs the database decides

- The number of tables to include in the database
- The number of columns in each table
- The way to relate a table to one or more other tables in the database

For example, a database that contains employee data may have a table that contains personal data about an employee, such as a home address and telephone number. Another table may be used to hold payroll data, and still another table might store employee insurance data.

Shop 101: Making your first table

Here's a common problem, and a question I'll pose to you. Suppose I want to modify the table that contains the addresses of my friends to include my friends' telephone numbers. How many columns should I insert into the Address table? I'll start the clock. You have two seconds to answer. GO!

Hmm . . . hmm. Time's up! If you say one column, I'm sorry to say you are wrong because most of my friends have more than one telephone number. And two isn't enough either. The correct answer is no columns should be added to the Address table.

Don't go scratching your head wondering if my answer was a mistake. The dilemma is that my friends can have any number of telephone numbers, including home phone numbers, work phone numbers, fax numbers, and mobile phone numbers.

No matter how many columns I insert into the Address table, Murphy's Law decrees that there will always be at least one of my friends who decides to have more telephone numbers than I have room for in my Address table. So why bother placing another column in the Address table when I know that I'll still run out of room?

The answer is to place all the telephone numbers in their own table and relate rows of my friends' telephone numbers to their data contained in another table. I called this new table the Telephone table.

I need to decide the number of columns to include in the Telephone table. I decided on four columns: two columns contain my friend's name, one column contains the telephone number, and the other column contains the type of telephone number (such as a home telephone number).

Let's join tables and sing

We can reduce the amount of data that we need to store by removing duplicate data using a technique called *normalization* (see Chapter 3 for more information). For example, my table duplicates my friends' names each time one of them sends me another telephone number. Using normalization, I can get rid of their duplicate names from the Telephone table.

Professional database designers relate one table to another table as a solution to the duplicate data problem. For example, all I need to do is to relate rows in the Telephone table with the appropriate row in the Address table, and then I'll be able to associate my friend's name with all her telephone numbers. A *relational database* is several databases that relate tables to each other.

Here's how the relationship is built. I need one column in both the Address table and the Telephone table that contain the same value. I could use the Last Name column, but someday I might meet Sam Jones and I wouldn't know which Jones is associated with the telephone numbers.

A better approach is to assign a unique number to each of my friends and create a column in both tables to store that number. Figure 1-2 shows you what I've done. The Num column contains numbers that I assigned to each of my friends. I placed my friend's number in the row of the Telephone table that contains my friend's telephone number.

Figure 1-2:
Each row in
the Address
table is
assigned a
unique
number. The
unique
number
matches
rows in the
Telephone
table.

Address Table

Num	First Name	Last Name	Street	City	State	Zip Code
1	Bob	Smith	121 Any Street	Some City	NJ	07777
2	Mary	Jones	10 Maple Street	Next City	NJ	08888

Telephone Table

Num	Telephone	Type
1	201-555-1234	Home
2	201-555-1321	Home
2	201-555-3542	Work
2	201-555-1165	Mobile
1	201-555-7765	Work
2	201-555-6354	Fax

Whenever I want to see my friend's telephone number, the DBMS and I take these steps:

1. **I send the DBMS my friend's first and last name.**

2. **The DBMS looks into the Address table for my friend's first and last name.**

3. **If there is more than one friend with the same name, the DBMS asks me to select the proper friend.**

4. **If there is one friend with the same name or if I selected the proper friend, the DBMS remembers the number assigned to my friend in the Address table.**

5. **The DBMS looks for all the rows in the Telephone table that match the number assigned to my friend in the Telephone table's Num field.**

6. **If the number assigned to my friend doesn't appear in the Telephone table, the DBMS tells me that my friend doesn't have a telephone number on file.**

7. **If the number assigned to my friend appears in the Telephone table, the DBMS displays all my friend's telephone numbers and the telephone number type (home phone number, for example).**

Notice that the Num column size in the Telephone table is much smaller than the two columns that contain my friends' names in the Address table. By relating tables using columns that contain the same values, I reduce the amount of data that the database needs to store.

A Database Model That You Won't Find on the Showroom Floor

When I was a kid, I liked to build model cars and airplanes. Today I build models of databases, commonly referred to as database models. A *database model* consists of tables that contain columns and rows of data.

A *relational database model* is the data model used in most computer applications, such as the applications used in your employer's company. A relational database model is so named because data is divided into two or more tables, and tables are linked together by a common column to form a relationship that's made in heaven.

Other kinds of database models exist, however. These include

✔ **Hierarchical database model:** A hierarchical database model arranges its files in a top-down structure. This is very similar to a family tree. This type of model doesn't use tables. The top file in the structure is called the root and the other files are called leaves. And just like my family tree, the top file is considered the parent and the lower files is the child. This model is one of the oldest database models and works well if information in the real world is organized in a hierarchical structure, which usually isn't the case most of the time. The hierarchical database model is rarely used anymore since the introduction of the relational database model.

✔ **Network database model:** Each file in a network database model (see Figure 1-3) can be associated with any number of files through the use of pointers. The network database model doesn't use tables. High-volume transaction-processing applications on mainframes, such as sales recording, use a network database model. Storage space and maintenance are two of the main drawbacks of using the network database model. More space is necessary to store data than with a relational database, and highly trained technicians have to maintain the data unlike a relational database model.

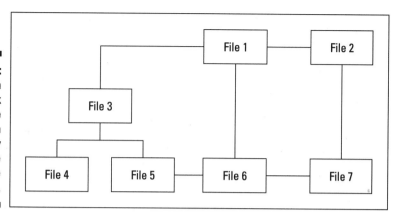

Figure 1-3:
A file in a
network
database
model can
relate to any
files in the
database
mode.

✔ **Object-oriented database model:** An object-oriented database model organizes information as attributes (see Chapter 2), which is similar to data members of a Java class. For more about Java in general, you might want to check out *Java For Dummies,* 3rd Edition, by Aaron Walsh (Hungry Minds, Inc.). This model is also how data is associated with real-life objects. For example, a person's first name and last name are data associated to the object we know as a person. Objects can inherit data from other objects. For example, just like a student is a person, therefore data associated with a person is also data associated with a student (see Figure 1-4). Object-oriented database models are new and not widely adopted when compared with the relational database model. However, keep an eye on this model because it can handle complex data — such as graphics, video, and sound — better than other database models.

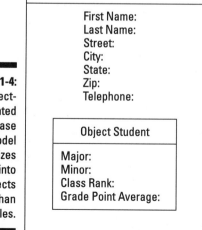

Figure 1-4:
The object-
oriented
database
model
organizes
data into
objects
rather than
tables.

Chapter 2

Designing a Database with an Artist's Eye

So you want to create a super database system to help track your hot clients or some other important information. However, before you can use Java to crunch the database for information, you need to store data in the database. Where do you get the data?

You can ask a friend for data, look in the attic, or even search the Web. Chances are pretty good that you won't find the data that you need for your database system in any of those locations. Instead of approaching your search for data in a haphazard manner, you can use the technique adopted by professional system designers:

   ✔ Look for entities in the system

   ✔ Identify attributes for each entity

   ✔ Translate attributes to data that you can use in your database

Simply use your common sense and follow along with the techniques shown in this chapter, and you'll be able to identify data for your database system in no time.

The System of Understanding Systems

When I began learning about computers I became confused whenever anyone spoke about a "system." My brother-in-law would call me, telling me that he found a great system I should buy. It was just what I needed to get started on my computing career. Of course, he was talking about computer hardware.

Then there was the geek at work who said she could build me a super-efficient system to automate my job. She was talking about building a computer application system that consists of many programs and a database (see Chapter 1).

It's no wonder anyone can be become disoriented when hearing the term *system* batted around in a computer book. So, let's set the record straight and avoid confusion. A system is an interrelated set of components that work together for some purpose.

The computer on your desk fits this definition because it contains electronic components that run computer programs. A computer application system, sometimes called a computer application, also fits the bill because the system also has components called programs and a database, which together enable you to do something with your computer hardware.

In this book I talk about two types of systems: a manual system, such as the system used by a bookkeeper to record business activities in ledger books, and a computerized system that uses programs and a database much like the system you use at work.

The labor-intensive manual system

Throughout this chapter I show you how to convert a manual system into a database system. A manual system consists of procedures that you perform manually, using data to conduct business.

Let's say that a customer wants to purchase goods from your business. Your sales representative helps the customer make a selection from your product line, and then she fills out an order form.

She gives the order form to the office staff for processing. There might be several manual steps to process the order. (The accounts receivable department records the order, for example, and then sends the customer an invoice. The warehouse staff reads the order form and picks the desired products from the warehouse shelves. And, finally, the shipping department packs the items and sends them to the customer.)

Your job is to streamline business operations by transforming the manual system into a computerized system that uses computer programs and hardware. You'll place all the data used in the manual system into a database and translate all the manual steps you'd use to process the order into Java statements.

In many situations you'll be upgrading an existing computerized system to a new and improved computerized system. The same procedures used for transforming a manual system to a computerized system are also used to upgrade an existing computerized system.

The magnificent database system

Manual systems have two components: data and procedures. *Data* is the smallest piece of information that is needed by the business, such as a customer's first name or last name (see Chapter 1 for more information about data). *Procedures* are the steps used to do something with the data. Processing data is a procedure, for example.

When converting the manual system to a computerized system, you must write procedures in a programming language to process data. I use Java in this book to write those procedures. A database permanently stores data for the computerized system (see Chapter 1). Any computerized system that stores data in a database is commonly called a *database application* or a *database system*.

The True Story of Entities

An entity may sound like a nerdy term for something inside your computer or a reference to an abstract concept that requires a Ph.D. to understand. An *entity* is a person or thing. In the context of your database application, it's a person or thing that is a part of your database application. This can be a customer, an invoice, or a purchase order. Practically anything can be an entity.

It's your job to identify all entities associated with your database system. Once you identify your entities, you can track down information that describes each entity, which you'll then translate into data.

Hunting for entities

All database applications begin with the hunt for entities, conducted with the same enthusiasm as seen in the flick *Hunt for Red October*. The hunt is more like a turkey shoot than combat since entities aren't dogging detection but are sitting out in the open.

You can guarantee a successful hunt for entities by following the time-tested strategy used by professional systems designers. These men and women come up with ideas for large computer systems like the ones used by major corporations. Here are the steps they follow to identify entities:

1. **Make a list of all the kinds of people and things that are used by the manual system that you are converting to a computerized system.**

   These may include order forms, customers, and invoices.

2. **Enter the names of these people and things into your word processor.**

   Using a word processor is easier than writing the names on paper — inserting new names and deleting those you don't think are entities is a snap! The word processor also checks your spelling.

3. **Review the list and check it twice, just like Santa, to make sure that you identified all possible entities.**

4. **Remove any entities that you don't want to use in the computerized system.**

Don't be concerned if you left out an entity. Those entities that you've overlooked will grab your attention as you continue to analyze the manual system for entities and procedures. You can always include new entities on the list as you uncover them.

Thinking logically

Entities don't have labels saying, "Hello. My name is Entity," so expect to use common sense when looking for entities in the manual system and when choosing entities for your computerized system. Ask yourself, "What people or things already exist in the manual system?"

Next, ask yourself, "What people or things do I need for the computerized system?" Make a list of them and compare this list to the list of entities for the manual system. Insert or remove items from the list of entities for the new computerized system as needed.

Here are common entities:

- Forms, such as an order form, regardless if the form is on paper or appears on the computer screen
- Customers or clients
- Employees, such as a sales representative
- Products, such as milk or an automobile

Making a list of entities from the manual system is always a good place to begin the hunt for entities because the computerized system probably uses most, if not all, of the same entities. These entities may be in a slightly different form, however.

For example, the manual system might have an order form printed on paper while the computerized system will have an order form displayed on the screen. You can call both entities "Order Form."

Attributes: The Best Part of Any Entity

Each entity has one or more attributes. An *attribute* is a piece of information that describes an entity. That's simple enough, right? A customer, for example, is an entity of a business, and an attribute for the Customer entity is the customer's name.

An entity typically has many attributes that help describe it (see Figure 2-1). Your job is to identify all the relevant attributes for the entities found in the manual and computerized systems. This isn't as difficult as you might first believe. All you need is to put your common sense to work for you.

Here are a few ways to identify attributes of an entity:

- Look carefully at each entity for the manual system.
- Enter information that is contained in the entity, such as a product number.
- Enter information that describes the entity, such as a customer's name.

Don't go crazy trying to identify entities and attributes for the computerized system. Simply use the entities and attributes of the manual system.

Looking for attributes in an instance

Identifying attributes of an entity is intuitive most of the time. For example, intuitively you know that a customer has a name, an address, a telephone number, and a customer identification number.

Some attributes aren't as intuitive as others to identify. For example, a shipping form may have a space on the form to permit the customer to write special shipping instructions. Unless you knew customers occasionally request special shipping instructions, you would probably overlook these instructions when compiling attributes for the Shipping Form entity.

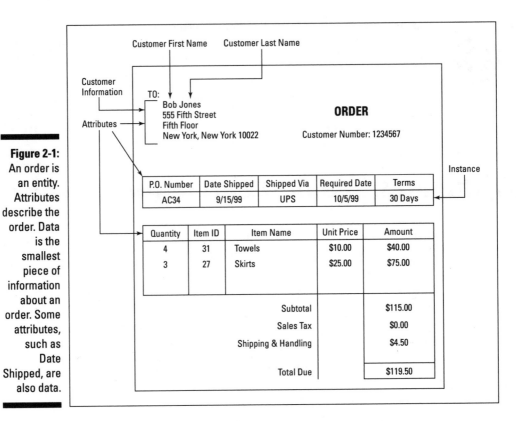

Figure 2-1:
An order is an entity. Attributes describe the order. Data is the smallest piece of information about an order. Some attributes, such as Date Shipped, are also data.

You can avoid missing an attribute by looking at an instance of the attributes for each entity. An *instance* is an entity that contains values for all the entity's attributes (see Figure 2-2).

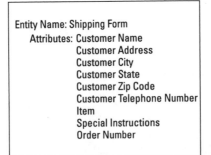

Figure 2-2:
An instance (right) is an entity (left) that already has some data assigned to it.

Entity Name: Shipping Form
    Attributes: Customer Name
             Customer Address
             Customer City
             Customer State
             Customer Zip Code
             Customer Telephone Number
             Item
             Special Instructions
             Order Number

Instance of Shipping Form: 1052

Instances of Attributes: Bob Smith
             1 City Center One
             Pittsburgh
             PA
             15212
             555-1212
             Product 5234
             Two-day delivery
             1052

Let's return to the shipping form in Figure 2-1 to see how looking at an instance helps you identify attributes. The shipping form for the manual system is a document printed on paper; it has text that describes information and blank spaces for writing in the information. The text that describes the information on the form is an attribute. Information entered into the blank space is an instance of that attribute.

Letting instances help you

Some entities have broad attributes, such as shipping instructions on the shipping form. A customer can write anything in the blank space alongside the Special Instructions attribute on the shipping form. Nerds call this *free-form text*.

Free-form text isn't a problem for people to understand, but it can become an issue for a computerized system. You probably want the computerized system to handle the special shipping instructions without human intervention, which is unlikely to occur if the special shipping instructions are in free-form text.

For example, the customer might write "Breakable. Handle with Care" as a special shipping instruction. This requires the shipping department to label the package accordingly. However, a shipping clerk must read the text written by the customer to know to label the package.

You probably want the shipping clerk to have minimal contact with the package in a computerized system. Maybe you want an industrial robot to package and label the product. Unfortunately, the robot cannot read the special instructions on the shipping form — at least not yet. This may change in the future.

The solution is to create new attributes based on common special shipping instructions requested by customers. You need to review all the instances of the entity's attribute and identify common requests. Those common requests become new attributes.

Here is a way to find new attributes by using instances:

1. **Obtain copies of entities where possible.**

   Collect real order forms, invoices, customer information forms, and the like.

2. **Write down common values of instances for each attribute.**

   You need to use your common sense for this. Only perform this task on attributes that use free-form text such as special instructions. Don't perform this task on attributes that have expected values, such as customer names, product identification numbers, telephone numbers, and so on.

Test your newfound knowledge

1. What are attributes?

a. Part of a manual system

b. Part of a computerized system

c. Something said at a retirement party

d. Part of an entity

2. What are entities?

a. People or things of a system

b. Computer hardware used to run a computerized system

c. A technique of reverse engineering

d. The main course at a wedding reception

Answers: (1) d. (2) a.

---

3. **Insert the common values into your list of attributes.**

For example, you might insert "Breakable" and "Handle with Care" as new attributes. "Yes" or "No" would become an instance of these attributes that enable the computerized system to easily identify the customer's request.

Some entities don't have new attributes hidden in free-form text attributes. So don't go crazy looking for them because they may not exist. One review of each attribute is sufficient to determine whether you can create new attributes from an existing attribute.

From Attributes to Data, The Decomposing Tale

Many attributes are too broad for the computerized system to use because they simply don't provide sufficient detail to properly describe an entity efficiently. And, of course, computerized systems always want to do things, such as look up data in a database, efficiently.

Suppose you want to use the computerized system to retrieve a customer's telephone number. First, you enter the customer's name into some kind of form on the computer screen that prompts you for the customer's name. You've probably done something like this many times at work.

The customer's name is the attribute, and the name you enter is an instance of the attribute. You enter "Bob Kirchoff." When the search begins, the computerized system searches for all the Bobs, and then within the Bobs, it looks for Kirchoff. This really isn't efficient because there is likely to be many more Bobs than Kirchoffs in the database. A better way is to search for all the Kirchoffs and then look for Bob.

The problem with our database is that the Customer Name attribute doesn't break out first and last names of the customer. Therefore, you need break the attribute into smaller pieces of information — data — such as the customer's first name and last name. This process of breaking down information into smaller pieces is called *decomposing an attribute.*

Getting a beat on decomposing

Decomposing attributes is the process of breaking down attributes into data. Data is more than just a *Star Trek* character. It's the smallest piece of information that a computerized system can use. A customer's first name, last name, and, in some cases, middle name, if the computerized system uses a customer middle name, make up a decomposed customer name.

A customer's name is an attribute of a customer. Customer first name, customer middle name, and customer last name are data in the Customer Name attribute. A computerized system stores and uses data, not attributes.

One of your jobs when designing a database system is to identify data that is associated with all the attributes of the system. Here are a few steps to follow that will help you identify data:

1. **Make a list of all the entities.**

2. **Make a list of all the attributes for each entity.**

3. **Look at each attribute and ask yourself if you can break the attribute into smaller pieces of information.**

4. **If so, list of the smaller pieces of information. They are data.**

5. **If not, list the name of the attribute. This is also data.**

   Some attributes cannot be broken down into smaller pieces. Therefore, the attribute itself is data used by the computerized system.

Decomposing in action

The best way to learn how to decompose an attribute is by working through an example. I'll use the Customer entity and Customer Address attribute as the example. The manual system contains information about each customer. It's obvious to me, and probably to you, that a customer is an entity of the manual system.

Tools of the trade

A word processor or paper and pencil and common sense are all you really need to analyze a manual system or computerized system to identify entities, attributes, and data. However, software is available that is specifically designed for analyzing manual systems and that simplify the process, which can become complicated in large computerized systems. This type of software is called a Computer-Aided Software Engineering (CASE) tool. Oracle Designer/2000, Rational Rose, and Together J are several of the better CASE tools on the market.

A CASE tool automates the process of taking apart a manual or computerized system to see how it works. You then use this information to build a new, computerized system. Here are some of the things a CASE tool can do for you:

- List entities

- List attributes

- List data

- Show relationships among entities, if any

- Show functionality of the manual system, such as the steps necessary to process an order

You still must enter information such as entities, attributes, and data into a CASE tool. However, the CASE tool has the know-how to crunch this information and produce various charts that help you understand how the manual system works.

Next, I review all the information about the Customer entity that is contained in the manual system. I notice the Customer entity has a

- Customer identification number
- Customer name
- Customer address
- Customer telephone number

These look like attributes because each is information used by the manual system to describe the Customer entity and also helps identify and separate the Customer entity from similar entities. I type them into a list in my word processor because I can always insert new attributes in case I miss one and I can delete information that I think might be better listed under a different entity.

Sometimes you may come across information associated with one entity but find it really belongs to a different entity. For example, I discovered a customer order number as information stored with customer information in the manual system.

At first I thought the customer order number is information associated with the Customer entity. But then I asked myself, "Does the customer order number describe the customer?" The answer is no. But the customer order number does describe an order. Therefore, the customer order number belongs as an attribute of the Order entity rather than the Customer entity.

Once I sort out the attributes, I turn my attention to decomposing each attribute. In this example, I decompose the Customer Address attribute. I ask myself, "Are there any smaller pieces of information contained in the Customer Address attribute?" Sure, there are! Here are the smaller pieces that I found:

- ✔ Street Address 1
- ✔ Street Address 2
- ✔ City
- ✔ State
- ✔ Country
- ✔ Country Code
- ✔ Zip Code
- ✔ Home Address
- ✔ Business Address

These data make up the Address attribute of the Customer entity. Home Address and Business Address data tell you whether the address data is a home or business address. Normally the values assigned to the data are Yes or No.

Hitting the decomposing barrier

You can't decompose every attribute into smaller pieces. A Customer Address attribute can be decomposed, but a customer identification number, such as a Social Security number, cannot be broken down into smaller pieces.

There isn't a Magic 8 ball that will tell you whether you can decompose an attribute. You need to use common sense to determine whether there are more pieces to an attribute than what you already have listed.

Don't worry if you miss decomposing all the attributes. You'll realize that you need to decompose attributes you missed when you get to the programming phase of the project.

You still must list the attribute name as data if you cannot decompose the attribute. Figure 2-3 lists the data for the Order Form entity.

| TO:
Bob Jones
555 Fifth Street
Fifth Floor
New York, New York 10022 | | **ORDER**

Customer Number: 1234567 | | | **Data for the Order Form Entity**

Customer First Name
Customer Last Name
Customer Street 1 Address
Customer Street 2 Address
Customer City
Customer State
Customer Zip Code
Customer Number
P.O. Number |

P.O. Number	Date Shipped	Shipped Via	Required Date	Terms
AC34	9/15/99	UPS	10/5/99	30 Days

Quantity	Item ID	Item Name	Unit Price	Amount
4	31	Towels	$10.00	$40.00
3	27	Skirts	$25.00	$75.00
		Subtotal		$115.00
		Sales Tax		$0.00
		Shipping & Handling		$4.50
		Total Due		$119.50

Data for the Order Form Entity

Customer First Name
Customer Last Name
Customer Street 1 Address
Customer Street 2 Address
Customer City
Customer State
Customer Zip Code
Customer Number
P.O. Number
Date Shipped
Shipped Via
Required Date
Terms
Quantity
Item ID
Item Name
Unit Price
Amount
Subtotal
Sales Tax
Shipping & Handling
Total Due

Figure 2-3:
List all the data from each entity. Here is the data list for the Order Form entity.

Data is the only piece of information that the computerized system you are creating can use. An attribute and data are the same thing when you cannot decompose the attribute, but they are different things when you can decompose the attribute.

A customer identification number, therefore, is an attribute and data. A customer address is an attribute but not data (see "Decomposing in action" for more about data associated with the customer address).

Describing Data to Your Friends and to the DBMS

You need to uniquely identify each data item so that you can use Java to ask the computerized system to retrieve that data later.

Suppose that you want to receive the address of the customer whose customer identification number is 555-55-5555. You need to tell the computerized system two things. You need to specify

- ✔ The name of the data you want to retrieve. (I show you how to do this in Chapter 13.)

✔ The value of the data that you want to match in the database. In this case, it's the customer identification number of 555-55-5555.

You'll say something like "Bring me the street address 1, street address 2, city, state, and Zip Code for the customer identification number that has the value 555-55-5555." Notice that I was specific about the data I want to see.

You need to review data that you identified for each attribute and uniquely describe the data so that the computerized system can use it. Java database programmers and others who design computerized systems review each attribute and describe data in three ways:

✔ **Name of the data:** For example, a customer's first name is data.

✔ **Type of data, called the data type:** The data type of a customer's first name is Text.

✔ **Size of the value that can be assigned to the data:** The size of a customer's first name can be 40 characters, although you can use any number of characters that you feel is sufficient to represent the longest first name of a customer.

Choosing a name

Each data has a unique name, and you have the privilege of specifying the name that the computerized system will use to identify the data. Don't rush out to name data after your family members. I'm sure that they'd appreciate the recognition, but that's not how professional system developers name data.

Professional system developers follow a general guideline to help them select names for data for a computerized system:

✔ **The name must be unique and cannot be used by any other data in the computerized system:** For example, you shouldn't use "firstname" as the name for the customer's first name data. You could have other entities, such as Employee, that also have a first name. Therefore, you'd probably want to call the generic "firstname" something like "customerfirstname." This name clearly identifies the customer's first name.

✔ **The name must describe the data:** You could use the letter X as the name for customer first name data, but you'll probably quickly forget that X represents the customer first name. Giving the data the name "customerfirstname" implies that the data contains first names of customers.

✔ **The name must be a single series of characters without any spaces:** The database management system (DBMS) may require that data names not contain spaces (see "Getting around the no-space problem").

Getting around the no-space problem

Don't go scratching your head to come up with data names that don't contain spaces. You can use the tricks of the trade to create names. Here's what to do:

1. Reduce the number of words needed to a minimum number of words.

   Don't say "the customer unique first name" for the customer first name data. Instead, use "customer first name" as the name for the data. This is short, yet still implies the nature of the data.

2. Remove spaces between words in the name.

   While "customer first name" is a good name for the data, it contains two spaces, which may not be permitted by the DBMS.

Remove the spaces between words, and you'll have a name like "customerfirst name."

3. Make the name of the data readable to people.

   A DBMS won't have any problem reading "customerfirstname." The same cannot be said for your coworkers. These three words run together, making them difficult to read without the spaces between the words. You have two choices to make the name more readable: You can capitalize the first letter of each word, such as "CustomerFirstName," or you can place an underscore between the words, such as "customer_first_name."

Assigning a data type

Besides providing a unique name for each data that you identified for use by the computerized system, you have to determine the type of data. Geeks call this the data's *data type*. You can simply think of this as another piece of information that you must provide the DBMS about each data.

Data type is a term that describes a technical concept people rarely consider when looking at data. However, you need to think about data types when you identify data for your computerized system because the DBMS running on your computerized system requires this information before it will manage your data. The data type tells the DBMS how to store the data in the database.

Each piece of data has one data type. Here are common data types to choose from:

✔ **Character, also referred to as alpha:** These are alphabetical characters and special characters, such as a hyphen, that you find on your computer keyboard. Numbers are excluded. The Character data type is perfect for the customer's first name because first names consist of all characters. However, the Character data type won't work for the customer's street address because a street address can be a mixture of characters and numbers.

✔ **Alphanumeric:** The Alphanumeric data type is similar to the Character data type in that characters of the alphabet and special characters on the keyboard can be used as values for fields. You can use numeric values, too. Therefore, a customer's street address can be an Alphanumeric data type. Numbers used in an alphanumeric type cannot be used for calculations.

✔ **Numeric:** A Numeric data type is used for data that will represent only numbers. Characters aren't permitted. Numbers used in a Numeric data type typically are used in calculations, such as the total dollar amount for an order.

✔ **Date:** A date is a combination of numbers and characters that have a special meaning. You tell the DBMS that data that is assigned a date has special meaning by making it a Date data type.

✔ **Logical, also referred to as Boolean:** Data that is a Logical data type can have one of two possible values. These are typically True or False, although sometimes the values can be Yes or No, depending on the DBMS. For example, the home or business data (see "Decomposing in action") should be defined as Logical data types because the value is either True or False. Either the address is a home address or it's not a home address. The same holds true for the business data.

Most DBMSs accept these data types, while other DBMSs will use other, more specialized data types. I don't cover the specialized data types in this book because of a lack of room. You can learn about specialized data types in the documentation provided by your DBMS.

Choosing the right data type for your data

The challenge, should you accept it, is to correctly assign data types to the data that you plan to use with your new computerized system. You can figure the correct data type to use without expert advice; all you need to do is follow the guidelines used by professional systems designers.

Here is a series of questions that you must ask yourself whenever you're deciding on data types:

1. **Will the value assigned to the data contain only characters?**

   If yes, the Character or Logical data types are good candidates.

2. **Will the value assigned to the data contain one of two values?**

   In other words, will it be choosing between values like True or False? If yes, a Logical data type is the best candidate.

3. **Will the value assigned to the data contain numbers not used for calculations?**

   If yes, an Alphanumeric type will do the job.

Test your newfound knowledge

1. What data type would you select for the customer identification number data?

a. Numeric

b. Alphanumeric

c. One of those special data types not mentioned in this chapter

d. Logical

2. What data type would you select for the ZIP Code data?

a. Numeric

b. Alphanumeric

c. One of those special data types not mentioned in this chapter

d. Logical

Answers: (1) b. (2) b.

4. **Will the value assigned to the data contain a mixture of numbers and characters?**

If yes, an Alphanumeric data type is your choice.

Introducing even more data types

Most DBMSs use the data types I mentioned earlier. However, some DBMSs also have other data types. If your system uses these data types, you can learn more about them by reading the documentation that came with your DBMS:

- **Currency:** This data type is used for data that is assigned currency values, such as the price of a product.

- **Integer:** This data type is used for data that is assigned whole numbers — that is, numbers that don't have a decimal value.

- **Float:** This data type is assigned to data with mixed values — numeric values with a decimal value.

Choosing the correct data size

Besides picking a name for the data and determining the data type of the data, you also need to decide the maximum size of the information that can be assigned to each data. The maximum number of characters that can be assigned to the data determines this data size.

Sometimes deciding on the size of data is easy. In fact, the DBMS probably makes the decision for you. The Date data type and the Logical data type, for example, have a fixed size — ten for the Date data type (the full century is used in the date) and one for the Logical data type. Numeric data types also don't require a size because the DBMS determines the size.

Alphanumeric and Character data types are another story, however. You're on your own to determine the correct size for these data types because the DBMS won't help you. You need to estimate the maximum number of characters that will be assigned to the data.

Selecting the proper size for data is a bit tricky. Pick too small of a size, and the computerized system won't be able to assign all the value to the data. Some of the value will be lost.

The best way to determine the size of data is to review the size of real-life data. Examine the size of customer last names in the manual system. Your job is to find the customer with the longest name. Count to see how many characters his or her name contains. This becomes the size that you assign to the data.

Putting the Pieces of Data Together

You probably have a good understanding about entities, attributes, data, data names, data types, and data size after reading this chapter. Now it's time to see how everything comes together to form the foundation for your new computerized system.

Your objective is to create a list of data and data descriptions (see "Describing Data to Your Friends and to the DBMS"). You then use the list of data to create the database for your new computerized system. I'll talk more about how to create the database in Chapter 3.

Here's what you need to do to create the list of data:

1. **Examine the manual system that you are computerizing for data used by the manual system.**

   You don't have to be creative to find data for your new computerized system when most, if not all, of the data you need is also used by the manual system.

2. **Identify and list entities of the manual system and of the new computerized system.**

   An entity is a person or thing that is used by the system (see "The True Story of Entities"). Customers, employees, order forms, products, and invoices are all examples of entities. The new computerized system uses most, if not all, of the entities of the manual system as entities.

3. **Identify and list attributes that are associated with each entity.**

An attribute is information used to describe an entity (see "Attributes: The Best Part of Any Entity"). Customer name, employee number, product identification number, and shipping address are all examples of attributes. I like to think of attributes as data in the rough, because you still need to do something to them before they become data.

4. **Decompose each attribute into data, and make a list of the data.**

Data are raw facts about an entity. Customer first name, customer middle name, and customer last name are examples of data decomposed from the Customer Name attribute (see "From Attributes To Data, The Decomposing Tale" for more about decomposing attributes).

5. **Describe each data.**

You must give each data item a unique name and data type, and specify a data size (see "Describing Data to Your Friends and to the DBMS"). This information enables the DBMS to find exactly what you want when you use Java to request data. I show you how to do this throughout the remainder of the book.

Dealing with Duplicate Data

Don't be surprised if the same data shows up in more than one entity, because sometimes multiple entities use the same information. For example, customer first name and customer last name are data associated with the Customer entity, the Order entity, and the Invoice entity to identify the customer who placed the order and who is to receive the invoice.

Customer first name and customer last name, along with any other repeated data, is duplicate data. *Duplicate data* must have the same data name, data type, and data size because the data is assigned exactly the same information.

Professionals don't design databases or computerized systems with duplicate data. That's a big no-no. Duplicate data

✔ Wastes valuable storage space in the database

✔ Increases the likelihood of errors because the same data is in more than one place

The DBMS must remember to update the data in more than one place whenever you change the value of the data. If you don't update one of the duplicate data, the database has incorrect information.

✔ Confuses you when you use Java to request data

Do you want the customer last name that is associated with the customer or the invoice? All you really want is the correct customer's last name without being concerned about where the information comes from.

You must remove duplicate data from the data list that you created for the new computerized system. I introduce the process of removing duplicated data, called normalization, in the next chapter.

Chapter 3

There's Something Normal About All Data

- -

In This Chapter
▶ Normalizing data

▶ Working with the first normal form

▶ Reorganizing data with the second normal form

▶ Fine-tuning data with the third normal form

▶ Using keys

▶ Maintaining integrity

- -

*Y*ou have a great idea to use a computer to organize data about your clients and the products that you sell in your business. You plan to enter data, such as your clients' name and their order information into the computer, and then let the computer crunch the data and spit out a report that tells you who your best customers are. You envision this as only one of many types of reports your computer could generate for you.

To get started with your grand plans, you begin by listing on a sheet of paper all the data that the computer needs to analyze your business (see Chapter 2). The list is probably longer than you originally anticipated because you need a lot of data to run your business.

Then the moment of truth arrives. You need to reorganize the list of data into something more manageable, something where customer data is in one place on the sheet and customer purchases are in another place. You also need a way to join customer data with customer purchases, so you can reconstruct a customer's order whenever you get a call from him.

What started out to be a straightforward task becomes complicated. Every day, professional database designers face the same kind of challenge — how to organize data efficiently. To do this, they do more than simply group related data together. They also

- ✔ Remove repeating data
- ✔ Uniquely identify each group of related data
- ✔ Make each group of related data independent of other groups of related data

The good news is that you don't need to call a professional database designer to help you organize your data. In this chapter, you'll learn the techniques to organize your data in the most efficient way possible, allowing your computer to help you manage your business better.

Simplifying Things with Normalization

Database designers must organize information so that their computer program can access data quickly and easily. They use *normalization* to reduce a long list of data into groups of data, and then they relate those groups to reconstruct the data. Normalization is a way to convert a complex organization of data into a more simple organization of data. That sounds simple enough, huh?

I like to think of normalization as the way my wife makes sense out of our weekly grocery list. We begin the week by posting a blank shopping list on the refrigerator door. As we finish the last container of milk or eat the last chocolate chip cookie (which, incidentally, usually goes hand in hand), we write the names of the items on the grocery list. As you can imagine, the grocery list is quite long by the end of the week.

My wife works smarter than I do when we go grocery shopping. Instinctively I grab the grocery list from the refrigerator and head for the supermarket. I go a bit crazy running up and down the aisles, trying to find all the items on the shopping list.

My wife, however, uses her own normalization technique. Before leaving for the supermarket, she rewrites the grocery list, organizing groceries into groups that coincide with their location in the supermarket. In a sense, my wife relates groups of groceries on the list to groups of groceries on the supermarket shelves.

Database designers follow a strict rule for reorganizing a long list of data into groups of data that can be used by a computer. The rule is called a *normal form,* and the process of applying the normal form to a list of data is called normalization.

The normalization process has many steps — too many, in fact, to discuss in this book. It's best to leave those finer points to professional database designers. However, database designers do use three normalization steps all the time to organize data into a database:

- **First normal form (1NF):** The first normal form requires you to remove repeating data from the list of data. By removing repeating data, you cut down the amount of data that you need to store in the computer.

- **Second normal form (2NF):** The second normal form requires you to remove data that is partially dependent on other data. Don't feel bad if I just confused you. I'll explain the second normal form in the section "Identifying Dependent Data with Second Normal Forms."

- **Third normal form (3NF):** The third normal form requires you to remove data that is transitive dependent on other data. Hang in there. I'll go into much more detail about the third normal form in the section "Removing Transitive Data with the Third Normal Form" later in this chapter.

Removing Repeated Data with the First Normal Form

The first normal form (1NF) focuses on removing repeating data. Let me show you what I mean. Let's assume that you have five orders from the same customer. Each order has the customer's name and address information, such as:

- Customer First Name
- Customer Last Name
- Customer Street 1 Address
- Customer Street 2 Address
- Customer City
- Customer State
- Customer Zip Code

You need to know who made the five purchases, and you also need to know where that person lives so you can send him the bill. However, you don't need to repeat the customer's name and address for each of the five orders. Instead, you can follow the first normal form and place the customer's name and address in a different group from the other data.

I've done this in Figure 3-1, which shows two groups of data. One group of data contains data that is necessary to identify an order. The other group contains data necessary to identify a customer. I call the first group the Order Information Data group and the other group Customer Information Data. Notice that my groups' names describe the type of data contained in the group.

You can call groups of data by any name as long as the name reminds you of the type of data in the group.

Providing the missing link

Once you extract the customer data from the order data, you need a way to link that data back since the order data no longer contains any reference to the customer who made the purchase. A *key* links the data between two groups of data (see "Letting the Key Open the Door to Your Data" later in this chapter).

A key is data within a group of data that uniquely identifies other data within the group. The key in the Customer Information Data group is the Customer Number data. The key in the Order Information Data group is the Order Number data. Since each customer has a unique Customer Number and each order has a unique Order Number, these numbers uniquely identify the customer and order, and therefore make perfect key data.

Figure 3-1:
I divide data associated with a customer's order into two groups.

Order Information Data	Customer Information Data
Order Number	Customer Number
Customer Number	Customer First Name
Date Shipped	Customer Last Name
Shipped Via	Customer Street 1 Address
Required Date	Customer Street 2 Address
Terms	Customer City
Quantity	Customer State
Item ID	Customer Zip Code
Item Name	
Unit Price	
Amount	
Subtotal	
Sales Tax	
Shipping & Handling	
Total Due	
Salesperson	
Region	

For example, let's say that I assigned Customer Number 123 to my best customer, Bob Smith. No customer has the same Customer Number as Bob because that would confuse me. In fact, each customer has his own unique Customer Number.

I use Bob Smith's Customer Number whenever I need to look up his address because I'm sure that I'll find the correct Bob Smith. So far I have only one customer with the name Bob Smith, but Bob and Smith are pretty popular names, so I might have another customer with the same name some day. When that day comes, I'll assign the new Bob Smith a Customer Number too, which will be different than my existing Bob Smith's Customer Number.

In this scenario, Bob's Customer Number of 123 is the key that helps me extract information about his name and address.

Sharing the key

We can also use the Customer Number data to identify the customer in the Order Information Data group who placed an order. Simply place the Customer Number data in both the Customer Information Data group and the Order Information Data group.

Whenever a customer places an order, I ask the customer for his Customer Number. The customer either has a Customer Number or he doesn't have a Customer Number.

If the customer has a Customer Number, I

1. **Look up the Customer Number in the Customer Information Data group.**
2. **Verify the customer's name and address with the customer to make sure the information in the Customer Information Data group is current.**
3. **Ask the customer for his order.**
4. **Assign the next Order Number to the order.**
5. **Place the Customer Number and the order information in the Order Information Data group.**

If the customer doesn't have a Customer Number, I

1. **Ask the customer for his name and address.**
2. **Assign the next Customer Number to the customer.**
3. **Place the Customer Number, the customer's name, and address in the Customer Information Data group.**

4. **Ask the customer for his order.**

5. **Assign the next Order Number to the order.**

6. **Place the Customer Number and the order information in the Order Information Data group.**

The Customer Number data in the Order Information Data group can have the same Customer Number for different orders because a customer is likely to place more than one order. However, there can be only one order for each Order Number because the Order Number data uniquely identifies orders in the Order Information Data group.

Updating, the easy way

From time to time you need to update your data. Updating data can become a nightmare if the data is repeated within a group of data because you must change each occurrence of the data. Miss updating in one spot, and you'll have both correct and incorrect data, but you won't know which one is which.

Let's say that we didn't apply the first normal form to the list of data that is necessary to record an order. This means that a customer who placed five orders has his name and address repeated five times, one for each order. We would need to change the customer address in five different places if the customer changes his residence.

However, we were smart and applied the first normal form, which separated the customer's name and address from the order information (refer to Figure 3-1). Any changes to the customer address are made only once, even if the customer placed five orders, because all the customer data is in one place in the Customer Information Data group.

Playing hide and seek: Normalization style

Sometimes identifying repeated data isn't so easy in a list of data because not all repeated data pops out at you. Take a closer look at the Order Information Data group and the Customer Information Data group in Figure 3-1. Can you find other data that is repeated?

Time's up! The Order Information Data group contains an Item ID, Item Name, and Unit Price for items purchased by the customer. Item ID, Item Name, and Unit Price probably will be repeated as more than one customer purchases the same item. Therefore, they must be placed in their own group, which I did in Figure 3-2.

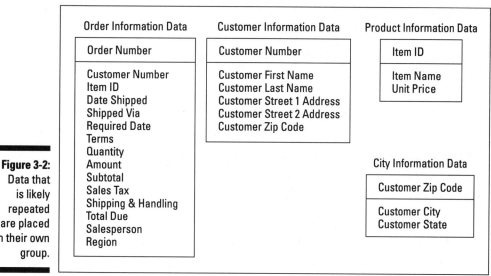

Figure 3-2:
Data that
is likely
repeated
are placed
in their own
group.

Let's take a closer look at Item Name and Unit Price:

✔ An item name might be the book *Java 2 Database Programming For Dummies.*

✔ The unit price is the price of one copy of the book.

Five customers can order *Java 2 Database Programming For Dummies.* This means that the Item Name *Java 2 Database Programming For Dummies* and the Unit Price for the book appear five times in the Order Information Data group.

Following the first normal form, I remove Item Name and Unit Price and place them in their own group, which I call Product Information Data group. I also assign a unique number to the item, and I call the number Item ID, which is the key to the Product Information Data group. The Item ID appears in the Product Information Data group and in the Order Information Data group.

When I look up an order in the Order Information Data group, I note the Item ID and then look up the Item ID in the Product Information Data group, so I can retrieve the Item Name and Unit Price.

I also need to modify the Customer Information Data group. The Customer Information Data group (refer to Figure 3-1) contains Customer City and Customer State. There could be more than one customer who lives in the same city and state, which means that the Customer City and Customer State data are repeated.

In Figure 3-2, I remove Customer City and Customer State and place them in a separate group called the City Information Data group. Customer Zip Code data is now the key for the City Information Data group. I use the Customer Zip Code data from the Customer Information Data group to find the customer's city and state in the City Information Data group. Customer Zip Code is a perfect key because the customer's Zip Code refers to only one city or a portion of the city where the customer resides.

Identifying Dependent Data with Second Normal Forms

By complying with the first normal form, I can remove all repeating data from the original list and place it in separate groups (refer to Figure 3-2). And, as a side benefit to organizing data into the first normal form, the data also complies with one requirement for the second normal form. That is, the data must be in the first normal form.

The second normal form focuses on functional dependencies of data in each group and requires that nonkey data (see "No independence") be functionally dependent on key data, as is shown in Figure 3-2. Data shown in Figure 3-2 complies with both the first normal form and with the second normal form because all data is either key data or dependent on key data.

A *functional dependency* means that one or more data exists only if the data is associated with another data. Sound confusing? If you read previous sections in this chapter you can set your mind at ease. I show you the concept of functional dependency, but I don't use the term functional dependency to avoid clouding the concept.

Let's see how functional dependency works by looking at the Customer Information Data group. A customer's name and address cannot be placed in the Customer Information Data group unless the customer has a Customer Number.

Professional database designers call this relationship a functional dependency because the customer data is dependent on a Customer Number.

No independence

Nonkey data is data that is functionally dependent on other data; key data is the other kind of data. The value of key data uniquely identifies nonkey data and must be unique. This means that each value of key data must be different from other key data within the same group.

Let's take a closer look at the Customer Information Data group in Figure 3-1 and identify key data and nonkey data.

The Customer Number is the key data because the Customer Number uniquely identifies a customer in the Customer Information Data group. That is, each customer has his or her own Customer Number.

The nonkey data are

- Customer First Name
- Customer Last Name
- Customer Street 1 Address
- Customer Street 2 Address
- Customer City
- Customer State
- Customer Zip Code

Each Customer Number must be unique because it's the key data to the Customer Information Data group. Customer First Name, Customer Last Name, and all the other nonkey data can have duplicate values because they are functionality dependent on the Customer Number. So, for example, you may have two customers with the same address, but because you have a Customer Number assigned to each, you can figure out which one will receive your shipment of pink flamingo lawn ornaments.

Functional dependency shorthand

Professional database designers use shorthand notation to indicate functional dependency among data. You'll find the shorthand technique useful whenever you review a long list of data, looking for key data and dependent data.

The shorthand technique is easier to learn than the shorthand techniques used to take down dictation because the shorthand used by professional database designers uses only one symbol.

Let's say that you want to write the functional dependency of Customer City and Customer Zip Code Data, which is shown in Figure 3-2. Here's what you need to do:

1. **Write the key data.**

   The key data is Customer Zip Code. It contains a unique value that identifies other related data such as a particular city.

Test your newfound knowledge

1. What is the first normal form?

a. The shape of the model on the cover of *Vogue*.

b. All data must be dependent on other data.

c. All repeating data must be removed.

d. Key data must be functionally dependent on nonkey data.

2. What is the second normal form?

a. All repeating data must be removed.

b. Functionally dependent data must be associated with key data, and data must conform to the first normal form.

c. The shape of the number two.

d. Functionally independent data must be associated with key data, and data must conform to the first normal form.

Answers: (1) c. (2) b.

---

2. **Draw a line ending in an arrow pointing to the right.**

   The right arrow signifies that data written to the right of the arrow are functionally dependent on key data written to the left of the arrow.

3. **Write all the functionally dependent data, separated by a comma.**

   Functionally dependent data are Customer City and Customer State. They have values that may or may not be unique, but the existence of the data depends on the key data.

 It's always better to identify key data and functionally dependent data using shorthand notation than immediately creating relationship diagrams. You'll find it easier to change the shorthand notation than to redraw the relationship diagram.

Removing Transitive Data with the Third Normal Form

The third normal form focuses on transitive dependency. *Transitive dependency* is a functional dependency between two or more nonkey attributes. I'll admit the transitive dependency is a bit elusive at first, but you'll find it easy to understand the concept by looking at an example.

An example spells it out

Notice in the Order Information Data group, shown in Figure 3-2, I have Salesperson data and Region data. The Salesperson data identifies the person who made the sales, and the Region data identifies the sales regions assigned to the salesperson.

Both the Salesperson data and the Region data have a transitive dependency because the Region data is functionally dependent on Salesperson data, and Salesperson data is functionally dependent on Order Number.

You must remove transitive dependencies to comply with the third normal form and make the database efficient. The Region data must be moved from the Order Information Data group to another group that will contain Salesperson data and Region data. The Salesperson data is key data in the new Salesperson Information Data group, and the Region data is nonkey data.

Once the long list of data complies with the second normal form and you remove the transitive data from the list, the list conforms to the third normal form.

Problems caused by transitive dependency

Transitive dependencies aren't obvious when you first look at the initial list of data, but they make themselves known at the worst possible time — when a DBMS stores data and you access the data.

Let's say that you didn't remove transitive dependent data from the Order Information Data group, as shown in Figure 3-2. And you want to

- **Assign a new salesperson to a region:** Because a salesperson is functionally dependent on an order, you cannot assign a new salesperson to a region until the salesperson finds a customer to place an order.

- **Remove an order from the Order Information group:** A salesperson doesn't exist without an order, so by deleting an order you could be inadvertently deleting a salesperson, especially if the salesperson has only one order.

- **Reassign a salesperson that is already assigned to a region:** Moving a salesperson to a different region poses a problem because you must change the value of the region on each order placed by the salesperson.

Compliance with the third normal form eliminates these problems because you can assign a new salesperson to a region without first having to place an order for a company. Likewise, you can remove a customer from Customer Information Data group and the salesperson information remains in the

Salesperson Information Data group. And only data in the Salesperson Information Data group needs to be changed to reassign a salesperson to a different region.

Letting the Key Open the Door to Your Data

The key to finding data quickly is to use a *key*. A key is similar to the key to the front door of your house. You could enter the house by breaking down the door, as they do in the movies, or you could use the less destructive method of unlocking the door with a key.

I like to think of the list of data as the door preventing me from finding the data that I'm looking for. Breaking down the door is like searching through all the data, which can be time consuming. However, I can unlock the data door by using key data and walk right in.

Key data is the unique value that identifies other data in a group of data. Key data can be

- ✔ Order Number
- ✔ Customer Number
- ✔ Item ID
- ✔ Customer Zip Code
- ✔ Salesperson

Here's how you can use a key. Instead of looking at Customer First Name, Customer Last Name, Customer Street 1 Address, Customer Street 2 Address, and Customer Zip Code, you can quickly find the customer by looking for a particular Customer Number.

Once the key data matches the information that you are looking for, you can look at all the data that is functionally dependent on the key data. This includes a particular customer name and address.

A key by any other name is still a key

The two keys used to find data with a list of data are the primary key and the foreign key. Both keys find data quickly within a list of data. However, a primary key and a foreign key do so in different ways.

✔ **Primary key:** You use a primary key to uniquely identify one or more other data. The other data have a functional dependency on the primary key. If the primary key is deleted, so are the functionally dependent data. A primary key can appear one time in a group.

✔ **Foreign key:** A foreign key is a primary key of another group that is used to draw a relationship between two groups of data. It can appear multiple times in a group because it is functionally dependent on the primary key of the data group.

You create a primary key and a foreign key when you place a list of data in the second normal form. The second normal form requires that data be functionally dependent on key data.

Turn the key and unlock data

Let's see how primary keys and foreign keys can unlock lists of data that comply with the third normal form. The value of a foreign key is a primary key of another data group. For example, Customer Number (see Figure 3-3) is the primary key of the Customer Information Data group and is also found in the Order Information Data group as a foreign key.

Suppose you want to find the customer's name on a particular order. First, you'd use the Order Number to search the Order Information Data group for the order. The Order Number is the primary key for the Order Information Data group.

Once you've located the order, you'll notice that you won't find any customer data except for the Customer Number. That's fine because if you found the customer name and address, the Order Information Data group won't conform to the first normal form — the Order Information Data group would have repeating data.

However, you can use the Customer Number to find the rest of the customer data in the Customer Information Data group because Customer Number is the primary key of that group.

You can use foreign keys to piece together all the data about an order. This relates groups of data together. Here's how to do it:

✔ **Customer Number:** The Customer Number in the Order Information Data group can retrieve a customer's name and address but not the customer's city and state.

✔ **Item ID:** The Item ID in the Order Information Data group can retrieve an item's name and unit price.

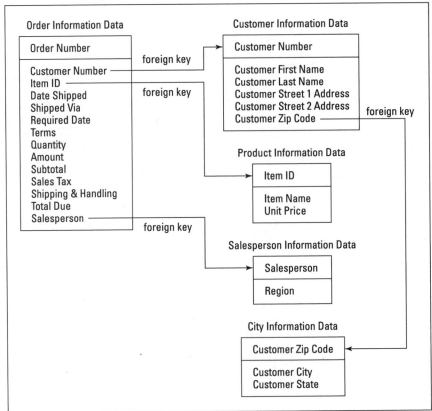

Figure 3-3:
Primary and
foreign keys
link together
groups of
related data.

  ✔ **Salesperson:** The Salesperson in the Order Information Data group can retrieve a salesperson's region.

  ✔ **Customer Zip Code:** The Customer Zip Code in the Customer Information Data group can retrieve a customer's city and state.

Integrity: The Honest Truth about Data

Once you normalize the original list of data into several groups, you must take special care to ensure the relationship between groups remain intact; otherwise, you won't be able to link together data from each group.

Referential integrity is the technique used to maintain references among groups. References are foreign keys within a group. A foreign key is a primary key of another group. For example, in Figure 3-3, Customer Number in the Order Information Data group is a foreign key and is also the primary key in the Customer Information Data group.

You maintain referential integrity by being careful whenever you delete data or modify the value of the primary key. Here's what you need to do:

✔ **Never delete data in a group that is referenced by another group unless you delete all references to the data in all the groups.**

This means that you cannot delete a customer from the Customer Information Data group if that customer's number is a foreign key of the Order Information Data group. If you do, you won't be able to find that customer's name and address when you look up the customer's order because you would have deleted him in the Customer Information Data group.

✔ **Modify all related foreign keys if you modify a primary key used as a foreign key.**

As a general rule, you rarely modify the value of a primary key because it links together two or more groups. However, you may need to modify the value of a primary key if an incorrect value is assigned to the key data. In this case, you need to correct the primary key and foreign keys that contain the same error. If you don't, one or more groups won't be able to link to the primary key.

Test your newfound knowledge

1. What is a foreign key?

a. Nonkey data for another group

b. A primary key of another group

c. The key that nonkey data is dependent on

d. A key that your grandmother brought over from the old country

2. What is referential integrity?

a. A technique used to maintain references among groups

b. A government background check

c. A technique used to remove repeated data from a list of data

d. A technique used to define a foreign key

Answers: (1) b. (2) a.

Chapter 4

Finding Data Quickly with an Index

• •

• •

A gents of the Federal Bureau of Investigation (FBI) seem to be able to locate anyone, anytime by making one telephone call to the FBI Command Center in Washington, D.C. The FBI Command Center uses indexes to find data in its many databases, so when an agent calls for data about a specific person, he can retrieve it quickly and continue his investigation.

An *index* is a shortcut to finding a piece of data among a large amount of data. Say, for example, Agent Williams needs an address for a Daniel Perkins. He would call the FBI Command Center, they would type in Daniel's state, city, last name, and then first name. (Isn't that the way you'd find an address of a long-lost friend on the Internet?) Up would pop Daniel's street address, and Agent Williams would be hot on his trail. This index includes the state, city, and first and last names.

But what would Agent Williams do if he was outside a house and he wanted to call the person inside? He doesn't know the guy's name, but he does know the street address, city, and state data. He could call up his buddies at the FBI Command Center and ask them to do another search using a different index. This time the index includes data for the state, city, and street address, and he could find out the person's first and last names.

Here Agent Williams used two different indexes and one database to find the data he was looking for. Programmers often create multiple indexes for a single database so that their users can look up data in various ways. Each index looks up data in one specific way.

Indexes make finding data in a database fast and easy, as long as you make the right choices when constructing your indexes. Index using the wrong data, and you'll never find the data you need. In this chapter, I show you

- ✔ How indexes work
- ✔ The various types of indexes that you can build
- ✔ How to select the best data for each index

Storing Data: First One in Is First in Line

Before you learn about indexes, you need to understand how a database stores data. A *database* is a collection of tables. Each table resembles a spreadsheet and contains columns of the same data and rows of related data (see Chapter 1).

For example, a table of a database may contain a person's name and address. All first names are contained in one column and all last names in another column. The same holds true for street address and Zip Code. Rows contain related data, such as one person's

- ✔ First name
- ✔ Last name
- ✔ Street address
- ✔ Zip Code

I left out the person's city and state on purpose because you can use the person's Zip Code to find a particular city and state. You can often find the Zip Code, along with the associated city and state, in a table other than the table that contains a person's name and address (see Chapter 3 for more information).

Each table typically contains many rows of data. The actual number of rows depends on the type of data you want to store in the table. For example, a table that contains Zip Codes and related cities and states will have a row for each Zip Code.

My auto mechanic doesn't believe in appointments. Instead, he tells all of his customers the same thing. The first car that is dropped off is the first car that gets repaired. He's very particular about this and assigns numbers in his parking lot to enforce his rule.

His parking lot has ten parking spaces, numbered one to ten. Each day, he can work on a maximum of ten cars. And on most days, customers arrive an hour before the shop opens in order to be ensured of getting one of those coveted parking spaces. No one wants to be the 11th car.

A database stores data in tables using a technique similar to my auto mechanic's. However, a table has rows instead of parking spaces and has more than ten spaces to "park" data.

Each row is numbered, although you don't actually see the row numbers when you look at the table. This is because the DBMS keeps track of row numbers internally.

The first row of the table stores the first set of data. A set of data consists of related data. I like to think of a set of related data as my mechanic's customers — one customer's data (name, address, and so on) fill the first row, or parking space. The second row, or parking space, stores the next set of related data, such as the next customer's information. This pattern continues, filling up subsequent rows similarly to how customers fill up my mechanic's parking lot.

When someone enters data into the *database application*, which is a program that collects and stores data, the DBMS stores that data in the order in which it was received. This is sometimes called *data-entry order* because data entry is the act of supplying data to DBMS.

Retrieving Data with the Index Table

An index is a small table that contains references to data in the large table much like an index of a book references words in the text of the book.

In a database, tables that contain actual data are like text in a book and the index table that contains data that you typically look up is like the index of a book. A table used to store data usually contains many columns, each used to store a particular type of data such as a person's first name or last name.

However, an index table contains only two columns, which the DBMS uses to quickly locate data in the corresponding data table. I'll show you how this is done in "Indexes work like a book index." Here are the two columns used in every index:

✔ Key
✔ Row Number

The Key column contains data that you want to look up in the database, and the Row Number column contains the number of the row in the table that contains the data. The DBMS uses the row number to quickly find the set of data related to the key data.

Indexes work like a book index

Suppose you are designing a database to hold data about the employees in your company. You will probably create a table to store each employee's name and address. And you will probably use an Employee Number to uniquely identify data about a particular employee (see Chapter 2).

You may want to use the Employee Number as a key to an index for the database, because no two employees will have the same Employee Number. Remember that the index should have two columns: one column should contain all the Employee Numbers and the other column should contain the row numbers that correspond to the row in the Employee table (see Figure 4-1). Whenever you want to find a particular employee, you give the DBMS the Employee Number of the employee whose data you want to see.

Figure 4-1: An index contains a search value called a key and a reference to the row number where the search value appears in the table.

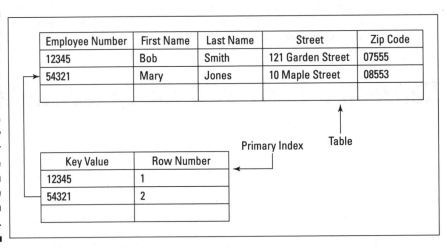

The DBMS compares the Employee Number that you've given it to the Key Value column in every row in the index. Either the DBMS locates the Employee Number or doesn't find the Employee Number in the Key Value column of the index.

> ✔ If the DBMS finds the Employee Number, it uses the row number in the Row Number column to find the appropriate row in the Employee table.

> ✔ If the DBMS doesn't find the Employee Number, it tells you that the Employee Number isn't contained in the Employee table.

When an index is initially created, the DBMS goes through each row of the table and copies the necessary information from the table to the index. Afterwards, the DBMS automatically updates the index whenever you insert or modify a row in the table.

Sometimes the terms index, table, and database can be confusing because whenever you look up data, you do so in a database using an index. However, an *index* references one table in a database and not the entire database. A *database* contains one or more tables (see Chapter 1). So you could say that you are actually looking up data in a table of the database rather than looking in the entire database and you'd be correct, but most of us simply say that we're looking up data in a database.

And the answer is . . .

Whenever you request data from a database, you give the DBMS the key data that identifies the data that you want to retrieve. You also give the DBMS the names of the type of data that you wish to see. These names are column names of the table that contains the data.

Suppose that you want to see the name and address of the employee who is assigned the Employee Number 55555. I'll show you the actual commands to use to do this later in this book, but for now here are the basic steps you need to perform to retrieve this data:

1. **Tell the DBMS the Employee Number, which is 55555.**

2. **Tell the DBMS the column names of the data about employee 55555 that you want to see.**

   These are First Name, Last Name, Street, City, State, and Zip Code.

3. **The DBMS searches the index that contains Employee Numbers, looking for the record with a key data of 55555.**

4. **You should receive the values of the employee name and address columns or a message saying that the employee isn't in the database.**

By returning to you the values of the employee name and address, the DBMS is saying, "Here it is. Do whatever you want with it." It's up to you to either display the values onscreen or use them for other purposes, such as printing mailing labels.

Not in the database? — Not necessarily true

When the DBMS reports that the search value isn't in the database, it really means that it couldn't find the search value in the index. The value still could be in the table. Remember that the DBMS looks for the search value in the index only and not in the table itself.

Whenever you insert key data into, modify key data in, or delete key data from the table, you also affect the corresponding key value in the index table. For example, when you delete an employee from the database, you must also delete the corresponding row in the index.

A table must be synchronized with each index used to locate data in the table. Most DBMSs maintain the integrity between indexes and tables. If an index gets off synchronization, the results of a search will be erroneous. Here's what could happen:

- The search value isn't found, but the row containing the value is in the table. The search value could be in the table, but wasn't inserted into the index when the row was inserted into the table (see Figure 4-2).

- The search value is found, but the DBMS doesn't return any values from the table. The row containing the search value was deleted from the table but not from the index.

The DBMS searches the index, not the database.

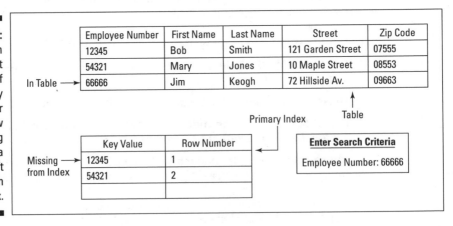

Figure 4-2: A row can appear lost in a table if the key value for the row containing the data isn't included in the index.

Employee Number	First Name	Last Name	Street	Zip Code
12345	Bob	Smith	121 Garden Street	07555
54321	Mary	Jones	10 Maple Street	08553
66666	Jim	Keogh	72 Hillside Av.	09663

In Table →

Table

Primary Index

Key Value	Row Number
12345	1
54321	2

Missing from Index →

Enter Search Criteria

Employee Number: 66666

Another way the search value could be in a table but not found by the DBMS is if the search value isn't a key to the table. The search value could be contained in a column that wasn't used to create the key to the index. Therefore, the search value won't appear in any index and the DBMS will report that it couldn't find the data. I show an example of this in Figure 4-3. I ask for the search value of Keogh, but the DBMS isn't going to find it in the index because it's not an Employee Number, which is the key value in the index.

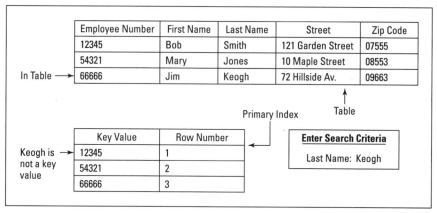

Figure 4-3:
A search
criteria
won't be
found
unless it's a
key value.

Typically, you choose which indexes to use when searching for data in a database, although some DBMSs are smart enough to choose indexes without receiving a hint from you. However, a full search of the database is necessary if the search value isn't a key to the database. Full searches take much longer than a search using an index because the DBMS must examine each column of every row.

Creating Primary Keys

Every table in a database has one or more columns whose values uniquely identify a row in the table. For example, the value of the Employee Number column is different for each row because each row contains data about a different employee. Therefore, the Employee Number column uniquely identifies each row in the table that contains employee data.

In contrast, the value in the employee's Last Name column may or may not uniquely identify data about an employee. A company could easily hire two or more employees who have the same last name. Likewise, two employees could have the same first and last names. This means that the value of the Last Name column or the combination of values in the Last Name column and in the First Name column wouldn't uniquely identify a row that contains employee data.

Combining values of two or more columns to uniquely identify a row in a table makes a *clustered index*. I discuss concatenating values to make a unique key in detail in the section, "Concatenating Is Like Matchmaking; It Brings Data Together."

A value that uniquely identifies rows in a table is called a *primary key*. A primary key is used in an index to locate data stored in a table. Each value in a primary key must be unique. That is, duplicate values cannot be used in a primary key because the same value cannot be used to identify more than one row of data in a table.

A primary key can be tricky to identify

Let's say that we design a table that contains customer data including a name and address. We'll probably have thousands of rows in the table because our business is bound to be an overwhelming success. So, we need a way to locate data in the table quickly. After all, we don't want to keep our customers waiting while the computer finds their data. We need to create a primary index for the table.

A primary index contains unique key values — no duplicates are allowed — and is the default index used to search for information in a table.

The Customer Data table will contain the following columns. Our job is to select one or more columns that can be used as the primary key to the table.

- Customer First Name
- Customer Last Name
- Customer Street 1 Address
- Customer Street 2 Address
- Customer City
- Customer State
- Customer Zip Code

You probably are unable to find a column or a combination of columns that meet the requirements of a primary key — that is, a column or combinations of columns must uniquely identify each row in the table. There could be a customer with the same first and last names that reside in the same town. And there is a chance, while somewhat remote, that two customers with the same name could live at the same street address.

When in doubt, create a new column

Sometimes you'll find that you are unable to use one or a combination of columns of a table to create a primary key because even a combination of all the columns in a row doesn't uniquely identify the row of data.

This is the case in the Customer Data table example earlier. Instead of scratching your head, trying to concoct a solution to this problem, you resolve this dilemma by creating a new column in the table.

You can assign a unique value to each row and place that unique value into a new column that can be used as the primary key to the table. In the case of the Customer Data table, we can create a Customer Number column and then assign a new Customer Number to each customer. You then store the assigned Customer Number in the Customer Number column of the row that contains the customer's data. In this way, you can uniquely identify each customer even if two or more customers have the same name and reside at the same address.

The primary key is a foreigner

The primary key of a table locates the key value, such as a Customer Number in an index. The primary key can also join two or more tables that contain similar data (see Chapter 17). Let's say that a customer database contains at least two tables. One of the tables contains the customer's name and address data. The other contains the customer's order data.

It doesn't make sense to place the customer name and address in the same table as the customer's order because this wastes disk space and isn't an efficient way to construct a database (see Chapter 3). A better approach is to place a customer's name and address in one table (the Customer Information Data table) and a customer's orders in another table (the Order Information Data table).

You need a way to link together rows of each table whenever you want to send the customer an invoice because you'll need to include the customer's name and address on the invoice.

Using the primary key of one of the tables links the tables (see Figure 4-4). In this example, the row that contains the customer's order has a column called Customer Number that has the same Customer Number that appears in the Customer Information Data table. Likewise, the Item ID in the Order Information table has the same Item ID number that appears in the Product Information Data table.

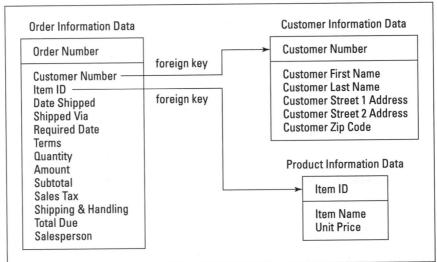

Figure 4-4:
Primary
keys link
together
rows of
different
tables.

Customer Number is the primary key in the Customer Information Data table and is a *foreign key* in the Order Information Data table. The primary key in the Order Information Data table is the Order Number because it uniquely identifies each row (that is, the order) in that table.

There can be many foreign keys in a table, each of which links a table to related data contained in other tables.

Test your newfound knowledge

1. What are the names of the columns in an index?

   a. Mo, Larry, and Curly

   b. Key Value and Row Number

   c. First Name and Last Name

   d. City and State

2. What is the purpose of a primary key?

   a. To uniquely identify each row in a table

   b. To prime the database before starting the search engine

   c. To restrict access to a table

   d. To sort data contained in a table

Answers: (1) b. (2) a.

Making Finds Faster with Secondary Keys

A table can have multiple indexes, each having a different key value. These *secondary indexes* and their secondary keys are nearly identical in concept to the primary index. Secondary indexes are small tables that contain two columns: the secondary Key Value and the Row Number that corresponds to a row in the main table (see Figure 4-5).

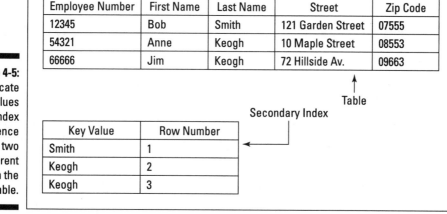

Figure 4-5: Duplicate key values in an index reference two different rows in the table.

The purpose of a secondary index is to provide a means for searching data in a table quickly without using the primary key value. For example, you may want to search the table using a customer's last name instead of using the Customer Number. This is a common practice whenever a customer makes an inquiry but forgets his or her Customer Number.

A secondary index is different from the primary index because it's not used to uniquely identify each row in the table. Instead, a secondary index can have duplicate key values, as is the case with using customer last name as the key value. There can be more than one customer with the same last name.

Secondary indexes and keys

- ✔ Offer a selection of search options.
- ✔ Narrow the choice of data to a smaller number of rows than the entire table.
- ✔ Don't uniquely identify each row of a table.

You normally don't have a limit on the number of secondary indexes you can create for a table, although each DBMS has its own set of rules that may limit you.

Performance of the database might be hampered if you have too many secondary indexes, because each index must be maintained whenever data changes in the database (see the "Too Many Indexes Can Cause a Slowdown" section later in this chapter).

Once you locate the caller's data, you can modify the address and tell the DBMS to update the Customer Information Data table with the new data (see Chapter 15 for more on how to do this).

Concatenating Is Like Matchmaking; It Brings Data Together

A key value of either a primary or secondary index can use the value in one column or values in multiple columns of the table. When you combine multiple columns into a key value, you are able to search for a combination of values. Combining values of multiple columns into a key value is called *concatenating*.

Concatenating values lets you

- Create a primary key using two or more columns
- Facilitate searching values of two or more columns using one index
- Create interesting ways to identify rows in a table

Concatenating sounds a bit techy for many of us, but this simply means taking the value of a column and placing it at the end of the value of another column when forming a key value. For example, many database designers concatenate Last Name and First Name columns to create a concatenated secondary key value for a secondary index.

I'll use my name to illustrate this concept. In my company's table of employees, you'll find a row that contains Keogh in the Last Name column and Jim in the corresponding First Name column.

If I concatenated the First Name column to the Last Name column, I'd end up with a key value looking like KeoghJim.

Notice that there isn't a space between the names. This is because I concatenated the value of the First Name column onto the value of the Last Name column — and most DBMSs remove any spaces that are used to pad the column before combining the first name and last name values.

Searching with clustered indexes

An index that uses a concatenated key as a key value is called a clustered index and has two columns. The two columns are

- Key Value
- Row Number

The Key Value column holds the concatenated value. This means Keogh and Jim, which are values of the Last Name and First Name columns, are combined together (concatenated) to form one new value, which is KeoghJim. You can find KeoghJim in the Key Value column of the index.

When I request data about Jim Keogh from the company's employee database, the DBMS concatenates the search value (Jim Keogh) to form a concatenated search value of KeoghJim.

Once the DBMS concatenates the search value, it goes about its usual business of comparing the search value with the key value of the index. In this case, the DBMS looks for the person with the strange name of KeoghJim.

Creating substrings

You can also create a key value that is a combination of parts of values in multiple columns by using a substring of those values. A *substring* is simply a piece of a full value.

Suppose that the network administrator of your company's computer network needs to create a database that uses an employee's network login ID as the primary key. The login ID would be a concatenation of parts of three columns. For the login ID, he would use

- The first letter of the value of the First Name column
- The first letter of the value of the Last Name column
- The value of the Employee Number column

Partial matching: How it works

I'm intrigued by the way a DBMS is able to find the data that I'm looking for even if I misspell the search value. The trick is with the way in which the DBMS compares the key value of an index. The comparison begins with the left-most characters of the search value and of the key value in the index. As long as one of the characters match, the DBMS returns data contained in the corresponding row as a match.

Let's say that I've mistakenly entered Mike Keogh as the search value, but I really want Jim Keogh. The DBMS concatenates the search value to create KeoghMike and then begins to compare KeoghMike to the concatenated key value of the index.

The search goes well because Keogh in the search value matches Keogh in the key value. However, the DBMS doesn't find Mike in the key value. Instead of telling me Mike Keogh isn't in the database, the DBMS returns all the Keoghs found in the database, one of which is Jim Keogh.

Some DBMSs require you to request that a search be made on a portion of the key value. You do so by specifying that you are looking for an inexact match or by using a wild card (see Chapter 13 for more about wild cards). A wild card is a character such as an asterisk (*). Different DBMSs have different wild cards.

I could use the wild card in a search value by placing the wild card after the characters that I want to match. For example, I'd use Keogh* as the wild card search value. This causes the DBMS to return data about any key value that has the first five letters of Keogh.

Some DBMSs even conduct a phonetic key search where they return key values that sound like the search value as matches. For example, the search value "fone" will match the key value "phone."

Therefore, the network login ID is the employee's initials followed by the Employee Number. For example, my Employee Number is 66666, so my network login ID is JK66666. The letter *J* is a substring of the First Name column. Likewise, the letter *K* is a substring of the Last Name column (see Figure 4-6).

Employee Number	First Name	Last Name	Street	Zip Code
12345	Bob	Smith	121 Garden Street	07555
54321	Anne	Keogh	10 Maple Street	08553
66666	Jim	Keogh	72 Hillside Av.	09663

Table

Primary Index

Key Value	Row Number
BS12345	1
AK54321	2
JK66666	3

Figure 4-6: The first letters of the first and last names are combined with the Employee Number to create a key value.

You can form a key value by concatenating substrings of any columns in a table. Use these key values as a primary key — just like in the login ID example.

Selecting Indexes: I Choose You and You

If you find yourself designing the database for your Java applet or application, you'll also have to decide on the number of secondary indexes to create and the values that you'll use for each index.

Your choice of indexes to create is sometimes intuitive based on the type of data stored in a table. For example, a Customer Number is a likely choice for the key to a primary index of a table that contains customer data. Likewise, an Order Number is the obvious choice for the primary key in a table that contains orders.

However, sometimes selecting an index and a key for the index can be tricky. What would be a good secondary key for a business that has a telephone catalog order service? Here are a few factors to consider when trying to answer this question:

- **An index must be a logical alternative to the primary index:** A primary index uses a primary key, such as a Customer Number that uniquely identifies a row in the table. Your choice for a secondary index must use a key value that is commonly used to find similar data. For example, a customer's first name and last name are logical alternatives to using the Customer Number. Using a customer's home address isn't a logical alternative to the primary key.

- **Data used in the index must be contained in the table or derived from data contained in the table:** This means that you can't choose key values that aren't included in the table or that you cannot create by using substrings of values in the table. For example, you cannot use the state in which the customer resides as a secondary key if the state isn't in a column in the table. Typically, a customer table contains a Zip Code column rather than a State column.

- **Only a reasonable number of indexes can be created:** Avoid creating unnecessary secondary indexes by limiting yourself to the most commonly used search values. For example, it doesn't make sense to create indexes using a first name, street address, city, or state as key values in a customer table. Rarely do you look up data by those values. Instead, you'd probably use a Customer Number, Zip Code, or the concatenated last name and first name values as index keys.

Test your newfound knowledge

1. What is a substring?

a. A term referring to using two column values as a key value

b. A combination of two indexes' values

c. Shoelaces used by the crew of a submarine

d. A portion of a value in one or more columns of a table used to form a key value

2. How is a wild card used in a search value?

a. It indicates that only characters up to the wild card need to match the key value.

b. It indicates that only characters after the wild card need to match the key value.

c. It indicates that none of the characters in the search value need to match the key value.

d. It indicates that you're a wild and crazy guy.

Answers: (1) d. (2) a.

There isn't a foolproof method to use to choose the proper number of indexes and the proper key values for those indexes. The best approach I found is to use common sense. Don't create an index unless you have a good reason for creating it.

The only good reason to create an index is to increase the performance of using the database. Performance is measured as response time, which is the time lapse between making a request for data and when the DBMS returns the data.

It's time to create a new index using the appropriate key value whenever you notice that it takes a while to retrieve data from the database.

The lack of an index isn't the only reason for seeing poor performance from a database. Hardware and network conditions also influence database performance. Make sure you confer with your company's hardware and network experts to eliminate hardware and network operations as a cause of poor performance.

Too Many Indexes Can Cause a Slowdown

Too much of a good thing isn't good for you, and no truer words have ever been spoken about indexes. The purpose of an index is to increase the performance of looking up data in a database. However, creating too many indexes can actually slow down performance.

Each index contains two pieces of data about a table in a database: the key value and the row number. Each time a change is made to the table that affects the key value, the DBMS must make the same change to the corresponding index.

Here are the events that occur to a table that could cause changes to an index:

- **Insert a new row:** Whenever you place a new row into a table, the DBMS must copy key values from the row and insert the key value, along with the corresponding row number, into each index that uses the key value.

- **Delete an existing row:** Deleting a row in a table requires the DBMS to delete the corresponding key value in all the indexes that are associated with the table.

- **Change the value of data used in the key value:** A change in a value in the table that makes up the key value must also be made in indexes that use that value.

Failure to make these adjustments to the indexes will cause the indexes to be out of synchronization with the table. This can result in erroneous searches for data (see Chapter 3).

Fortunately, the DBMS takes the time to keep indexes and tables synchronized. However, that time can negatively impact the performance of the database.

Whenever a change is made to data that is part of a key value, the change isn't completed until all the appropriate indexes are updated. Typically, the DBMS sends a confirmation to whomever made the change.

The time lag between making the change and receiving confirmation is a few seconds, even if the DBMS has to update three or four indexes during the process. However, the time lag can become noticeable if the DBMS must maintain many indexes.

The question that you are probably asking is, "How many indexes can you create before you experience degradation in performance of the database?" The honest answer is, it depends. It depends on

- **Number of rows in each index:** The greater the number of rows in the index, the longer it might take to update the index.

- **The type of key value that is used to create the index:** More time is necessary to update a key value that is comprised of concatenated values than the actual value of a column.

✔ **The power of the computer hosting the DBMS:** Computer power is measured as the number of instructions the computer can process in a second. A computer hosting the DBMS must be able to process millions of instructions per second so there isn't a degradation of database performance.

The best approach to take when deciding on the number of indexes to create for a table is to follow my earlier recommendations. Gradually create indexes as you need them and then monitor the performance whenever you make changes to the database. Delete the least necessary indexes should you experience a slowdown in performance.

Chapter 5

Client/Server Architecture for Snappy Service All the Time

Do you know where your database is? You probably don't if you work for a larger company, and you probably don't care as long as you can access data whenever you need it. Many, if not all, businesses and government agencies store data in databases that are located miles away from the employees who use that data for their jobs. And yet, employees have the feeling that their computers store these databases.

This bit of deception is made possible through the implementation of distributive data architecture, network architecture, and client/server architecture. Don't be concerned if these terms sound foreign to you because you'll probably understand their concepts once I explain these terms in everyday language, which I do in this chapter.

A database that is operated by a database management system (DBMS) stores your data. A server, which is a powerful computer, holds the DBMS. Your computer — the client — contacts the server over your company's computer network whenever you request to see data. You can think of your computer as a business client of the server. It's the server's job to satisfy your request for data, which is similar to how your business must make your business clients happy.

Nearly all Java database applications or applets use client/server architecture to store and retrieve data. It's for this reason that you need to have a good understanding of client/server architecture before I show you how to use Java to work with data.

You'll learn all you need to know about client/server architecture in this chapter. The good news is you don't need to become a client/server expert to build Java database programs — you can leave those skills to the database professionals in your company — however, you will need to know

- ✔ How using a client/server architecture is different from using a local database
- ✔ The benefits of using remote data access
- ✔ How to make requests that any client/server database will understand

Client/server architecture is at the heart of every corporate Java application, including those that run on the Internet, an intranet, or extranets.

The Lonely Standalone Database Application

Many databases that are shared among employees have their origins as a lonely, standalone database. A *standalone database* is the term given to any database that isn't shared. Sometimes this is called a local database because the database resides on one user's computer.

Years ago, I developed a standalone database application for the Mergers and Acquisitions group at Salomon, Inc., a major international investment banking firm. The database was located on the hard drive of a personal computer in the department and contained the status of the entire firm's pending deals.

Executives had their assistants walk over to the computer and access the database whenever they needed a status on a pending deal or they needed to update data about a deal. As you can imagine, conflicts arose whenever two executives required deal data at the same time.

These conflicts are common with standalone databases and are the reason why companies tend to redevelop standalone databases as a client/server database application. Typically, a standalone database application

- ✔ Starts as an employee's way of organizing and tracking business data
- ✔ Resides on one computer
- ✔ Isn't accessible to other computers over a network
- ✔ Contains critical business data that isn't secured

You build standalone databases using DBMSs. They are capable of processing the same requests that a client/server database application would receive.

Some programmers use a standalone database to initially create their database application, and then they re-create the database as a client/server database application once the bugs have been worked out of the application. You should follow this approach whenever possible. The examples in this book use a standalone database.

Advantages of standalone databases

Executives have a tendency to hoard data because it gives them the edge in their business to make the right decision in critical times. And they like to store their private stash of data in a standalone database.

Standalone databases offer advantages that aren't available in a client/server database application. These advantages tend to encourage executives to store mission-critical data on their own computers rather than to give up the data to a remote database.

Here are the important benefits of using a standalone database:

- **Recognizable ownership of the data:** The executive who creates and maintains the standalone database is responsible for ensuring that that data is current and accurate. In contrast, it's typically unclear who is responsible for data that is shared among employees in a client/server application.

- **Reliability of the data:** One employee who can easily institute and enforce quality-assurance procedures usually maintains the data in a standalone database. This assures executives of a predictable level of accuracy of the data. However, this also means that the employee must be around to maintain the data.

- **Availability of the data:** The database is always ready to respond to an executive's request for data as long as the computer is operational and the executive is physically present at the computer. A standalone database practically eliminates the risk that the database is unavailable because of network problems or because a technician has brought down the database for maintenance.

- **Control over the database:** Changes to the data and modification of the database are under the executive's direct control, which means the executive determines what changes need to be made to the database and when to implement them. In contrast, executives must deal with the technology department of the company to implement changes to a client/server database application.

- **No need to negotiate with other users for data:** The standalone database owner unilaterally determines the design and modification of the standalone database. Client/server databases are frequently designed to accommodate multiple departments within a corporation, which tends to require executives to jockey for changes they want to the database.

Disadvantages of standalone databases

Executives and others do run into a few drawbacks with a standalone. One of which is the inability to easily share some of the data.

Old timers in the computer industry coined the term *sneaker net,* which graphically depicts how computers, in the days before computer networks abound in offices, shared data. Employees would copy the data to be shared onto a floppy disk and then walk the disk over to another computer to load the data onto its hard drive.

Sharing data this way became a hassle whenever the size of data exceeded the available space on a floppy disk. Multiple disks had to be used, and eventually a compression program had to be used to collapse the data into a smaller size, which meant the data had to be restored to its full size once it was copied to the other computer.

However, sneaker net was the smallest worry for executives using a standalone database. Here are other drawbacks that make a standalone database less than an ideal choice for storing a company's mission-critical data:

✔ **Lack of security:** A standalone database is vulnerable to theft or vandalism because it resides on a computer that is typically in an unsecured area of the building — not in a well-protected data center.

✔ **Redundancy of data:** Data stored in a standalone database becomes valuable to executives other than the executive who created the database. This results in the data being shared throughout the organization by replicating the entire database on other computers. A company doubles the cost of storing the database each time someone places the database on another computer.

✔ **Accuracy of data:** A replicated standalone database exposes a company to the risk that not all copies of the database will have the latest data. For example, a change to data in the original database must be manually changed in all the copies of the database. This can easily lead to decisions being made based on erroneous data contained in the database.

✔ **Loss of data:** An executive or an assistant can easily enter the wrong command and corrupt data in the database. Many times, a current backup copy of the database isn't available to repair the damage. All too often employees see backing up the database as grunt work. Client/server databases are automatically backed up daily — sometimes twice a day — and a secured data library stores the backup tapes and CDs.

TECHNICAL STUFF

Files and databases: Viva la difference

It's easy to confuse a file that contains data with a database, because both seem to have a similar purpose.

However, a *file* contains data that isn't typically used to search for data. Although you can use the Find feature in a word processor to locate data in a word processing document file, this is not as efficient as finding data in a database.

Likewise, data is stored in a spreadsheet and can be searched using the Find command. Spreadsheets organize data into rows and columns, which is similar to a database. In fact, spreadsheets contain database-like capabilities to organize data, but spreadsheets are more like files than a database.

A database contains one or more tables divided into rows and columns (see Chapter 1) and indexes that help you quickly find data that you need (see Chapter 4). A database may consist of multiple files, such as the database itself and related indexes. It can also have report files that contain data organized into printed reports, such as invoices.

Typically, files such as a word processing file or spreadsheet file are small in size, so you can easily copy them onto a floppy disk and share them with another computer. In contrast, a database is often very large — too large to store on a floppy disk and therefore difficult to share with another computer.

Your Serve to Serve Up the Database

A primary disadvantage of a standalone database is the inability to easily share data stored in the database. Some companies overcome this limitation by placing the database on a file server that is accessible by many computers over a corporate computer network.

You can think of a *file server* as a computer that shares files on its hard drive with other computers. When a computer needs data from a file, the file server copies the file from its hard drive to the computer that requested the file. Once the computer receives a copy of the file, it then processes the file as it normally would if the file was stored locally on the its hard drive.

For example, data stored in a standalone database could be stored in a database on a file server. Whenever an executive needs to search for data in the database, she would copy the database from the file server to her computer.

You should use a file server for a database when

- ✔ Several employees must share data.

- ✔ Copying the database or remotely accessing the database doesn't impede other traffic on the corporate computer network.

✔ A professional must back up and restore the database.

✔ You need to secure the database with a login ID and password.

Everyone can share in the data

Storing a database on a file server has a number of advantages over using a standalone database. The most obvious is the elimination of sneaker net. You no longer need to go through the hassle of squeezing a database onto a floppy disk and then copying the database onto the hard drive of another computer.

A database that was initially developed by an executive to satisfy her own need to organize and access data quickly migrates to a file server when colleagues seek to use her data. Instead of continually bothering the executive's assistant for copies of the data, other executives can directly access the data from the file server.

Besides the benefit of easily sharing data, housing a database on a file server provides

✔ **Professional maintenance:** Someone usually places the file server in a data center where professional computer technicians, who follow standard operating procedures to ensure safe operation of the file server, can watch it.

✔ **Unlimited access to data:** You can typically connect to the file server using a computer at your desk, using a computer located elsewhere in your company, or using a computer in your home. This is something nearly impossible to do with a standalone computer. Of course, the computer used to access the database must have the appropriate DBMS to process requests for data.

✔ **Data security:** A network administrator or other computer professionals can limit access to files on the file server to only those employees who are authorized to use those files. This includes files that contain the database. Standalone databases, on the other hand, lack professional data security.

Who changed the data?

Conflicts always arise whenever more than one person has the capability to modify the same data. One executive typically makes changes that are disagreeable with her colleagues or makes changes without notifying other executives. This usually leads to finger pointing and unnecessary fighting.

These disagreements can easily overshadow the advantages of storing data on a file server. Many of these disadvantages aren't obvious. Here are a few of the most important disadvantages, so you'll know the pitfalls of using a file server:

- ✔ **Timing:** You can't be sure that data retrieved from the database is the latest data because another executive might modify data at the same time as you receive it.

- ✔ **Overwriting data:** The value of data represents the value last saved to the file server. Suppose that you and I are updating the database to show my new salary. You set my salary at $20,000, and I set my salary at $150,000. If you save my salary to the file server first, my $150,000 salary will overwrite yours when I save my version to the file server — but I really don't mind.

- ✔ **Audit trail for changes:** The file server doesn't record who changes what in the database. Some DBMSs do keep track of requests and changes using *transaction logs*. The transaction log lets you examine all changes made to the database.

Whose data is it anyway?

Once someone transfers a standalone database to a file server, there is a tendency for the data in the database to be in the public domain. That is, no one in the company feels ownership of the data. Instead, the data sits somewhere on the network, and "the company" is responsible for maintaining the accuracy of data in the database.

It doesn't take long before checks and balances that were once in place to enforce data integrity for the standalone database disappear from the file-server version of the database. This can lead to people entering erroneous data into the database, which could lead executives into making business decisions based on faulty data.

You can prevent a database from becoming orphaned by restricting rights to access database files. A network administrator can limit the type of access each person has to the database files and thereby reduce the likelihood that erroneous data will find its way into the database. The three general kinds of file rights are

- ✔ **No access:** A person isn't granted access to the file.

- ✔ **Read only:** Grants a person the right to look at the contents of a file but not be able to change the file.

- ✔ **Read and write:** Grants a person the right to look at the contents of the file, modify the data, and insert new data into the file.

Test your newfound knowledge

1. How does a database differ from a file that contains data?

a. A database is an organization of data into tables, columns, and rows. A file may not have any formal organization.

b. A file is used on a desktop computer, and a database is used on a network computer.

c. A file is insecure, and a database is secure.

d. A database contains data, and a file is something used to break out of jail.

2. Why would you choose to create a stand-alone database?

a. You don't want the guys in the IT department to interfere with your business.

b. So you can process corporate-wide transactions.

c. You want to share the data with others in your office.

d. Data stored in the database is unlikely to be used by anyone but you.

Answers: (1) a. (2) d.

When you first move the database files to the file server, no one except the owner has access rights. Anyone wishing for access rights must receive permission from the owner. Normally, only two or three people who are under the owner's direct control have read-and-write access. All others have read-only access.

Many DBMSs have a rights' management feature that enables the owner of the database to restrict access without having to use the file access rights of the network.

I'm Your Server, You're My Client

The most efficient way to manage data required to run a typical corporation is to use client/server architecture. *Client/server architecture* is a way authorized users can request corporate data from any computer as long as the computer is connected to the corporate network. This is also a way for a corporation to centralize data and data processing to a limited number of powerful computers, located strategically throughout the company.

Technologists find that client/server architecture is the most efficient way to control the integrity of data and yet make that data freely available to those who need access to it. Client/server architecture

✔ **Reduces or eliminates redundant data:** A central database holds the data, and the data isn't replicated on many computers throughout the company.

✔ **Provides consistency in data:** The same type of data is standardized throughout the company.

✔ **Centralizes processing power:** You find high-powered computers, specifically designed to process large amounts of data, in data centers rather than on every desktop.

✔ **Offers data flexibility:** You can easily transform data into various formats for reports and analysis through the proper formulation of a request using Structured Query Language (SQL).

Client/server architecture in action

Imagine that you work for an automobile manufacturer, and you need to have a list of all the customers who live within ten miles of a particular car dealership. You can use your computer and make this request to a customer database.

A database server in one of the company's ten data centers holds your database. But you don't really care where the database is as long as you receive a response to your request quickly.

The DBMS runs on the database server rather than on your computer. This is an important distinction between a client/server architecture and a stand-alone database or a database housed on a file server.

Your computer is a client, and the database server is the server in the client/server architecture. The client is responsible for properly formulating the request for data, and it's the server's job to translate the request into procedures that are used to search the database.

These clients don't need a lawyer

A *client* is any computer application that requests data from a database server, such as a Java application or an applet that you build using techniques that I show in this book. The database server does all the processing and returns the requested data to the client.

Computers that are used to request data don't need to be powerful because clients don't directly search through thousands or millions of rows of data to fulfill the request. Instead, clients can be standard desktop computers.

This is one of the important benefits of client/server architecture. Companies don't need to invest large sums of money to place powerful computers on every desktop. Instead, a company should invest heavy-duty computer power on database servers since this is where you need the horsepower to crunch large amounts of data.

There are two kinds of client/server architecture: thick clients and thin clients. A thick client has special software to access the database. A thin client uses a browser and related Web pages to access the database.

Clients focus on three tasks:

✔ Formulating the request for data from the database

✔ Analyzing data supplied by the database server

✔ Presenting data and the results of the analysis on the screen or in a report

Clients aren't concerned about the location of the data or how the database server finds the data that is used for analysis and presentation. It's the database server's job to track down the necessary data.

Server up the data

A *server* is a powerful computer designed to quickly respond to requests made by clients over a computer network. A computer network has various kinds of servers connected to it, and each server has a specific job.

Your company's computer network probably has some or all of these servers working behind the scenes. These include

✔ **Domain server:** Coordinates network operations such as logins and routing requests to the proper server

✔ **E-mail server:** Manages your company's e-mails

✔ **Print server:** Coordinates the printing of documents sent by clients

✔ **Database server:** Fulfills a request for data stored in one or more databases

The database server is used in client/server database architecture; it runs the DBMS and houses database files on its hard drive.

Sometimes the database server is called the database engine because, like the engine of your car, it's the workhorse of the client/server database system. And, like your car, the more powerful the engine, the better the database server will perform its job.

More than a servant to clients

A database server is the central source for data in a company. Companies can use the database server to enforce rigid data standards and security to ensure data integrity. *Data integrity* describes the reliability of data. A high degree of data integrity means that users can trust that the data is accurate.

Data standards are one of those lesser-known factors of working with a database that strongly influence data integrity. Let's say that one of the columns in your new table contains the dates of orders. How would you represent the date in the column? I can think of several formats:

- 1/1/02
- 1/1/2002
- January 1, 2002
- Jan-1-02
- 02-1-Jan

You probably had no trouble reading the date in any of these formats. Most DBMSs can store dates in these formats. However, a client needs to know the date format used for the Order Date column to form the request for the date, to properly analyze the date, and to present the date onscreen.

Centralizing databases to one or a few database servers enables a company to standardize data, such as the format of commonly used dates. Anyone in the company wishing to create a database or modify an existing database asks a database administrator to fulfill the request using standardized data formats.

A *database administrator* is a technician who is responsible for creating and maintaining a database stored on a database server. This is the person who will be creating your databases when you begin to build your own database applications using Java.

You'll be the database administrator for the databases used in this book because we'll be using a local DBMS, such as Microsoft Access, to get you started programming.

I was here first. No, I was!

Sharing resources, such as a printer or a database, can be a tough job, especially when deadlines loom over you and your colleagues. And client/server architecture doesn't eliminate competition for the database. Fortunately, database servers manage conflicts for resources effectively.

Database servers can handle receiving multiple requests at the same time. Database servers and the DBMSs running on them utilize several techniques to process requests quickly. Some of the common techniques are

- ✔ **Placing incoming requests in a queue:** Requests from clients are organized into a line. This *queue* is much like the line that you stand in at the supermarket checkout counter.

- ✔ **Processing higher priority requests first:** Some database servers enable the database administrator to give certain requests priority over other requests. So requests from the president of your company jump the line and get processed by the database server before everyone else's.

- ✔ **Processing low-priority requests in the order in which they were received:** Requests that don't have priority are processed in the order in which the database server received them. Think "first come, first served."

- ✔ **Identifying and allocating resources such as databases and indexes based on each request:** The DBMS that runs on the database server analyzes each request from a client and determines the most efficient way to process that request.

- ✔ **Assigning processes to the appropriate computer processor or co-processor:** Database servers typically have more than one processor inside the computer. The processor (CPU) is the chip inside the computer that actually crunches the data. Multiple requests can each be sent to one of the processors onboard the server. This means that the database server can process more than one request at the same time — this is called parallel processing.

The database administrator, network technicians, and hardware technicians tweak the DBMS; the network operating system, which is the software that operates the computer network; and the server hardware, to get the best possible performance from the database server.

Replication servers love to copy other people's work

Even with sophisticated tweaking of the database server, sometimes the demand for access to the database can overwhelm the database server's capacity to provide timely responses to requests. This is especially true for transactional databases.

A *transactional database* records and reports on business transactions, such as sales at a supermarket checkout counter or stock trades in a brokerage house. At peak times, thousands of transactions could be inserted as new rows into a transactional database. There could also be hundreds of requests for transactional data from users throughout the company. The combination of new transactions and requests can bring the fast-moving database server to its knees, leaving it chugging along like an old car.

Designers of client/server database applications overcome this problem by using a combination of a replication server and reporting servers. A *replication server* copies new transactions from the transaction server to several reporting servers. A *reporting server* is a database server that contains databases used solely for processing requests for data.

Here's how this divide-and-conquer strategy works. When a user adds new data or updates existing data, transactions are inserted into the transaction database. After each transaction is written to the transaction database, the replication server makes a copy of the transaction. The copy is then inserted into all the reporting databases located on one or more reporting servers. The database server forwards the requests from clients for transactional data to one of the reporting servers for processing.

Here are the basics of replication servers:

✔ They provide a fast response to clients regardless of the volume of transactions.

✔ They provide redundant data. If one database server fails, a duplicate database is always available.

✔ They require duplicate storage capacity for databases because the same data is stored in multiple locations.

Scalability is the key to success

Using multiple databases for receiving new transactions and reporting on existing transactions distributes the data-processing workload among several database servers. This results in an acceptable response time, regardless of an increase in transactions or requests for data.

Response time is the amount of time that passes from when a client inserts a new transaction or requests data to the time when the database server responds. This is simply the amount of time you wait for the database server to return the data that you requested.

Typically, response time decreases to a level of unacceptability when the demand for database server services is greater than the database server's ability to respond adequately. However, the use of a replication server and reporting servers enables the database system to be scalable.

Scalable means that adjustments can be made to the system to meet the current demand for services. For example, you can install another reporting server whenever response time becomes unacceptable. Likewise, a company can reallocate a report server should one less report server satisfy a drop in demand.

Speaking the Server's Language

Any client can request data from a database server. However, the owner of the database must authorize the client to access the data. The client must also write the request for the data in a language understandable by the DBMS that runs on the database server.

A DBMS understands requests that are written in Structured Query Language (SQL). SQL uses English-like expressions to tell the DBMS

- The rows of data that you want to see
- The columns of data within the rows that you want to see
- The columns and rows you want to modify
- The rows that you want to insert into the database

I'll show you how to write SQL requests throughout the remaining chapters of this book and how to send those requests to the DBMS from within your Java application or applet.

Requesting data from any database

An advantage of using SQL to view or modify data in a database is that as a client you don't care about the type of database or DBMS that is used to manage the data. Computer technicians call this *data independence* because these database operations, such as fulfilling requests, are separate from clients requesting data.

Companies use a number of DBMSs, and each DBMS understands the same SQL request if the request identifies the proper database, tables, and columns that contain the data. Here are the popular DBMSs that you'll be able to access using your Java application or applet:

- Microsoft Access
- IBM's DB2
- Sybase
- Oracle

> ✔ MS SQL Server
>
> ✔ Informix

Each DBMS has its own way of processing requests, but you don't need to concern yourself about it. All you need is to properly write the SQL request. And to do this, you'll need to know the location of the data. Specifically you need to know

> ✔ The name of the database
>
> ✔ The name of the table(s)
>
> ✔ The name of the columns

Of course, if you design and create your own database, as I show you later in this book, you'll already know the location of the data. If you're developing a Java database application or applet for a business, the database administrator who maintains the database can give you the names of the database, tables, and columns that you'll need to access the data.

Making the middleware connection

Programs that you build using Java don't make requests for data directly to the database server. Instead, an intermediary called middleware must process requests.

A *middleware driver* is a utility program that translates a low-level request from your application into low-level instructions that the DBMS understands. Similarly, it also translates low-level instructions from the DBMS back to instructions the Java application or applet understands.

I like to think of middleware as the service advisor in the service department of a car dealership. I tell the service advisor the trouble I'm having with my car. The service advisor translates the problem into technical terms that the mechanic understands. The mechanic then uses technical jargon to tell the service advisor what he fixed on the car. The service advisor finally translates that into plain, simple English for me.

You write your request using the Java Database Connectivity application program interface (JDBC API) that has the necessary Java classes to handle the grunt work of communicating with the DBMS.

Java Database Connectivity (JDBC), which is a middleware driver, connects the DBMS and your application or applet. JDBC does practically the same job as the service advisor. Most DBMS manufacturers provide their customers with a JDBC middleware driver for their product. You need only be concerned that the proper JDBC middleware driver is installed for the DBMS that you are using. Chapter 7 explains JDBC in detail.

Test your newfound knowledge

1. What is a client?

   a. Any computer that requests data from a server

   b. Someone who pays a lawyer's bill

   c. Any computer that supplies data to another computer

   d. A person for whom you build a Java database application or applet

2. What is a server?

   a. A star tennis player

   b. Any computer that fulfills a request from another computer

   c. A computer that requests data from another computer

   d. A Java API

Answers: (1) a. (2) b.

Chapter 6

The Setup: Planning a Database Application

*E*very Java database application begins with a plan that describes in detail how the application will work when you finish coding. The plan is the moment of truth when you put your ideas down on paper and see if you have addressed all of the various facets of the project.

Your plan is a road map that shows everyone involved in the project the steps that must be accomplished to make your Java database application a reality. You can think of the plan as an architect's drawings of an office building that depicts what the building will look like and how it will function when completed.

I'll take you through every phase of the planning in this chapter. You'll learn about

✔ The components of a plan

✔ The business rules

✔ Data dictionaries

✔ The functionality requirements of the application

Java database programmers tend to begin writing code once they have come up with an idea for a database project. However, you need to avoid this knee-jerk response and instead carefully think through all the aspects of the database project before writing the first line of code. You'll find that by first developing a thorough plan, you'll make fewer programming errors.

Whenever I use the term Java application in this chapter, I also mean Java applet and servlets.

Planning Your Database Application

The plan for your Java database application must contain all the information necessary to create the database and to write the Java code that will interact with the data stored in the database.

Some Java programmers refer to the plan as "specifications" for the project. Specifications are precise descriptions of every component of the application — much like a recipe for your favorite cake. The recipe for your Java database application requires

- **A description of each component needed for the project:** For example, you need to identify data elements such as a person's first name, middle name, and last name. This is the same as listing the ingredients for making a cake.

- **A definition of each component needed for the project:** For example, data must be defined according to size and type of data (see Chapter 2). This is like describing the quantity of each ingredient you need.

- **Sequencing of tasks:** List the steps needed to incorporate each component into the application. You'll find this similar to identifying the order in which to introduce each component into the mix.

You place your specifications in a written document that everyone can reference. I like to call the plan the "bible" of the project because it steers everyone in the right direction.

You probably don't need to develop a formal plan for the examples I show you in this book because they are small projects. However, a team of professionals creates most Java database applications that larger companies need. Therefore, you'll need a plan to keep everyone on track.

Failure to be meticulous with details of the plan can cause bugs in the program.

Components of a database application plan

Every plan for a database application must contain sufficient data about the application's design for the database administrator and programmers to translate the plan into working code and a working database.

You'll need to include in your plan:

- ✔ **A database schema:** This is a diagram that shows all the tables that comprise the database and shows how tables relate to each other (see Chapter 3). This is also called a data model.

- ✔ **Data dictionary:** You must create a listing of all the columns in each table, along with a definition of the data stored in each column.

- ✔ **Indexes:** You need to include the names and keys to all the indexes that are necessary to find data in the database. These include primary and secondary indexes (see Chapter 4).

- ✔ **Methods:** A *method* is a specific way of processing data, such as making a request to the DBMS for particular data. The plan must identify each method along with the steps that are executed within the method.

Database schema, data dictionary, and indexes

Your plan must contain the details about the database that the Java application will use. This includes a list of all the data and tables of the database. You don't need to use a lot of words to describe the database. You can just use a few well-designed illustrations with labels instead.

Here's what you need to do:

1. **Follow the guidelines in Chapters 2 and 3 to develop a list of data.**

   These guidelines also show you how to organize data into the most efficient table structures for the database.

2. **Create a database schema diagram (see Figure 6-1).**

   This diagram shows all the tables, their columns, and the foreign keys that are used to link tables together.

3. **Create a data dictionary for each table (see Figure 6-2).**

   Column name, data type, and size define the data (see Chapter 2).

4. **List all the indexes that are used to access data in each table.**

   You need to include primary indexes and secondary indexes along with key values for each index (see Chapter 4).

   Once you've finished drawing illustrations that depict your database, you've defined the database sufficiently for the database administrator and programmers to understand the data that you'll need for your Java application.

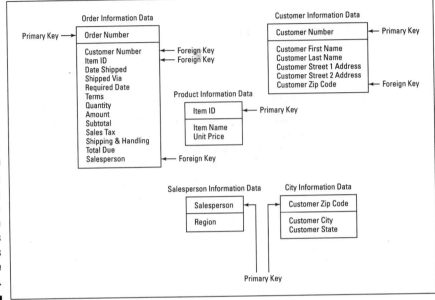

Figure 6-1:
A database
schema
diagram
contains
components
of the
database.

Description of Data for the Order Form Entity

Data Name	Data Type	Data Size
Customer First Name	Character	50
Customer Last Name	Character	50
Customer Street 1 Address	Alphanumeric	50
Customer Street 2 Address	Alphanumeric	50
Customer City	Character	50
Customer State	Character	2
Customer Zip Code	Alphanumeric	10
Customer Number	Alphanumeric	10
P.O. Number	Alphanumeric	10
Order Date Shipped	Date	10
Order Shipped Via	Alphanumeric	10
Order Required Date	Date	10
Order Terms	Alphanumeric	8
Order Quantity	Numeric	Set By DBMS
Product ID	Alphanumeric	10
Product Name	Alphanumeric	30
Product Unit Price	Numeric	Set By DBMS
Order Amount	Numeric	Set By DBMS
Order Subtotal	Numeric	Set By DBMS
Order Sales Tax	Numeric	Set By DBMS
Order Shipping & Handling	Numeric	Set By DBMS
Order Total Due	Numeric	Set By DBMS

Figure 6-2:
A data
dictionary
contains the
definition of
data used in
a database.

You'll find it easy to draw your database diagrams if you use graphical presentation software that enables you to draw boxes and move them around the page. I used Microsoft PowerPoint for the diagrams that you see in this book.

The method of developing methods

As a Java programmer, you probably have a good understanding of the meaning of a method. If you do, you can stop reading this section and jump to the next one. However, read on if you want me to refresh your memory and show you how methods are defined in a plan for your Java application.

A *method* is a task your application performs, such as calculating the number of products that were sold by your company last week. Database applications perform many tasks, each of which you must program as a method into the application.

Each task typically mimics one or more tasks that are performed in the operation of a business. For example, an employee might be assigned the task to review shipping orders for the previous week and then manually calculate the total units sold for each product.

To automate this manual task, create a method in your Java application to query the transaction database that contains shipping data. The Java application then would have the method calculate the number of units the company sold the previous week.

When planning a Java database application, you must review business operations and identify all the tasks that need to be performed by methods in your application. For each task you must

- **List the data and the source of the data required to perform the task:** Data can come from a database, can come from someone entering data into the application, or can be derived from calculating other data.

- **Identify processes that must be performed to complete the task:** A process is something done to the data, such as calculating an increase in salary.

- **List the processes in the order in which they must be performed:** I've found that a typical business task has several processes, each of which must be performed in succession.

- **Determine the types of results that occur after the task is completed:** You may have a number of conclusions once you complete a task. For example, the task might be completed error free or it may encounter an error during processing. For example, the database may not be available at the time data is needed for a process. You must identify all the possible results so that your Java application can respond properly to each one.

Write down each task. Once you define all the tasks, you must identify the order in which you would perform each task.

High-level tasks, such as those performed when someone chooses a selection from a menu, are independent from similar high-level tasks. That is, they aren't performed in a sequence. Instead, they are performed when an event occurs, such as a menu selection. These should not be connected with a line in your diagram.

Defining the Parts of Every Database Application

When you begin to create Java database applications, you'll soon discover a common thread among all applications. I discovered the similarities among database applications when I developed computer systems for the Wall Street investment banking firm Salomon, Inc.

After a while it seemed that I was building the same system over and over again with only the names of the columns changing within each database application. Although the business objective of each system was different, each database application employed the same basic four tasks:

 ✔ Inserting data into a database (see Chapter 12)

 ✔ Retrieving data from a database (see Chapter 13)

 ✔ Modifying data stored in a database (see Chapter 15)

 ✔ Deleting data from a database (see Chapter 16)

Take time to master these four common tasks found in every database application because you'll be using these tasks in every database application that you build.

Inserting data

The process of storing data into a database is called inserting data. Every database application has one or more methods that place new data into the database.

Sometimes new data is received directly from someone entering data into the application using the mouse and keyboard. This is referred to as data entry, which most of us have experienced whenever we order merchandise from an online store. The order form, shipping instructions, and other screens that pop up on our computer require us to enter data through these data-entry forms. The process of entering data is called data entry.

Other times, other applications transfer new data to the database. This is the method when your company directly deposits your pay into your checking account — and transfers some of your pay to the IRS database.

You must clearly identify the ways in which you intend to insert data into your database application and then write specifications for the Java method that will handle the task. Make sure that you consider

- **Validating data before inserting a new row of data into the database:** Don't assume the data that your application receives is accurate. Always set up a validation process that tests the accuracy of the data before you commit the data to the database (see the sidebar "Validation is more than stamping your hand" for more information).

- **Handling exceptions to the normal task of gathering and inserting data into the database:** Your application must be able to catch errors. Suppose that your application normally receives data electronically from another application in a data feed. However, there can come a time when the data feed doesn't send data because of a technical foul-up, a common experience in real-world applications. Your application shouldn't wait for the data feed. Instead, the application should signal an error and then continue with the next process that doesn't require the data feed.

Retrieving data

Probably one of the most important reasons for building a database application is to retrieve data you stored in the database. Your Java application must formulate a request using SQL and submit the request to the DBMS. The DBMS then searches the database and returns to your application just the data that you requested.

During the planning phase of your Java application, you must decide on the data that you'll need from the database and how you are going to formulate your request for that data. The nature of the business task will help you decide on the type of data you need to complete the task.

For example, if you want to count the number of widgets that were shipped last week, your application needs to see the quantity of widgets from each shipping order last week. The data is different for each application.

You must also determine in the planning phase how your application will obtain the data needed to build a request statement. For example, how will your application ask the database for last week's quantity of widgets that were shipped?

Validation is more than stamping your hand

A validation process catches errors in data that were destined to be inserted into the database before the insertion process begins. It's your job to devise rules that determine whether data is accurate; this isn't an easy job, as you'll discover.

Some rules are easy to enforce. For example, you need to determine whether data to be inserted into a Date column contains an actual date and appears in the date format required by the application. In this case, you can write Java statements to test the data.

Other rules are more difficult to enforce. Let's say that you want to prevent a large number from being inadvertently inserted into the Salary column of a database — unless that number correlates to my salary.

Here's the problem. The column that contains salary data will accept numeric data such as a salary or a large number. This means that the DBMS won't catch the error as it would when you insert a non-date into a Date column.

Here's the solution. Write Java statements that test whether the value of the data is reasonable — that is, does it make sense. Most salaries are within a range of values such as between $20,000 and $200,000. The actual salary range depends on your company. Therefore, your application can determine if the incoming salary data is less than $20,000 or greater than $200,000. If it is, the application should set aside the row of data that contains the salary as a possible error.

Typically, a database application uses an error table in the database to store questionable incoming data. A technician then examines the error table to determine whether the data really is in error. If it is, he corrects the data before resubmitting it to the database application for insertion into the database. If not, he inserts the data as is into the database.

Of course, you have no guarantee that the edits will prevent erroneous incoming data from being inserted into the database. For example, a salary could be within the acceptable range and still be incorrect. However, the validation process reduces the risk to an acceptable level.

Here are the common ways to gather data necessary for your application to create an SQL request:

- ✔ **Hard-code the request into your application:** *Hard-coding* is where you write specific search values directly into your program, such as specifying the date ranges that define last week. Avoid doing this because you'll need to change your program each time the search value changes.

- ✔ **Prompt someone to input the requested data into your application using the keyboard or mouse:** Search values can change each time the task is performed without you having to change your program. However, someone must be available to enter the data whenever the application retrieves data from the database.

✔ **Have your program calculate the search value:** You can write Java statements that let your application determine the search value without requiring input from someone or requiring you to change your program. For example, your application can determine today's date and calculate the beginning and ending date of last week, which it then can use as the search value for the SQL request to determine the number of widgets that were shipped last week.

✔ **Receive the search value from another application or from another method within your application:** Suppose your application must send delinquent notices to customers who have outstanding invoices. The accounts receivable system feeds the customer numbers of customers who should receive notices to your application. Your application must request the customer's name and address for each customer number so he or she can be sent a delinquent notice. This is an example of one application feeding data to another application.

Modifying data

Data in a database rarely remains unchanged because most data is fluid. You can expect data to change frequently for a variety of reasons — whenever a customer moves to a new address, changes his telephone number, or changes the name of his business.

Your application must be able to modify data in the database to reflect changes to the data. This ensures that you are maintaining an acceptable level of accuracy for the data stored in the database. Here are the steps that your application must perform to modify data:

✔ **Capture changes:** Identify how your application is going to receive new data. The two common ways are for someone to enter new data using a keyboard or mouse, or to receive updates from a feed from another application.

✔ **Retrieve the data currently in the database that is being updated:** This verifies that the modifications are actually updates to existing data rather than new data. Your application shouldn't assume that the update has a corresponding row in the database.

✔ **Validate changes:** Updates must also pass the same validation tests that you use to test new data before it's inserted into the database. Don't assume that updates are accurate. You can compare columns of current data to the updates as part of the validation test. Suppose that you're updating the Salary column of employees in the database. If the new salary is greater than 20 percent of the current salary, your application probably should hold off inserting the update until someone verifies the change.

✔ **Overwrite existing data with updated data:** Once the update passes the validation test, your application should replace the current data in the database with new data.

✔ **Record the update in a transaction log:** The application notes all changes to a database in a table called a *transaction log.* A transaction log contains a copy of the old data, a copy of the updates, the dates and times when it made the updates, and the login ID of the person or application who made the changes. You can use the transaction log to reverse changes to the database (see Chapter 22).

Some DBMSs automatically record changes to the database in a transaction log. In these cases, your application doesn't have to create and maintain a transaction log table.

Deleting data

You must prepare Java database applications to remove data from a table. Deleting data is a delicate task because it's often irreversible. That is, once you remove data from the database, you can't retrieve it later.

Your plan for your Java database application must establish rules for deleting data from the database. You should base these rules on the business rules you use to operate your business.

Here are some common factors that you need to consider when establishing rules to delete data:

✔ **Review your proposed rules with the appropriate business executives who will use your application:** I found that some data could freely be deleted while other data must be maintained for a fixed number of years or forever.

✔ **Determine who is authorized to delete data:** Very few employees should be authorized to remove data from a database because of the serious effect deleted data can have on business operations. Let the executive in charge of business operations tell you the names of employees authorized to remove data from the database.

✔ **Determine if data should be deleted or marked for deletion:** You can easily enable someone to recover deleted data if you mark data for deletion rather than actually deleting it. Create a Delete column in each table. Whenever a request is made to delete data, place an asterisk in the Delete column of that row. Ignore rows that contain an asterisk in the Delete column whenever a request is made to retrieve data. In this way, your application reacts as if the row was deleted, but your application can always recover deleted data by removing the asterisk from the deleted column. Deleted items can be recovered as well if the DBMS uses a transaction log.

Test your newfound knowledge

1. What is the purpose of validating data before the data is inserted into a database?

   a. It helps to maintain the transaction log.

   b. It demonstrates the power of being a programmer.

   c. It ensures that your boss will get his salary red-flagged when he tries to increase it in the database.

   d. It stops erroneous data from getting into the database.

2. What is a benefit of planning your Java database application?

   a. It shows your boss that you don't need help to build the Java application.

   b. It justifies a trip to the beach in Hawaii where you can kick back and think about the application.

   c. Most problems are resolved before programmers and other technicians begin to develop the application.

   d. A well-illustrated plan tells everyone that you know how to design a Java database application.

Answers: (1) d. (2) c.

A transaction log is a table in the database that contains rows of data that were modified or deleted before they were modified or deleted. You can use the rows in the transaction log to restore a modified or deleted row.

Some DBMSs may have the "marked for deletion" feature built into their databases.

Describing Your Plan for All to See

The plan for your database application should be written clearly so that programmers and technicians who will help you develop the application will know exactly how you want the database application to work.

The objective of your plan is to provide a recipe that describes in detail all the components necessary to build the application. Therefore, the plan must

> ✔ **Be written using words that everyone can understand:** Use the same terms that you use to tell someone about your idea for the database application. Programmers and technicians will be able to translate those words into technical concepts they need to carry out your plan.

✔ **Specify the details of every aspect of the application:** Avoid using vague terms because then you'll be leaving it up to programmers and technicians to interpret what you really mean. This tends to lead to confusion and results in the application not performing the way that you intended.

✔ **Use illustrations to convey complex concepts or ideas:** Tables, charts, and other types of illustrations make a plan easier to understand than if you try to describe an idea — such as a database schema — in words.

✔ **Use lists and steps rather than paragraphs:** Technicians and programmers can quickly comprehend the details of your plan if you minimize the number of words you use in your plan. I've found the best way to do this is by using bulleted lists rather than paragraphs.

Writing down business rules

Each method in your plan translates business rules into a specific sequence of Java statements that are executed whenever the method is called from within your application. Your job is to convey the business rules to the programmer without writing the program yourself.

You do this by writing a draft of each method using pseudo code. Pseudo code isn't a formal computer language. Instead, it's a combination of English sentences and fragments of sentences that organizes the method into specific tasks. Here is an example:

```
If ( NewSalary < 20000 || NewSalary >200000)
    {
        Insert incoming data into error table
    }
else
    {
        Insert incoming data into database
    }
```

You'll notice that I used a mixture of everyday English and statements such as the Java if statement.

You can probably read my pseudo code and know exactly how to translate it into Java statements because you already know how to write a Java program. Other programmers who may be helping you write your database application also know how to rewrite your pseudo code into Java statements.

Be sure that your pseudo code contains all the steps needed to perform the task required by the method and that each step appears in the order in which you want the application to perform it.

Giving everyone a paper and an electronic version

There isn't any special program that you need to use to create the plan for your database application. I use Microsoft PowerPoint because it lets me easily combine words and illustrations into one document. However, you should make your plan available on paper and electronically to accommodate everyone who works on the project with you. Some technicians prefer to have a printed copy so they read your plan whenever they are away from their computers. Others prefer to quickly bring up the plan on their computer screens.

Programmers find using an electronic copy of your pseudo code beneficial when converting pseudo code to Java code. They'll copy your pseudo code into a program file and then substitute appropriate lines of your pseudo code with the corresponding Java code. Coding an application goes much faster using this method than if a programmer has to write a method from scratch.

Calling in the Professionals

Building a professional database application requires the skills of many technicians, so you shouldn't expect to create a database application without help. The only exception is when you create the sample database applications in this book.

Companies purposely restrict database programmers from performing all the chores necessary to build a database application. The reasons are many, but these restrictions are primarily to achieve the most efficient performance from a database.

A database programmer is restricted to

- Planning for the database application
- Inserting data into a database
- Retrieving data from a database
- Modifying data contained in a database
- Deleting data from a database

Rarely will a company tell a programmer of these limitations. Instead, the database administrator simply restricts the programmer's access to the database to only those features mentioned above.

The DBMS controls the databases. A DBMS is a complex product that typically needs to be tweaked and tuned to deliver the best response to users throughout the company. A specialist called a database administrator has the skills that are necessary to finely adjust the DBMS.

The database administrator has the job of making sure that the database is operational during business hours and properly maintained so that no one needs to wait too long for their request for data to be fulfilled.

Here are the common roles that a database administrator will perform in the creation of databases for your application:

- Advise you on the most efficient database scheme
- Advise you on the selection of indexes and index keys
- Build the database
- Build tables, although you'll be able to build tables yourself for your own database
- Drop (remove) tables
- Drop (remove) the database
- Back up the database
- Restore the database from a backup database

Part II
Java Database Connection

The 5th Wave — By Rich Tennant

"I STARTED DESIGNING DATABASE SOFTWARE SYSTEMS AFTER SEEING HOW EASY IT WAS TO DESIGN OFFICE FURNITURE."

In this part . . .

It's amazing how a Java application or applet can connect to practically any database located on a corporate computer network, the Internet, an intranet, or an extranet. If you have ever wondered how this is done, you'll find this part fascinating.

This part presents the steps necessary to open a database so a program can retrieve and manipulate information stored in the database without someone having to intervene. You'll also learn how to use this bit of cyber-magic in your own Java program.

Nearly every Java program needs to access data. After reading this part, you'll know how this is done and how to link your Java application or applet to any database around the world that you are authorized to access.

Chapter 7

JDBC in English

In This Chapter

▶ Looking inside at JDBC

▶ Introducing the types of JDBC drivers

▶ Checking out the three-tier database application

▶ Working with JDBC and ODBC

*J*DBC is unlike many computer terms that you've learned in that JDBC is an acronym that you don't pronounce. It isn't like DOS, which sounds like a real word although it's an acronym for disk operating system. Instead, you simply say the letters in JDBC. And those letters are the most important letters that you need to know when building a Java database application because JDBC connects your application to the database.

A Java database application is unable to directly communicate with a database management system (DBMS) because it doesn't know all the idiosyncrasies of each DBMS. Rather than teach these subtle differences, DBMS manufacturers provide an interface between their product and Java applications called the JDBC driver.

The JDBC driver is a program that

✔ Creates a connection between a Java database application and the DBMS

✔ Translates SQL statements between the Java database application and the DBMS

✔ Returns data from the database to the Java database application

✔ Closes the connection between a Java database application and the DBMS

I'll give you an insider's look at JDBC in this chapter and show you how to find and install the JDBC driver for your DBMS.

Whenever I use the term Java application throughout this chapter, I also mean Java applet.

JDBC: A Word You Can't Pronounce

Back in 1996, Sun Microsystems expanded their Java programming language to include database connectivity. Until then, Java applications were unable to interact with any DBMS. This meant that you could build a fancy Java application, but the application couldn't interact with a database.

Engineers at Sun Microsystems remedied the problem with the creation of the JDBC specification that describes all the details on how the Java programming language will connect to and communicate with a database. The JDBC specification has since become the standard for Java database connectivity.

You don't need to learn the JDBC specification unless you're going to build a JDBC device driver for a DBMS product. Very few programmers actually do this, so I don't think you'll be building a JDBC device driver anytime soon.

However, I'm sure you'll find the concept of the JDBC specification interesting since you can use this knowledge to show off in front of your colleagues.

The driver

A driver, such as the JDBC driver, is similar to the rubber molding that fits between your car body and the car door. Different machinery manufactures the car body and the door based on the automobile designer's specifications.

The specifications fit within a range of acceptable measurements called *tolerance*. As long as the size of the body and door are within tolerance, the rubber molding will fill any gaps between the body and the door. A gap will appear if either the body or door is outside the tolerance range.

A *driver* is a program that fills the gap between applications or devices. For example, a printer driver fills the language gap between the computer's operating system and the software that runs the printer. The JDBC driver has a similar role between the Java application and the DBMS (see Figure 7-1).

The specification

Engineers at Sun Microsystems wrote the specifications for the JDBC driver. The specifications define the format Java uses to present queries and statements to the DBMS. Likewise, specifications also describe the format of the response that Java expects from the DBMS.

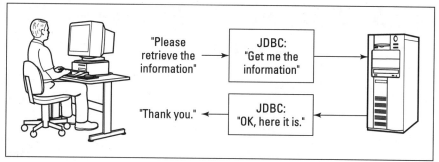

Figure 7-1: A driver translates statements into commands understood by a database.

This situation is similar to how your boss tells you to write a program. She tells you the data that will be input into the program and the data that she expects to receive from the program. Your boss doesn't care how you fulfill her request.

Each DBMS manufacturer is responsible for building a JDBC driver that translates data given to the driver by the Java application into a format that the DBMS needs to process the request.

The driver then formats the results of processing into the form of data that the Java application expects to receive. As long as the driver conforms to the JDBC specifications created by Sun Microsystems, the DBMS can be used in any Java application.

JDBC is independent

JDBC makes the Java database application totally independent from the DBMS since the burden of interfacing with a Java application rests with the manufacturer of the DBMS.

You use standard SQL statements to make your requests for data. You embed the SQL statements into the Java application (check out Chapter 8 for more on this). Java sends the SQL statements to the JDBC device driver that handles communications with the database.

The Java application doesn't care what kind of DBMS is being used to store and retrieve data. This feature enables Java database applications to use any database as long as

- The manufacturer of the database has created a JDBC driver.
- The JDBC driver is installed on the computer used to access data from the database.
- The JDBC driver conforms to standards set down by Sun Microsystems.

Inside JDBC: An Application Programmer's Guide

JDBC is more than a driver that connects a Java application to a database. It's also an *application program interface (API)*. An API consists of classes that contain methods and data members that a Java programmer can use to interact with the JDBC driver.

You can get the Java JDBC application program interface with the Java Software Development kit that you can download from the Sun Microsystems Web site or purchase from third-party vendors such as Borland's J Builder.

I show you how to use the Java JDBC application program interface in the next chapter. For now, simply understand that the JDBC API will let you create Java statements that

- Identify the database to use with your application
- Log into the database using a user ID and password
- Send SQL statements to the database
- Retrieve results by querying the database

The JDBC API has two layers. The first layer is the API you use in your Java application to interact with the database. The other API is the JDBC manager driver API, which is responsible for sending SQL statements to and receiving responses back from the JDBC driver. Don't concern yourself with the JDBC manager driver API because this is transparent when you use the JDBC API.

Introducing the JDBC driver types

The Sun Microsystems JDBC specification classifies JDBC drivers into four groups called *types*. Each group addresses a specific need for communicating with various kinds of DBMS.

- **Type 1 JDBC to ODBC driver:** JDBC translates requests from the application to the format required by *Open Database Connection* (ODBC), which in turn communicates the request to the DBMS (see "Understanding the differences between JDBC and ODBC" for more on ODBC). The other name for Type 1 JDBC drivers is a JDBC/ODBC bridge (see Figure 7-2). The Java Software Development Kit gives you a Type 1 JDBC driver.

  The JDBC/ODBC bridge is fine to use when you're developing a database application. In fact, you'll use the bridge in examples throughout this book. However, I suggest that you avoid using the bridge in a mission-critical database application because of possible performance problems. Instead, use one of the other types of drivers from this section.

✔ **Type 2 Java/Native Code driver:** Type 2 JDBC drivers use a combination of Java classes and platform-specific code, which means that you need to use a class provided by the DBMS manufacturer along with Java classes for the library. Your database administrator can help you obtain the necessary classes if the database uses a Type 2 JDBC driver. The disadvantage is that you may lose some portability of your code due to the platform-specific code.

✔ **Type 3 Java Protocol:** Type 3 JDBC drivers translate queries into JDBC-formatted statements, which are then converted to the format required by the DBMS (refer to Figure 7-1). This is the most commonly used JDBC driver.

✔ **Type 4 Database Protocol:** Type 4 JDBC drivers forgo converting Java statements into JDBC-formatted statements. Instead, Java statements are translated directly into the format understood by the DBMS.

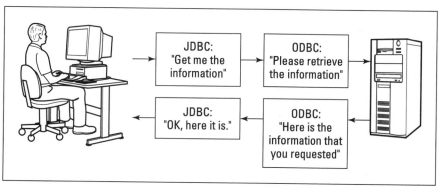

Figure 7-2:
The
JDBC/ODBC
bridge
connects
JDBC to
ODBC.

Understanding the differences between JDBC and ODBC

The concept of using a driver to make a database application independent of the DBMS wasn't conceived by Sun Microsystems. It was an outgrowth of Microsoft's desire to enable applications written in the C programming language to connect to various databases.

Microsoft created the *ODBC*, which became the general model used for Sun Microsystems' JDBC driver. ODBC defines how to ask for data from a database or how to update or delete data in a database from applications written in the C programming language. ODBC has since been used to connect applications written in other languages to various databases.

You're probably curious to know why Sun Microsystems simply didn't decide to adopt the ODBC specifications rather than create their own. Some say that Sun Microsystems felt that the ODBC command set was limiting and couldn't handle complex queries.

Another reason for not adopting ODBC was because it uses conventions that Java doesn't use. For example, ODBC uses pointers, which you won't find in Java. The C and C++ programming languages use pointers to reference memory addresses.

Of course, some programmers believe that the rivalry between Sun Microsystems and Microsoft probably had more to do with Sun Microsystems skirting ODBC than technical considerations.

Using JDBC

You can use JDBC for applications, applets, and servlets. However, applets can access databases that are located on a server but not on the local drive. This is because a computer that uses the applet will consider it untrustworthy by default.

You also must be aware of a future restriction involving JDBC. The database must reside on the same server as the applet; otherwise, the applet won't be able to connect to the database once the browser downloads it.

Typically, the location of the database can become a problem with Web-based database applets. However, you can work around the location problem by using a proxy server. A *proxy server* creates the appearance that applets, databases, and other files are located on it when these files are really on other servers.

Here's how you can dupe Java. Assign the URL for the Web site to the proxy server. Let the proxy server reroute requests to the appropriate server, such as the database server. The browser will assume that all files downloaded to the browser are coming from the same server.

Java database applications don't have the restrictions found in a database applet. Therefore, I suggest that you build a Java application instead of an applet whenever possible to avoid the hassles of working around the applet restrictions.

The network and database administrators in your company can set up the proxy and database servers to work around the limitations posed by database applets.

The Three-Tier Database Application Model

With the onset of Web technology, an alternative to the client/server model arose: *the three-tier database application model*. The three-tier database application model has, well, three tiers that work together:

- **Client:** The client is typically the PC running the browser or another computer that the end user of the data works with.

- **Middleware:** Middleware is another application — such as a servlet, JavaBeans, or Common Gateway Interface (CGI) program — that is called by the client.

  A *servlet* is a Java program that runs on a server. A *CGI program* is a program running on a server that is typically written using a scripting language such as Perl.

- **Database server:** A database server is a computer connected to a network that stores the database and responds to requests for data from clients.

Here's how the three-tier database application model works:

1. **A Java program running on a client needs data from the database.**

2. **A client requests data to the middleware program.**

3. **The middleware program creates an SQL request.**

4. **The middleware program sends the SQL request to the database server.**

5. **The database server returns the results of the query to the middleware program.**

6. **The middleware program forwards the results to the client.**

Sometimes the middleware program might process the results before sending them to the client. For example, the client may want to summarize sales data from three regions. Each region has its own database. The middleware can retrieve sales data from each of the three regional databases and then combine them into a final result before passing the data to the client.

The three-tier database application model might also use remote-method invocation technology (RMI) to either retrieve data or process retrieved data.

Let me quickly review a couple of basic Java terms to refresh your mind before I explain remote-method invocation. Real objects, such as an order form, are defined as a Java class. A Java class has two general components: data and methods.

Data consists of data elements that are used by the class methods for processing. A class method defines functionality that is associated with the class. Let's say that an order form class defines the data and functionality (methods) that are associated with an order form. The order form number is an example of data, and the search method is a functionality that locates a particular order form in the database.

Keep in mind that a class is like a template in that it's a description of something. However, a class isn't alive. A class comes alive when you create an instance of a class. The instance is referred to as an object that can be used in your program.

I'll stop my thumbnail review of Java here. You can further brush up on your Java basics by reading *Java 2 For Dummies,* 3rd Edition, by Aaron Walsh (Hungry Minds, Inc.).

A remote-method invocation is the technology that enables your program to call a method of an object that is located on a computer other than your own computer. Let's say that your Java program is a client that needs to retrieve data on a particular order form. Your application can call the search method of the order form object that is located on middleware using RMI.

Basically, the client in a three-tier architecture can get information from the database server in two ways: through servlets on the middleware or through RMI.

The technique for making a remote-method invocation is beyond the scope of this book. I suggest that you visit www.java.sun.com for details.

Test your newfound knowledge

1. What is a JDBC/ODBC bridge?

a. It's a new laser dental replacement technique.

b. It enables ODBC to use JDBC to connect to a database.

c. It enables JDBC to use ODBC to connect to a database.

d. It's a connection between a database and an index.

2. What is a driver?

a. A program that converts data between formats required by two other programs.

b. A kind of golf club.

c. A request for data from a client to a database.

d. A result of a query.

Answers: (1) c. (2) a.

Getting Started with JDBC

You need to make a few preparations before you can write your first Java database application (see Chapter 8). Whenever I hear the term "preparations" used in the context of my computer, I cringe at the thought because it seems to be a euphemism for getting down and technical with my computer.

Chances are good that you also have similar feelings, especially if you ever installed new software on your computer that didn't work well. You had to back out the software and hope that there wasn't any permanent damage to your computer.

The preparations for writing your first Java database application aren't this drastic. I prepared several computers and didn't run into any problems. Here's what you need to do to set up your computer for a Java database application:

1. **Install JDBC.**

    JDBC comes with the JDK, which you can download from www.java. sun.com. You can also download JDBC separately from the same site if you already have an older version of the JDK installed on your computer or if you are using Java application development software that doesn't come with JDBC. Follow the directions that come with the JDBC to install it on your computer.

    I've found that most Java application development software comes with at least the JDBC/ODBC bridge. You can also obtain JDBC from the manufacturer of the DBMS that you are using for the database for your application.

    The JDBC/ODBC bridge works within Windows and the Solaris operating system, but doesn't support Microsoft J++ and JDBC2.

2. **Install a database.**

    You must have access to a database. I'll be using Microsoft Access for the examples in this book. You can use a database such as Oracle, Sybase, or others that might be available on your company's network. Contact your company's database administrator for details on how to locate these DBMSs and how to obtain authorization to use them.

If you don't have a database available to you, you may want to download an evaluation copy of the PointBase database, which is used in a variety of applications including wireless applications. Visit www.pointbase.com to find out more data about this database.

Is JDBC installed?

You might be scratching your head wondering if you already have JDBC installed on your computer. The quickest way of finding out is to use the Find feature in Windows if you are using a Windows-based computer.

The Find feature will search the hard drive or those drives that you select, looking for the search value that you enter into the Find dialog box. The bottom of the Find dialog box will display any file or folder that contains JDBC in the name.

Once you're sure that JDBC resides on your computer and that you have a working database, you're ready to write your first Java database application and connect to the database. I'll show you how to do this in the next chapter.

If you're working on any computer other than a Windows computer, ask your database administrator to help you determine whether you have JDBC on your computer.

Chapter 8

Having the Right Connections Gets You to the Database

*W*ith the right connections, your Java database application can tap into a wealth of data stored in online databases within your company or around the world. As long as your application has the proper authorization, it can access practically any type of data available, including financial and personnel data.

Your job is to connect your application to a database using the correct Java statements. Making the connection between the database and your application involves the clever use of many of the concepts you learned when you first began programming in Java, so expect to see some familiar terms and concepts.

Once you connect your application to the database, you can

✔ Create a query using SQL

✔ Insert the query into a statement that requests data from a database

✔ Retrieve the results of a query

✔ Display the results onscreen

In this chapter, I show you how to write a Java program that performs these functions. You can then use the program to test the connection to the database.

Using JDBC to Program

Database programming is made easy with the use of the JDBC classes from the java.sql package. Engineers who built the JDBC classes have written most of the code that you need to perform the grunt work of database programming — that is, the low-level programming necessary to connect to a database, transmit SQL queries, and manipulate data returned from a database.

With all the nitty-gritty work done for you, you just need to create objects from the JDBC classes and then call methods associated with these objects in your Java application to interact with the database. You use the JDBC classes to

- Create a connection to the database
- Create statements
- Execute queries
- Display metadata — information that describes data, such as names used as column headings in a table
- Display values of rows
- Move among data returned from the database
- Terminate the connection to the database

Once data is retrieved from the database, your application is able to use the data with standard Java features, similar to how you use data stored in variables. For example, you can place the results of a query in a table onscreen.

Looking at the database programming big picture

Let's take a cook's tour of the steps involved in writing a Java database program before you get down and dirty writing code. The first component of a Java database program is the data necessary for the program to open a connection with the database.

Typically, you need three pieces of data:

- **The location of the database:** The location is the Uniform Resource Locator (URL) that points to the database that the program needs to access.

✔ **The user identifier:** The user identifier is the user ID that identifies your application to the security program that protects the database from unauthorized entry. You can program the user ID directly into your program. Alternatively, your program can prompt the user for a user ID, which is then passed along to the security program. In rare situations, such as a personal database, a user ID isn't required.

✔ **The user password:** The user password functions similarly to the user ID and can be hard-coded into the program or dynamically created by prompting the user for the password. Likewise, a password may not be necessary for personal databases.

You use the URL, user ID, and password along with the getConnection() method to open a connection to the database. Once the connection is successful, your program creates an SQL expression as a Java String. The query is made part of a JDBC database statement, which is then sent to the database using the executeQuery() method.

The database returns data in a ResultSet. You can think of a ResultSet as a table that contains columns and rows of data retrieved from the database. The ResultSet is assigned to elements of a Vector, which is an array whose size changes dynamically as data is assigned to the array. The Vector then displays all or selected columns and rows on the screen.

Receiving errors

Your Java database program can't assume that everything works perfectly when connecting to and retrieving data from a database. Sometimes you'll find that the database or the computer network isn't cooperating as you had hoped when you wrote the program.

Examples of database programs shown in this book use a local database that doesn't require you to connect to the database over a network. However, in the real world, a database server may store many databases, and you need to access those databases across a computer network. This can pose problems since the database and the network are under someone else's control, such as the database administrator and the network administrator.

What this means to you is that the database and/or the network may not be available when your Java database program needs to access the database. Therefore, your program may receive an error instead of the data it expected.

Many methods of classes in the sql package throw an SQLException whenever an error occurs. You must build contingencies into your program to catch errors when they occur and then properly respond to these errors. Chapter 9 shows you how to catch and handle SQL errors.

Stepping through the results

After your program calls the executeQuery() method and passes the SQL expression defining the data that you want to retrieve from the database to it, JDBC submits the query to the DBMS and returns the results.

A Java database program accesses one row at a time from the ResultSet, beginning with the row before the first row that contains data. A virtual cursor points to the current row. I call the cursor "virtual" because it's hidden from view but functions similarly to a cursor in a spreadsheet program.

Your program can move the virtual cursor to the next or previous row in the ResultSet by calling the appropriate method (Chapter 9 explains this). You can't use the traditional cursor keys on the keyboard to move the virtual cursor because SQL objects, not keyboard commands, control cursor movements.

Once your program positions the virtual cursor on the row you want, your application can reference data in each of the columns for use in your program. For example, your program could determine if a customer account is overdue by referencing the invoice data in a column in the customer's row using a method of an SQL object. Your program could then subtract the invoice date from the current date to determine if the account is overdue.

Creating the Database

Before writing your first Java database program, you must prepare by creating a database that you can use to test whether or not you are able to connect your program to the database. You can use any database for this purpose. I use Microsoft Access throughout this book because many readers have Microsoft Access already installed on their computers if they have the Professional Edition of Microsoft Office.

If you don't have Microsoft Access on your computer, you can choose to use any database to test your first Java database program, including

- ✔ Oracle
- ✔ DB2
- ✔ Sybase
- ✔ Informix

I strongly urge you to contact your database administrator for assistance connecting to any database that is located on a network. The database administrator knows whether JDBC is installed and, if not, knows how to install it.

Furthermore, the database administrator is likely to be the only person who can create a new database and give you access to that database. So you can avoid any hassles by asking for help now, before you begin writing your Java database application.

Making the sample table

Create a table similar to the one I built for Figure 8-1. I call the database *customers* and the table *customername*. The table has two columns: FirstName and LastName. Both columns are of the Text data type and can have a maximum of 50 characters.

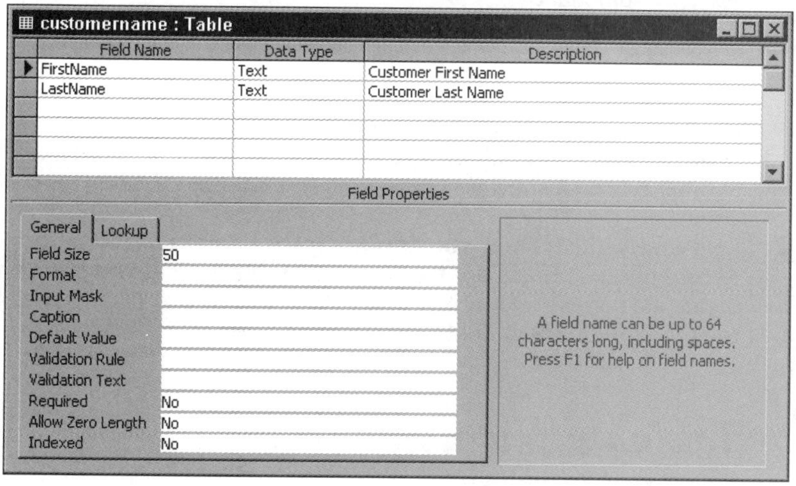

Figure 8-1:
Create a
database
called
customers
and a table
called
customer-
name that
contain
these fields.

We'll be using the database to test the connection between the database and your first Java database program. Therefore, you can call your database, table, and columns anything you wish and you can use more than two columns in your table.

I'll be more particular about the name of database, tables, and columns in the other examples in later chapters because you'll need to have the proper database structure to learn how to retrieve and manipulate data in a Java database program. But, for now, you'll be using the same database to retrieve all the rows and columns.

Once you create the database and table, insert data into two new rows in the table so you'll have data to retrieve from the database. I placed the names Bob Smith and Mary Jones in the table (see Figure 8-2). You can insert these names into your table or create your own names for this exercise.

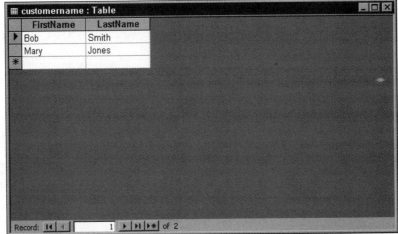

Figure 8-2:
Enter data
into two
rows of the
customer-
name table.

Don't be concerned about creating a primary key or secondary keys for this table because you won't be searching for particular data or linking the table to another table. I'll show you how to do this later in the book (see Chapter 11).

I purposely didn't show you how to create a database and table in Microsoft Access because that's not the purpose of this book. If you don't know how to create a database and table, I suggest reading a copy of *Microsoft Access For Dummies,* by John Kaufeld (Hungry Minds, Inc.).

Taking a few notes

Whenever you create a database and tables, you should write down key data about them so you can easily reference the data when writing your Java database program.

Normally I jot down:

- ✔ The database name
- ✔ The table name
- ✔ The column names
- ✔ The data type of each column
- ✔ The size of each column
- ✔ The names of primary and secondary indexes
- ✔ The key values of primary and secondary indexes
- ✔ The directory path to the database

Some DBMSs have a built-in report feature that prints a copy of this data so you don't need to make a hand-written copy. In either case, you'll find that having this data handy will save you time looking up the data in the DBMS while you're in the middle of creating your Java database program.

Connecting the Database to ODBC

Since you are using Microsoft Access or a PC database as a local database on a PC, you will need to use the JDBC/ODBC bridge to connect the Java database program to the database (see Chapter 7). I'll show you how to use the JDBC/ODBC bridge in the sample program in Chapter 9.

Before you can use the JDBC/ODBC bridge, you must define the database so that the ODBC driver can locate the database when requests for data are made from your Java database program. You use the ODBC Data Source Administrator to define the database to the ODBC driver.

The *ODBC Data Source Administrator* is a utility program that is part of Windows and is used to associate ODBC files with the ODBC driver. Once ODBC "knows" of a file that you'll be using for the connection test, such as the Microsoft Access database file, the ODBC driver is able to locate the file when an application program calls for it.

Here's how the ODBC driver connection works:

1. **Your Java database application opens a connection to a database by sending the JDBC/ODBC bridge data about the database, such as the database name, user ID, and password.**

2. **The ODBC driver receives this data and looks up the data source reference in a file maintained by the ODBC Data Source Administrator.**

3. **The data source reference contains the complete path and the database file name, which is used by the ODBC driver to communicate with the database.**

You don't need to define the database to the ODBC driver if the DBMS you are using came with a JDBC driver. In this case, you can directly reference the JDBC driver in your Java database program.

Define a database to the ODBC driver

Once you have created the database, you need to use the ODBC Data Source Administrator to define the database to the ODBC driver. I found this process to be fairly direct, since the ODBC utility walks you through each stage of the process.

Before you begin, you need to know the name of the database and the directory path with the location of the folder that contains the database. You can manually search your hard drive for the location of the database or ask your database administrator for help if you are using a networked database.

Here's how to define the database to the ODBC driver:

1. **Select ODBC 32 from the Windows Control Panel to display the ODBC Data Source Administrator.**

2. **Select the Add button to add a new User Data Source (see Figure 8-3).**

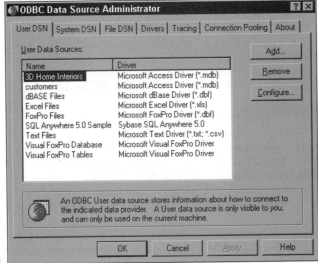

Figure 8-3: Select the ODBC Data Source Administrator from the Control Panel.

3. **Select the drive that you wish to update.**

   I selected the Microsoft Access Drive because I'll be using a Microsoft Access database, but you should select the appropriate driver for your database (see Figure 8-4).

   You'll need to install the driver for your DBMS if you don't find the driver on the list.

4. **Enter the Data Source Name in the ODBC Microsoft Access Setup dialog box (see Figure 8-5).**

   This is the name that you'll use in your Java database program when you connect to the database. You can enter a description of the data source to remind you of its purpose (optional).

5. **Click the Select button and locate the directory path and the name of the database. When you click OK, you'll see the directory path and database name appear on the ODBC Microsoft Access Setup dialog box.**

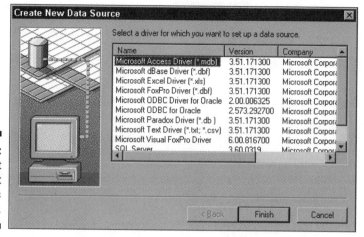

Figure 8-4:
Select
Microsoft
Access
Driver.

Figure 8-5:
Enter the
Data Source
Name (used
by program)
and
description.
Then click
the Select
button.
Locate and
select the
database.

6. **Click the Advanced button to display the Set Advanced Options dialog box. Enter the login name and password, and click OK.**

   Make a note of your login name and password because you'll need to include them in your Java database program whenever you open a connection to the database.

7. **Click OK when you see the ODBC Microsoft Access Setup dialog box.**

8. **Click Finish when you see the Create New Data Source dialog box.**

Test your newfound knowledge

1. What is the purpose of defining a database to ODBC?

   a. Because it's the polite thing to do.

   b. So the ODBC driver knows where to look for data when it receives a request from JDBC.

   c. So JDBC knows how to translate a request into a format the ODBC understands.

   d. So you can determine whether the database is Microsoft Access.

2. How is the Data Source Name used by ODBC?

   a. It identifies the program that makes the request for data from the database.

   b. It identifies the type of database that is being used by the program.

   c. It's the name your program uses to identify the database connection to open.

   d. It's the name of the person who entered the data into the database.

Answers: (1) b. (2) b.

Chapter 9

Writing Your First Java Database Program

In This Chapter

▶ Connecting to a database

▶ Requesting data from a database

▶ Handling errors

▶ Displaying data from a database

L adies and gentlemen, start your editors!

Your first Java program will retrieve all the rows from the customers database that you built previously in Chapter 8. This may not seem very useful, but you must admit this exercise is better than writing a program that displays "Hello, World."

You should write this program for three reasons:

✔ You get your feet wet writing a Java database program.

✔ You test whether you have the JDBC driver, the ODBC driver, and the JDBC/ODBC bridge installed properly on your computer.

✔ You learn the basic components of a Java database program.

The program is called conxtest.java, which is short for connection test. This chapter lists the code for reference, so I'll explain how the program works. You can enter the code into your editor for testing or you can download the program from www.dummies.com/extras/Java2DataProg.

The Program: Piece by Piece

The conxtest.java program uses what I like to call the "divide and conquer" approach to programming. That is, the program is grouped into logical components with each one handling a specific functionality necessary to access and interact with a database.

Each functional group within the program becomes a method, which the program defines. As each of these functionalities is needed, the appropriate method in the program calls them.

Here are the methods I used for the conxtest.java program because they handle functionality that is common to Java database programs:

✔ Connecting to the database and sending the query

✔ Displaying the results on the screen

✔ Moving down the ResultSet

✔ Disconnecting from the database

Some Java database programmers might use groupings that are different from those I present here. You can create your own groupings, depending on the needs of your program.

Study and experiment with the conxtest.java program before creating your own functional groupings. The conxtest.java program gives you a good foundation from which you can build your own Java database program.

In this chapter I review each method separately. The complete working program appears at the end of this chapter.

Connecting to the database and sending a query

The constructor of the Java database application carries out the database connectivity and execution of the query. The constructor is the first method executed whenever an object of the constructor's class is created.

A *constructor* is the method of a class that is called automatically whenever an object of the class is created.

The constructor has three segments (see Listing 9-1). Each segment handles a particular step in the process of connecting to the database and requesting data from the database. Here are the segments:

base

showing the results of the query

uctor

```
                          jdbc:odbc:customers";
                       = "jim";
                     d = "keogh";
                   Request;
                   lts;

                   ame( "sun.jdbc.odbc.JdbcOdbcDriver");

                   ager.getConnection(url,userID,password);

                   tFoundException error) {
                   .println("Unable to load the JDBC/ODBC
                   + error);
                   (1);

                   tion error) {
                   .println("Cannot connect to the
                   + error);
                   (2);


                 y = "Select * FROM customername";

                 = Database.createStatement();

        Results = DataRequest.executeQuery (query );

        Display (Results);

        DataRequest.close();
    }

    catch ( SQLException error ){
        System.err.println("SQL error." + error);
```

(continued)

Listing 9-1 *(continued)*

```
        System.exit(3);
    }

    setSize (500, 200);
    show();
}
```

The Constructor walk-about: Making the connection

The first three lines in the constructor assign data needed to access the database to `String` objects, which are later used to connect to the database. The `url` String contains a reference to the data source (`jdbc:odbc:customers`).

If you're using a database on a network, you'll be using something like `JDBC:oracle:customers`. Contact your database administrator for the specific syntax to use with your database.

The first reference tells the program that you'll be using the `jdbc` driver, which will be the `odbc` drive. You'll notice that this is really the JDBC/ODBC bridge (see Chapter 7). The last reference is the name of the Data Source Name that the ODBC Data Source Administrator defined (see Chapter 8). Likewise, the ODBC Data Source also defines the user ID and password.

The program then tries to connect to the database by initially loading the database driver. The `Class.forName("sun.jdbc.odbc.JdbcOdbcDriver")` performs this. `JdbcOdbcDriver` is a class contained in the `sun.jdbc.odbc` package.

A *package* is a collection of Java classes. You must import the appropriate packages into your program for every class that is not defined within the program. See the `import` statements in the full listing of the code at the end of the chapter.

The program also tries to connect to the database using the `getConnection()` method. The `getConnection()` method is a member of the `DriverManager` class, which you can find in the java.sql package.

The `getConnection()` method uses the `url`, `userID`, and `password` to connect to the database. A reference to the database is assigned to the Database object. The `Database` object is an object of the `Connection` class.

The `Database` object is defined outside the constructor as a private member of the `conxtest` class. You can see the definition in Listing 9-5 at the end of this chapter.

Two errors can occur: one when the constructor tries to load the database driver and another when the constructor tries to connect to the database. The constructor traps both errors by using the catch{} block.

The first catch{} block traps the ClassNotFoundExeception that will occur if the program is unable to load the database driver. The java.lang package defines the ClassNotFoundException. When the program detects this error, it displays a message telling you about the error. The program then closes and returns a value of 1 to the operating system. The variable error contains the actual error that occurred.

Traditionally, programmers send a value to the operating system whenever a program stops running. If the program ends successfully, it returns a value of 0. The program returns a value other than 0 if it detects an error. Each program has unique error code values. In the conxtest.java program, a return value of 1 means the JDBC/ODBC bridge couldn't be loaded. A return value of 2 means that a connection cannot be made to the database. I'll tell you about the other return values when I describe them in the program.

The second catch{} block traps an SQLException, which occurs whenever there is a problem using an SQL command or query. In this example, the command to connect to the database failed. The java.sql package defines the SQLException.

The Constructor walk-about: Sending the query

Once the program has successfully connected with the database, it creates and executes an SQL query to retrieve data from the database. First, the program creates two objects that are needed to execute the query: the Statement object and the ResultSet object. The java.sql package defines both objects.

The program uses the Statement object as a kind of envelope for the query, and the ResultSet references data returned from the database. DataRequest is the name of the Statement object, and Results is the name of the ResultSet object.

Within the try{} block, the program assigns the SQL expression to the String query object. Words and characters within the SQL expression String query consist of SQL language syntax. In this example, I tell the database to return all the columns and rows from the customername table of the database using the connection we established in the previous segment of the constructor (see "The constructor walk-about: making the connection").

The SQL expression contains the SQL query. Here's what the SQL expression means:

✔ The SELECT statement defines the columns that you want to retrieve from the database.

✔ The asterisk is a wild card indicating any column. In later examples in the book you'll replace the asterisk with the names of columns that you want to see.

✔ The FROM clause specifies the table from which the columns are to be retrieved.

Next, the program uses the createStatement() method of the Database object (see "The constructor walk-about: Making the connection"), which returns a reference to the new statement (DataRequest). The executeQuery() method of the new statement passes the String query to the database.

The DBMS receives and processes the SQL statement and then returns the requested data, which is assigned to the Results object. The Results object is passed to the Display() method. The Display() method is another functional grouping that I'll describe later in this chapter (see "Displaying the results"). Then the close() method closes the SQL statement.

The Java compiler doesn't perform a validation on the SQL commands. The executeQuery() method can send any characters to the DBMS, which means the SQL expression can have words or characters that the DBMS doesn't recognize.

The DataRequest object automatically detects errors returned by the DBMS. These errors are in the form of SQLException errors and are caught by the catch{} block. Once caught, the program displays a warning that an SQL error has occurred and exits the program with a value of 3.

The Constructor walk-about: Displaying a window

The last segment of the constructor creates and displays a window where data returned from the database will display. You construct the window using two methods: setSize() and show().

The setSize() method defines the width and height of the window in pixels. In this example, I made the width 500 pixels and the height 200 pixels. This is sufficient size to display column names and a few rows on the screen. The show() method actually builds the window on the screen.

Displaying the results

To display your results in the window created by the constructor, you use the Display() method (see Listing 9-2). This process has two segments:

> ✔ Gather data in a row

> ✔ Insert data into a table

The first segment positions the virtual cursor into the next row of data in the database and then displays the title of the table (see Chapter 8 for more about the virtual cursor). The last segment inserts data from each row into a table, which will display onscreen.

Listing 9-2:   The Display() Method

```
private void Display (ResultSet DisplayResults)throws
        SQLException
{
    Vector ColumnNames = new Vector();
    Vector rows = new Vector();
    boolean Records = DisplayResults.next();
    if (!Records )
    {
        JOptionPane.showMessageDialog( this, "End of data."
          );
        setTitle( "Process Completed");
        return;
    }

    setTitle ("Customer Names");

    try {
            ResultSetMetaData MetaData =
        DisplayResults.getMetaData();

        for ( int x = 1; x <=
        MetaData.getColumnCount(); ++x)
            ColumnNames.addElement
        (MetaData.getColumnName ( x ) );

        do {
            rows.addElement (DownRow( DisplayResults,
        MetaData ) );
            } while ( DisplayResults.next() );


        DataTable = new JTable ( rows, ColumnNames ) ;

        JScrollPane scroller = new JScrollPane (
        DataTable ) ;
          getContentPane(). add ( scroller,
        BorderLayout.CENTER );

          validate();
```

(continued)

Listing 9-2 *(continued)*

```
        }

        catch (SQLException error ) {
            System.err.println("Data display error." +
            error);
            System.exit(4);
        }
    }
```

The Display () walk-about: Gathering data

The first thing the program does is move the virtual cursor to the first row in the table using the DisplayResults.next() method. DisplayResults is a ResultSet object that passes from the constructor to the Display() method.

DisplayResults contains all the data that was returned from the database. The virtual cursor points to the beginning of the table, which is above the first row of the table. This is why you must move the virtual cursor to the first row before you gather data from the ResultSet.

The DisplayResults.next() method returns a Boolean value of either true or false. You get a false value if the virtual cursor points to the end of the ResultSet after you move the virtual cursor from its initial position. Otherwise, you get a true value. In this example, the program assigns the return value to the Record variable.

The program calls the showMessageDialog() method if the Record value is false. The dialog box contains the message "End of data.". The program leaves the Display() method once the user clicks the OK button to exit the dialog box.

However, if the virtual cursor doesn't point to the end of the ResultSet, the program sets the title of the window to "Customer Names." The program then moves to the next segment of the Display() method.

The Display () walk-about: Inserting data into the table

At the beginning of the Display() method, you declare the two Vector objects. The ColumnNames Vector contains names of the columns of the table and the rows Vector contains values of each column, organized by rows.

The program tries to collect the column names from the ResultSet using the getMetaData() method, which the java.sql package defines. *Metadata* is data that describes data. In this case, metadata contains the column names. Metadata also contains the size and data type of the column and other data that describes data in a database.

The getMetaData() method returns the MetaData object that is used to reference metadata of the ResultSet. The metadata reference is the number of columns that are contained in the ResultSet. The getColumnCount() returns the number of columns, which the for loop uses to retrieve each column name.

For each column, the program calls the getColumnName() method and passes the number of the column to the method. The program identifies the first column as column one. The getColumnName() returns the name of the column; the addElement() method inserts the name of the column into the ColumnNames Vector.

Once the program collects the column names, it enters a do...while loop that retrieves the data stored in rows of the ResultSet. The program calls the DownRow() method to move to the next row in the ResultSet. I'll show you how the DownRow() works later in this chapter (see "Moving down the ResultSet").

The DownRow() method is passed the reference to the MetaData and DisplayResults ResultSet and returns a reference to a new row. The addElement() method inserts the data from the new row into the rows Vector.

The do...while loop continues until the DisplayResults.next() method returns a false value, at which point all the rows have been inserted into the rows Vector. This means that the data is ready to display in a table onscreen.

Next, the program creates a new table and places the data now stored in the Rows Vector and the ColumnNames Vector in the new table. The JTable() method builds the table and returns a reference to the table, which this program calls DataTable.

The new JscrollPane() method, which is referenced by the scroller object, places the table onscreen within a new scrollable container called a pane. The add() method defines the layout of the pane.

The program calls the validate() method to determine whether the graphical user interface (GUI) portion of the program is correct or whether the program found an error. The catch{} block finds any error that happens while the Display() method is being executed. If it finds an error, it displays the "Data display error." message and exits the program, returning a value of 4.

Moving down the ResultSet

The program must move the virtual cursor to each row of the table and then copy data from each column into memory before the data displays onscreen. The copying process is tricky because the program must use the proper method to read data from the column.

Listing 9-3 uses the getString() method to retrieve String data from the column. However, the program must determine the data type of the column before copying the data so that it uses the correct method to copy the data.

Here's what the program needs to do:

✔ Create a new Vector to temporarily store data copied from columns.

✔ Examine each column's data type.

✔ Use the property method to copy the data and insert the data into the Vector.

ON THE WEB

Listing 9-3: The DownRow() Method

```
private Vector DownRow ( ResultSet DisplayResults,
        ResultSetMetaData MetaData )
    throws SQLException
{
    Vector currentRow = new Vector();

    for ( int x = 1; x <= MetaData.getColumnCount(); ++x )
    {
        switch ( MetaData.getColumnType ( x ) ) {
            case Types.VARCHAR :
                currentRow.addElement(
            DisplayResults.getString ( x ) ) ;
                break;
        }
    }
    return currentRow;
}
```

The DownRow() method needs a temporary place to store data copied from the row, so the program creates a Vector called currentRow. Once the method finishes, this Vector will no longer be accessible. But that's not a problem because the contents of the Vector are returned to the Display() method, which called the DownRow() method.

The program enters a for loop where it uses the getColumnCount() method to determine the maximum number of columns in the row. For each column, the program retrieves the data type of the column using the getColumnType() method. The getColumnType() requires that you pass the number of the column that you want retrieve. I pass the getColumnType() method the current incremental value (*x*) from the for loop.

The switch statement compares the data type of the column to known data type values. Since I know that the database contains only text, I need to use only the Types.VARCHAR value. VARCHAR is JDBC's data type for Strings. In other examples throughout the book, I'll show you the other data types (see Chapter 10 for more about data types).

The program passes the getString() method the incremental value (*x*) to identify the column whose data will be copied to the currentRow Vector using the addElement() method. The program then returns the value of the currentRow Vector to the Display() method.

Disconnecting from the database

The final process of the program is to break the connection with the database. You do this with the Disconnect() method (see Listing 9-4). The Disconnect() method contains two statements. The Database.close() method performs the disconnect.

The catch{} block catches any errors that occur with the Database.close() method, displays the error message "Cannot break connection." onscreen, and then exits the program with a return value of 5.

Listing 9-4:   The Disconnect() Method

```
public void Disconnect()
{
   try {
       Database.close();
   }

       catch (SQLException error) {
          System.err.println( "Cannot break connection." +
       error) ;
          System.exit(5);
   }
}
```

The Complete Program

It's time to put together all the pieces of the program and see how the program works in real life. The program listing begins with import statements, each of which tells the Java compiler to use specific Java packages when compiling the program.

The program begins execution with the main() method, which is the standard starting point for every Java application. The first statement creates an object of the conxtest class. The conxtest class is the class defined in the code listing.

The constructor of the conxtest class is automatically executed (see "Connecting to the database and sending a query"). The constructor or methods called by the constructor then call the other methods discussed in this chapter.

The `main()` method then creates a WindowListener that monitors the windowing environment for messages from the operating system. Each time the user of the application moves or clicks the mouse and presses a key on the keyboard, the operating system records an event.

The operating system sends a message to the application telling the application about the event. The WindowListener is the object in the Java application that receives the message. Every application should react to messages received from the operating system.

The application ignores some messages, such as an irrelevant movement of the mouse. Other messages, such as the application closing, cause the application to take action. In this example, the WindowAdapter must react to messages from the operating system.

A standard method in every Java application is the `windowClose()` method, which executes whenever the WindowAdapter receives a message saying that the user closed the application. Statements within the `windowClose()` method then execute.

In this example, the program calls the `Disconnect()` method to break the connection with the database. Afterward, the `System.exit()` method ends the application. The `System.exit()` method returns a 0 value to the operating system, indicating that the application ran without errors.

ON THE WEB

Listing 9-5:   The Complete Listing

```
import java.sql.*;
import javax.swing.*;
import java.awt.event.*;
import java.awt.*;
import java.util.*;
import java.lang.*;

    public class conxtest extends JFrame
    {
        private JTable DataTable;
        private Connection Database;

        public conxtest()
        {
            String url = "jdbc:odbc:customers";
            String userID = "jim";
            String password = "keogh";
            Statement DataRequest;
            ResultSet Results;

            try {
                Class.forName( "sun.jdbc.odbc.JdbcOdbcDriver");
```

```
                Database =
            DriverManager.getConnection(url,userID,password);
        }
        catch (ClassNotFoundException error) {
            System.err.println("Unable to load the JDBC/ODBC
            bridge." + error);
            System.exit(1);
        }
        catch (SQLException error) {
            System.err.println("Cannot connect to the
            database." + error);
              System.exit(2);
        }

        try {
            String query = "Select * FROM customername";
            DataRequest = Database.createStatement();
            Results = DataRequest.executeQuery (query );
            DisplayResults (Results );
            DataRequest.close();
        }
        catch ( SQLException error ){
            System.err.println("SQL error." + error);
            System.exit(3);
        }

        setSize (500, 200);
        show();
    }

private void DisplayResults (ResultSet
        DisplayResults)throws SQLException
{
    boolean Records = DisplayResults.next();

    if (!Records ) {
        JOptionPane.showMessageDialog( this, "End of
            data.");
        setTitle( "Process Completed");
        return;
    }
    setTitle ("Customer Names");
    Vector ColumnNames = new Vector();
    Vector rows = new Vector();

    try {
        ResultSetMetaData MetaData =
         DisplayResults.getMetaData();

        for ( int x = 1; x <= MetaData.getColumnCount();
        ++x)
```

(continued)

Listing 9-5 *(continued)*

```
            ColumnNames.addElement (MetaData.getColumnName
        ( x ) );

        do {
           rows.addElement (DownRow( DisplayResults,
        MetaData ) );
        } while ( DisplayResults.next() );


        DataTable = new JTable ( rows, ColumnNames ) ;
        JScrollPane scroller = new JScrollPane ( DataTable
           ) ;
        getContentPane(). add ( scroller,
         BorderLayout.CENTER );
        validate();
     }
    catch (SQLException error ) {
       System.err.println("Data display error." + error);
       System.exit(4);
     }
  }

private Vector DownRow ( ResultSet DisplayResults,
       ResultSetMetaData MetaData )
     throws SQLException
{
   Vector currentRow = new Vector();
   for ( int x = 1; x <= MetaData.getColumnCount(); ++x )
      switch ( MetaData.getColumnType ( x ) ) {
      case Types.VARCHAR :
         currentRow.addElement( DisplayResults.getString
        ( x ) );
         break;
      }
   return currentRow;
}

public void Disconnect()
   {
   try {
      Database.close();
   }
   catch (SQLException error) {
      System.err.println( "Cannot break connection." +
         error) ;
      System.exit(5);
   }
 }

public static void main ( String args [] )
```

```
{
    final conxtest link = new conxtest();

    link.addWindowListener (
            new WindowAdapter() {
        public void windowClosing(WindowEvent WinEvent )
        {
        link.Disconnect();
        System.exit ( 0 ) ;
        }
    }

);
    }
}
```

Windows versus non-windows

A Java application can be written to work in a graphical user interface (GUI) windows environment or in a console environment. A GUI windows environment has all the buttons and images that you find on a typical application running in Microsoft Windows or on the Mac. An application running in a console environment is found running in the MS-DOS Prompt windows or in a Unix environment that is not running a GUI interface.

Applications that run in a windows environment are referred to as event-driven applications. This is because the application responds to events that occur within the windows environment, such as scrolling a list box, clicking the OK button, and all the other niceties that are found in most user interfaces.

In contrast, an application that runs in a console environment isn't dependent upon most events

that occur outside of the application. Most console applications fully control their own user interfaces and control how users' responses are detected and how the application reacts to those responses.

Whether you build your Java database application for a windows or console environment depends on the nature of the application. As a general rule, any application that doesn't require interaction with the person who uses the application should be written as a console application. Otherwise, write the application as a windows application.

You'll need to use Java Swing classes to build a state-of-the-art user interface. I show you how to create simple user interfaces using Swing in examples in this book.

Part III
Database
Interactions 101

The 5th Wave — By Rich Tennant

BEAL & WASP
DATABASE
CONSULTANTS

"Your database is beyond repair, but before I tell you our backup recommendation, let me ask you a question. How many index cards do you think will fit on the walls of your computer room?"

In this part . . .

The most important aspect of using a Java database applet or application is to be able to store information into a database, update information in a database, retrieve information from a database, and delete information from a database. I call these tasks *database interactions*. This part covers how to incorporate these database interactions into your own Java database applet or application.

Chapter 10

Table Manners: Creating and Dropping Tables

*W*ithout a table, you cannot have a useful database. You're responsible for creating tables for the database, regardless of whether the database is local to your computer. When you create a table, you need to

✔ Have a plan so each table you create enhances your Java database application

✔ Identify the type of data that you want to store in the table

✔ Know how to use the `Create` statement within your Java database application to create the table

Once you create the table, you can insert new data (see Chapter 12) and retrieve data from the table (see Chapter 13). You'll also have the capability to remove a table from the database once your Java database application no longer needs it (see "Drop By and Drop a Table").

Database Management from a Distance

The tasks of creating and dropping tables are called *database management* because they are necessary to keep your Java database application operating efficiently. Your company's computer network stores nearly all the databases that you'll be using for professional database applications (see Chapter 5).

This is unlike Microsoft Access, which you probably have installed on your computer. You can run Microsoft Access and then use its graphical user interface (GUI) to create and drop tables interactively. In fact, you can run a macro that asks you a few questions and then creates tables for you. However, there isn't a macro that will drop tables. You must to do that yourself by selecting the table and then pressing the Delete key on your keyboard.

Some database management (DBMS) software have a graphical user interface. However, most do not, which means that you must create and drop tables by embedding SQL expressions within your Java application.

You probably won't have rights to create or drop tables if a database administrator is managing the DBMS that you're using. Typically, the database administrator will create or drop tables, or assign you rights to do so.

Need to create new tables

You'll find that most Java database applications are fluid. Changes in the marketplace typically require a change in the business operations, and that means you need to make changes to the database applications used to run your business.

Therefore, you should expect that your carefully designed database application will change and that you will likely need to change the number of tables in the database. For example, your company may expand into a new distribution channel for your products that requires you to create a new table to hold data for the new distribution channel.

Each time there is a need to create new tables for the database, you should revisit and, if necessary, modify your plan for the database (see Chapters 1 and 2). In this way, you can be sure that the changes have been efficiently integrated into your original design.

Need to drop existing tables

Removing a table from a database is called *dropping* a table. You should drop any table that your Java database application is no longer using. Tables that are not being used waste resources, such as disk space and time, when backing up the database.

Some programmers get lazy and forget to drop an unused table, especially if the unused table doesn't affect the program. If the program works fine, they tend to not touch something that isn't broken.

Once a year you should revisit all your database applications and audit the database. *Auditing* is a simple process of reviewing all the tables that are in the database to determine whether the database application is still using each table. Your database administrator can help you with this task.

Before Creating a Table

Don't be in a rush to create a table because you can make inadvertent errors. Instead, refer to the database schema that you developed for the application (see Chapters 1 and 2). The database schema contains all the data you need to create tables for your Java database application.

Here are the pieces of data that you need to create the database:

- ✔ Name of the table
- ✔ Name of each column in the table
- ✔ Data type of each column in the table
- ✔ Size of each column in the table

I normally copy the data I need to be in the table from the database schema onto scrap paper. In this way, I can focus on the data I need to create the table and I'm not distracted by other data contained in the database schema.

The rules of the table

Just like there are rules you follow at the dinner table, there are also rules that apply when creating a table for your database. The DBMS has the role of your mother and will correct your errors — although you won't be grounded for violating them. Instead, the DBMS simply won't create your table until you conform to the rules.

The rules for creating a table are straightforward and easily understood:

- ✔ Every column must have a unique name in the table.
- ✔ Duplicate column names can be used but only in different tables.
- ✔ Every column requires a data type.
- ✔ You can require that data be entered into a column by using the NOT NULL clause.
- ✔ A column can be assigned a default value. A default value is automatically placed in the column if the program doesn't provide a value for the column when a row is inserted or updated.

Know your data types

You probably remember learning about data types when you studied how to program in Java. A data type is a description of the data. The description tells either the Java compiler or the DBMS how much room to reserve in memory to store the data successfully.

For example, a person's first name is almost always a Character data type. In contrast, the quantity of a product in a purchase is an Integer data type. You need simply to choose the data type that is sufficient to store data used by your Java database application. Table 10-1 contains the common data types used in SQL. You can use them when you're creating your table.

SQL data types are a standard. However, not all DBMSs adhere to these standards. This means that some data types will not work with all DBMSs. Contact your database administrator if you receive a data type error when trying to create a table. He or she will be able to provide you with an alternative data type that is acceptable to your DBMS.

Table 10-1	Common SQL Data Types
Data Type	**Description**
BLOB	A binary large object, such as a picture.
BOOLEAN	True or false.
CHAR (n)	Fixed-length string of length where *n* is the maximum length.
CHARACTER (n)	Fixed-length string of length where *n* is the maximum length.
CLOB	A character large object, such as a text.
DATE	A date.
DEC(m, n)	A number with a decimal value where *m* is the total number of digits in the number and *n* is the number of digits following the decimal point.
DECIMAL(m, n)	A number with a decimal value where *m* is the total number of digits in the number and *n* is the number of digits following the decimal point.
DOUBLE	A very large or very small number.
FLOAT(n)	A number with a decimal value where the precision is specified. Precision is the number of decimal values.
INT	A number without a decimal value.
INTEGER	A number without a decimal value.

Data Type	Description
NUMERIC(m, n)	A number with a decimal value where m is the total number of digits in the number and n is the number of digits following the decimal point.
REAL	A number with a decimal value.
SMALLINT	A number without a decimal value.
TIME	A time.
TIMESTAMP	The current date and time.
VARCHAR (n)	Variable-length string of maximum length n.

Know your data size

Besides specifying the data type of a column, you might also need to specify the size of the column, depending on the database. For example, the Character data type needs a size value such as CHARACTER (30), which tells the DBMS to create a column that will hold no more than 30 characters.

In contrast, some data types don't require you to specify a size. Time and Date are examples. The DBMS already knows how much space it needs to store a time or a date in a column.

You can determine the size of a column by referencing the data schema that you created when designing the database for your application (see Chapters 1 and 2).

Creating a Table from Afar

You create a table by writing an SQL expression and embedding the statement into your Java database application. Once you've placed the SQL expression into your code, you need to compile and run the application.

Here are the steps that you need to perform:

1. **Make sure you know the name of the database to use when creating the table.**

2. **Write Java statements to link your application to the database (see Chapter 9).**

3. **Assign the SQL expression to create a table to a** String **object in your application.**

4. **Insert the SQL expression into an SQL statement.**

5. **Execute the SQL statement.**

Your application opens the connection with the database and sends the SQL statement to the DBMS, which creates the new table based on your specifications. Your application can begin to insert data into the table once the DBMS has finished creating the table.

Creating your first table

Enter Listing 10-1 into your editor, and then compile the code into an executable Java class. Alternatively, you can download the code from www. dummies.com/extras/Java2DataProg.

This sample application creates a table called *address* that has four columns. These are the customer number and the customer's address data. I purposely left out the customer's name because I'm assuming that another table stores that data and that you can link the two tables together (see Chapters 1 and 2).

You won't see much when this program runs because the DBMS handles most of the activity related to creating the table behind the scenes. You should hear your hard disk cranking away for a few seconds before returning to the prompt if you are using a local DBMS such as Microsoft Access. You won't hear the cranking if you are using a remote DBMS — unless, of course, you're sitting right next to the server.

An error displays when the program finishes. The error states that the DBMS didn't return a ResultSet. You can ignore the error message because we don't expect a ResultSet return when we create a table because we aren't asking for any rows of data from the DBMS.

Listing 10-1:   Creating a Table

```
import java.sql.*;

    public class createtb
    {
        private Connection Database;
        public createtb()
        {
            String url = "jdbc:odbc:customers";
            String userID = "jim";
            String password = "keogh";

            try {
                Class.forName( "sun.jdbc.odbc.JdbcOdbcDriver");
```

```
            Database =
        DriverManager.getConnection(url,userID,password);
        }
    catch (ClassNotFoundException error) {
        System.err.println("Unable to load the JDBC/ODBC
        bridge." + error);
        System.exit(1);
        }
    catch (SQLException error) {
        System.err.println("Cannot connect to the
        database. "+ error);
        System.exit(2);
        }

    Statement DataRequest;

    try {
        String query = "Create Table address (
        CustomerNumber CHAR(30), CustomerStreet CHAR(30),
        CustomerCity CHAR(30), CustomerZip CHAR(30))";
        DataRequest = Database.createStatement();
        DataRequest.executeQuery (query);
        DataRequest.close();
        Database.close();
        }
    catch ( SQLException error ){
        System.err.println("SQL error." + error);
        System.exit(3);
        }
    }

public static void main ( String args [] )
{
    final createtb link = new createtb();
    System.exit ( 0 ) ;
    }
}
```

Always place a space between the name of the column and the name of the data type; otherwise, you'll receive a DBMS error.

The Create Table walk-about

The code that creates a table might seem imposing at first glance, but after I walk you through each line I'm sure that you'll understand how the program creates the table. The program begins with the main() method, as with any Java program.

The main() method is near the bottom of the program because it uses the createtb() constructor defined at the top of the program. You must define classes, methods, and data members before your program can use them.

The main() method creates a createtb object. This is the name that I gave to the class that creates the table. You can rename this class if you'd like to, but for now I suggest using this name. The object of the createtb class is called link, which is not used too much in the program. This is because the constructor of the createtb class performs most of the work of creating a table.

The constructor automatically executes when an object of its class is created. The constructor uses the url, userID, and password to open a connection with the database (DriverManager.getConnection()). The Database Connection object contains a reference to the database if the connection is successfully opened.

If the database connection isn't open, the program throws an error, which is caught by one of the catch{} blocks. The first catch{} block displays an error if the application is unable to load the JDBC/ODBC bridge (see Chapter 7). The second catch{} block displays an error if the database connection doesn't open.

Each catch{} block displays an error message that I wrote into the program and the error message (error) that was thrown by Java statements in the try{} block. Once the error message displays, the program stops running (System.exit()) and returns a value (1 or 2) to the operating system. This value tells you where in the code the program ended.

After the database connection opens, the program creates the String (query) that contains the SQL expression needed to create a table. The Database.createStatement() statement creates the SQL statement object called DataRequest. The program passes the query String to the executeQuery() method of the DataRequest object. Then the statement and the connection to the database close.

The catch{}block detects any errors that occur when executing the SQL statement. Similar to the previous catch{} block, an error message that I wrote into the program and the actual error that was created by the SQL statement display onscreen. The program also stops running.

Once the constructor runs successfully, the program returns to the main() method and executes the System.exit() statement, which stops the program.

A closer look at Create Table code

The program uses the Create table statement to tell the DBMS that you want to create a new table. The name of the new table is *address*. Column names, data types, and sizes appear within parentheses.

A column name shouldn't have spaces because some DBMSs don't allow spaces for column names. You can use a combination of upper- and lower-case characters (CustomerNumber), hyphens (Customer-Number), or an underscore (Customer_Number) to separate compound column names without using a space.

You must have a space between the column name and the data type of a column. A comma separates columns.

Verifying that you have a new table

You might be scratching your head wondering if your program created a new table. I felt this way the first time I created a table because I heard my hard drive doing something, but nothing appeared on the screen of my computer — nothing was supposed to appear!

Here's a way of satisfying your curiosity and determining whether you have a new table. Open Microsoft Access and then the database that contains the new table. You should see the name of the new table listed on the screen (see Figure 10-1). If you don't see the name of the new table, review your program and make sure that your program resembles the example in this book.

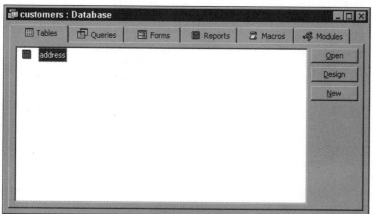

Figure 10-1:
Verify that your program created the new table by looking at the list of tables in Microsoft Access.

If you were using a DBMS other than Microsoft Access, you need to write a program that selects data from the table. I provide a sample program in Chapter 9 and more robust examples in Chapter 13.

Making code easier to read

I bet that you probably had a difficult time reading the String that contains the SQL expression in the previous program. That's because I placed all the statements into one String, and the String wrapped to the next line.

Here's a much better way write the String. Break up the String into several Strings and use the plus sign to concatenate the Strings into one. Notice that I placed each column in its own String, which is placed on its own line (see Listing 10-2).

Listing 10-2: Writing Clearer Code

```
try {
    String query = "Create Table address (
CustomerNumber CHAR(30)," +
                    "CustomerStreet CHAR(30)," +
                    "CustomerCity CHAR(30)," +
                    "CustomerZip CHAR(30))";
    DataRequest = Database.createStatement();
    DataRequest.executeQuery (query );
    DataRequest.close();
    Database.close();
}
```

You'll notice that I show just the `try{}` block rather than repeat the whole code each time that I want to show you a new feature. This saves you from becoming confused with a long listing of Java statements. All you need to do is replace the `try{}` block in the code with the new `try{}` block and recompile the program. You can then test out the new feature.

A mix of data types

You can create a table that contains mixed data types by specifying the data type you need in the SQL expression. Table 10-1 shows the SQL expression for the standard SQL data types. Simply place the SQL data type command after the column name in the SQL expression.

Your Java database program and the Java compiler don't validate the SQL expression in the SQL String. Instead, the SQL String is sent to the DBMS for validation and processing. This means that some DBMSs may not understand some standard SQL expressions such as data types because the DBMSs use syntax other than the standard SQL syntax.

In this case, you can ask your database administrator for the data type syntax that your DBMS requires and then substitute the standard SQL syntax shown in this chapter with your DBMS-specific syntax. Your Java database application will then be able to create a table.

You may find that other DBMSs accept standard SQL syntax and their own syntax for data types. Such is the case with Microsoft Access. You can use the CHAR( ) data type, which is standard SQL syntax, or use the TEXT data type, which is standard for Microsoft Access. Both work fine.

I suggest that you use standard SQL syntax wherever possible. This enables you to use your Java database application with any DBMS, without having to change your code except for the name of the database.

The NOT NULL keywords

You'll discover that there will be times when your Java database application requires certain data to be inserted into every row in a table. Let's say that you are creating a customers table that contains names of your customers. You probably want all rows in the table to contain a customer's last name and first name.

The easiest way to ensure that every row contains required data is to use the NOT NULL keywords when you create the table. NULL is a common term used to mean nothing or empty. If you use NOT NULL, the DBMS requires that you enter a value in a column designated as such.

If you attempt to leave the column empty, the DBMS won't insert any data and will return an error message back to your program. Listing 10-3 shows how to use NOT NULL in your SQL expression.

Listing 10-3:   Using NOT NULL

```
        try {
            String query = "Create Table customers ( " +
                            "FirstName CHAR(30) NOT NULL," +
                            "LastName CHAR(30) NOT NULL)";
            DataRequest = Database.createStatement();
            DataRequest.executeQuery (query );
            DataRequest.close();
            Database.close();
        }
```

Always place a space between the data type and NOT NULL.

You can verify that the DBMS implemented the NOT NULL restrictions by displaying the table in the Design mode if you are using Microsoft Access as your DBMS. Figure 10-2 shows how Microsoft Access displays the NOT NULL setting.

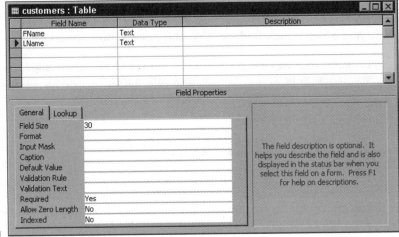

Figure 10-2:
Point to the
column to
verify that
the column
must have a
value.

You'll notice that you won't find NOT NULL displayed. Instead, you'll see the Required column attribute, which is set to Yes. This is Access' way of saying NOT NULL. Microsoft Access translates NOT NULL into the proper setting of Required.

If you're not using Access, insert a new row into the table leaving one or more Required (NOT NULL) columns empty (see Chapter 12). An error will be returned if the column is set to NOT NULL.

Ask your database administrator for help if you have problems verifying that NOT NULL has been set for a column.

I'll fill in the blanks

You can have the DBMS enter the most frequently used data into a column automatically by using the DEFAULT modifier. This is a valuable feature when you're building Java database applications that require someone to enter data from the keyboard to store in the database.

Let's say that you're building a table to hold customer names and the country in which the customer resides. Since your company is in the United States, most of your customers will live here. However, you might have a few customers who live abroad and have contacted you because you have a hot Internet site.

Your application must permit someone to enter a country designation, but you don't want the person to have to bother with entering USA all the time. Instead, you can have the DBMS enter USA for you by setting USA as the default value for the column.

Listing 10-4 shows how to set the default value for a column when you create the table. I include the NOT NULL keywords in the SQL String, but that's not necessary unless you want the column to become a required column. You don't need to use NOT NULL when you use DEFAULT.

Listing 10-4: Using Default Values

```
try {
    String query = "Create Table customer ( " +
                    "FirstName CHAR(30) NOT NULL," +
                    "LastName CHAR(30) NOT NULL,"+
                    "Country CHAR(30) NOT NULL
DEFAULT 'USA')";
    DataRequest = Database.createStatement();
    DataRequest.executeQuery (query );
    DataRequest.close();
    Database.close();
}
```

Always place a space between the keyword DEFAULT and either the data type or any other keyword(s) that follows the data type. Also, place the default value within single quotations.

Drop By and Drop a Table

Dropping a table destroys all the nice handiwork you built into your table. Yet, there is a time when every table must drop. Dropping a table is much easier than creating a table because you only need to use three magical words.

You must be careful whenever you write a program that drops a table because you can easily drop the wrong table by accident, which results in a loss of data and possibly causes your Java database application to not run properly.

You may want to drop a table when

✔ The application doesn't require the table any longer.

✔ You're replacing the table with a new and improved table — after you copy existing data into the new table.

✔ You're consolidating data into fewer tables.

You may not be authorized to drop tables — even tables that you created. Database administrators are cautious granting such authorization because of the impact a dropped table has on the database application.

Tim-ber! Down comes another table

The SQL statement `Drop Table` directs the DBMS to remove a specific table from the database. You specify the table to drop by placing the name of the table in the SQL expression, as is shown in Listing 10-5.

Don't expect to be prompted to confirm that you want to drop the table because that won't happen. Instead, the DBMS blindly follows the direction of your Java database application. The assumption is that the programmer knows what he or she is doing.

You can verify that the table is gone by opening the database in Microsoft Access and trying to locate the name of the table. The table name will be missing if the program has successfully dropped the table.

Alternatively, you can attempt to insert a new row into the dropped table if you aren't using Microsoft Access. You'll receive an SQL error if the table has been dropped.

Listing 10-5:   Dropping a Table

```
try {
    String query = "Drop Table address ";
    DataRequest = Database.createStatement();
    DataRequest.executeQuery (query );
    DataRequest.close();
    Database.close();
}
```

Test your newfound knowledge

1. What is the purpose of using a default value?

a. So the DBMS can enter frequently entered values.

b. So you can control all the data entered into the column.

c. So you can play a trick on the person who is entering data

d. So all columns are NULL columns

2. What does NOT NULL do?

a. Places NULL into the column

b. Enters a empty row into the table

c. Requires that data be placed into the column

d. Places required data into the column

Answers: (1) a. (2) c.

Chapter 11

Basic Index Etiquette

. . . .

. . . .

*N*eed to find data quickly in this book? Don't read every page! Use the index instead, but I didn't have to tell you that. You already know that an index is the best way to locate words and phrases in a book. An index is also a way database management systems (DBMSs) find data in a table.

Your job as a Java database programmer is to choose the best data to include in an index (see Chapter 4), and then write a program to tell the DBMS to create an index for the tables your Java database application uses.

Here are three reasons why you would use an index to search for data:

✔ An index contains words that you most frequently need.

✔ An index contains a reference of where important words can be found in a table.

✔ An index contains a smaller amount of data to search than a table.

DBMSs use an appropriate index to respond to a request for data only if the index exists. Otherwise, the DBMS searches the entire table for the requested data.

Maintaining Your Index

The way in which you create an index for tables used by your Java application is dependent on whether the DBMS sits on a remote database server or on your local disk drive.

Typically, you use a program to create an index for tables associated with a remote database. You can do the same with a local database, but you typically use the graphical user interface (GUI) supplied with the DBMS. In this chapter, I use a program to create an index on a local database rather than use the GUI, so I can show you how to write a program to create an index.

The company for whom you are writing the database application usually determines whether you use a local or remote database. Companies usually prefer to centralize data to a data center.

Need to create a new index

You may find yourself creating new indexes long after your Java database application is operational. This is because your application will, over time, gradually accumulate sizeable amounts of data — like so many database applications do.

The result is a large database of data that probably becomes laborious to search without an index. You can improve the performance of searching for data by creating a new index.

The amount of data is just one reason for creating a new index. Another reason is because there will be a need to search using various search criteria. Let's say that you have a table that contains customer contact data such as a customer's name, Customer Number, address, and telephone.

You probably plan on searching by Customer Number and by customer name, so you probably created an index for each when you designed the database. However, you receive frequent requests from the marketing department to find customers who reside in the same general area so sales reps can visit more than one customer per trip. This means that you need to create an index for the Zip Code as well.

Another reason why you should create a new index is because you notice the DBMS is slow in getting its responses back to you. The lack of an index doesn't cause all performance decreases. Other conditions influence performance, such as network responsiveness. Your network administrator can determine if the performance slack off is due to the network.

Need to drop existing index

An index is a very useful feature of a DBMS. However, too much of a good thing can impede the efficiency of the DBMS. Each index that you create must be maintained whenever the key value changes in the database (see Chapter 4 for more on key values).

This happens when

- You add a row into a table.
- You delete a row from a table.
- You change the key value of the index in the table.

Each time one of these changes occurs, the DBMS must stop processing a request and update each of the indexes. The more indexes that you create, the longer the DBMS will take to update the indexes.

Therefore, you'll find it necessary to delete indexes that are no longer being used, which decreases maintenance for the DBMS. We also refer to deleting an index as *dropping* an index.

Organizing Before Creating an Index

An index is a delicate thing — at least I like to think of it that way — because my choice of an index affects the performance of the DBMS. Therefore, you should plan carefully to create an index. You begin this process by analyzing the ways in which your application will probably need to search for data. Chapter 4 shows you how to perform this analysis.

Once you complete your analysis of the application, you will have a list of indexes that you need to create and the key value for each index. You need this data so you can enter the proper statements into your program to create the table.

Your list of indexes should also identify whether an index is a primary index or a secondary index (see Chapter 4).

Creating a Primary Index

Your Java database application sends an SQL expression embedded in an SQL statement to the DBMS to create the index. The DBMS then follows directions from your program and creates the index.

You need to make sure that

- You already have a database.
- You have a table that will be indexed.
- You know the name and path of the database.
- Your program can connect to and open the database.

Clustered keys are tricky

Pay careful attention to columns used as the key value to a clustered index so you can avoid conflicts before you write your program. A clustered index uses a combination of two or more columns to create the index key value.

A commonly clustered key is Last Name and First Name, which enables the DBMS to search on a combination of last and first names. In this example, Last Name and First Name are both the Character data type, which means they are the same types of data.

However, you can create a clustered index using columns of different data types. For example, you can use Last Name, First Name, and ContactDate columns for a clustered index key value. Last Name and First Name are Character data types and ContactDate is a Date data type. This means that you must temporarily change the data type of ContactDate to a Character data type before you can combine it with the Last Name and First Name columns to create the key value of the clustered index. I'll show you how to do this in "Converting data types" later in this chapter.

Your list of columns that you plan to use for a clustered index should list the data type of each column. In this way, you have all the data you need when you write the code to create the clustered index.

When you're using a remote database, you shouldn't assume that it's available because the database administrator may have taken the database off the network temporarily to perform maintenance on it. It's always best to call the database administrator before trying to create an index, so that you're sure the database is running properly.

Writing the code

Probably the first index that you'll create for a table is a primary index because it identifies each row uniquely. Listing 11-1 shows the Java program to create a primary index. You may notice that there isn't an SQL keyword called primary index. Instead, you use the SQL modifier UNIQUE to create the primary index. UNIQUE tells the DBMS to create an index that doesn't permit duplicate values, which is another way of telling the DBMS to create a primary index.

Before running this program, you need to include a CustomerNumber column and then populate that column with numbers. Also make sure that you exit Microsoft Access. Otherwise, Microsoft Access locks the table, preventing the program from creating the table.

Listing 11-1:   Creating a Primary Index

```java
import java.sql.*;

  public class createix
  {
    private Connection Database;

    public createix()
    {
      String url = "jdbc:odbc:customers";
      String userID = "jim";
      String password = "keogh";

      try {
            Class.forName(
        "sun.jdbc.odbc.JdbcOdbcDriver");

            Database =
        DriverManager.getConnection(url,userID,password);
      }
      catch (ClassNotFoundException error) {
        System.err.println("Unable to load the JDBC/ODBC
        bridge." + error);
        System.exit(1);
      }
      catch (SQLException error) {
        System.err.println("Cannot connect to the
        database. "+ error);
        System.exit(2);
      }

      Statement DataRequest;

      try {
            String query = "CREATE UNIQUE INDEX custnum "
        +
                          "ON customername
        (CustomerNumber) ";
            DataRequest = Database.createStatement();
            DataRequest.executeQuery (query );
            DataRequest.close();
            Database.close();

      }
      catch ( SQLException error ){
        System.err.println("SQL error." + error);
        System.exit(3);
      }

    }
```

(continued)

Listing 11-1 *(continued)*

```
public static void main ( String args [] )
{
    final createix link = new createix();

        System.exit ( 0 ) ;
}
}
```

The Create Primary Index walk-about

The program begins with the main() method, where an object of createix is created and called link. The class createix is defined at the top of the list and is an abbreviation for "create index." The constructor of the createix class is automatically called when the object is created.

The constructor performs all the work to create the index. First, it creates Strings to identify the url, userID, and password. The getConnection() method uses these to connect to and open the database in the try{} block.

Also in the try{} block is forName(), which you use to load the JDBC/ODBC bridge (see Chapter 8). If either forName() or getConnection() fail, the program throws an exception, which one of the two catch{} blocks that follow catches.

The first catch{} block displays an error message stating that the JDBC/ODBC bridge wasn't loaded and then exits the program. The other catch{} block also displays an error message, stating that the program is unable to connect to the database. It also exits the program.

Both catch{} blocks also display the actual error when your program detects the problem. The error variable contains the messages.

After the program loads the JDBC/ODBC bridge and makes a connection to the database, it executes the second try{} block. The SQL expression needed to create the index is assigned to a String variable called query, which is placed into an SQL statement and then sent to the DBMS by the executeQuery() method. The SQL statement and the connection to the database then close.

Statements within the second try{} block throw an error whenever the catch{} block finds a problem. The catch{} block then displays the SQL error. You'll see an error message on the screen after statements in the try{} block execute, indicating that the DBMS didn't return a ResultSet. A *ResultSet* is a reference to rows of data that we requested. However, since we didn't request any rows in this program, you can ignore the error message.

After the constructor finishes executing, the program returns to the statement in the `main()` method that is below the statement that created the `createix` object and exits the program.

A closer look at Create Index code

The program uses the `CREATE INDEX` statement to tell the DBMS that we want to create a new index. It uses the `UNIQUE` modifier to indicate that the index should include only unique values. This means that the key value used to create the index must be different in each row.

The name of the index is custnum, which follows the modifier `INDEX` in the SQL expression. The `ON` keyword specifies the name of the table. In this example, customername is the name of the table associated with the index.

The parentheses that follow the name of the table contain the key value of the index. CustomerNumber is the name of the column in the customername table that is used as the key for the index.

Make sure that you place spaces between keywords in the SQL expression. Otherwise, you'll receive an error message when the DBMS attempts to run your request.

Verifying that you have a primary index

You need to rely on error-trapping routines (`catch{}`) in your program to determine whether your program successfully created the index. However, if you're using Microsoft Access, you can verify that the index exists by using the Access graphical user interface (GUI). Here are the steps:

1. **Start Microsoft Access, and then open the customers database, if you are using the same database as I do in this book.**

2. **Select the customername table, and then click the Design button (see Figure 11-1).**

   You'll notice the Indexed property is set to Yes (No Duplicates). Your program successfully made an index! Congratulations!

If you are using a remote database, ask your database administrator to confirm that your program created an index.

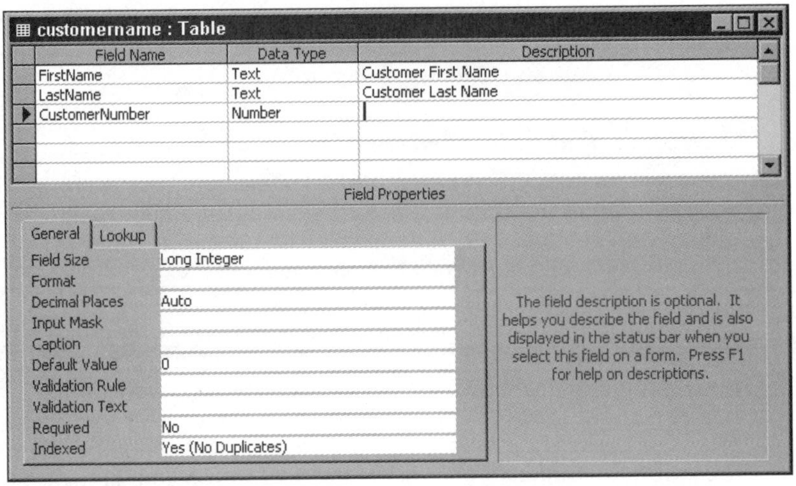

Figure 11-1:
Display the
table in
Design
view, and
then point
to the
Customer
Number
column.

Creating a Secondary Index

Creating a secondary index on a table uses practically the same code as the primary index, with one exception. You don't include the keyword UNIQUE in the SQL expression. By eliminating UNIQUE, you're telling the DBMS that the index can include duplicate values.

For example, you can use a customer's last name as a secondary index, but not as a primary index. The reason is that you could have more than one customer with the same last name. A secondary index permits duplicate last names to be included as the key to the index.

Writing the code

Listing 11-2 shows the segment of code that you use to create a secondary index. Simply replace the second try{} block in the previous program with the following code, recompile the program, and run the program to create the secondary index.

Notice that the SQL expression String is very similar to the SQL expression String in the previous program. This SQL expression tells the DBMS to create an index called custlname on the LastName column of the customer-name table.

Listing 11-2:   Creating a Secondary Index

```
try {
    String query = "CREATE INDEX cust1name ON
customername (LastName) ";
    DataRequest = Database.createStatement();
    DataRequest.executeQuery (query );
    DataRequest.close();
    Database.close();
}
```

Verifying that you have a secondary index

You can see that the program created the secondary index by using the graphical user interface (GUI) of Microsoft Access. Open the database in Microsoft Access and view the customername table in Design mode (see "Verifying that you have a primary index"). Highlight the LastName column.

Notice that the Indexed property is set to Yes (Duplicates OK), which means that the DBMS will use duplicate key values for the index (see Figure 11-2).

Figure 11-2:
Display the table in Design view, and then point to the LastName column.

Field Name	Data Type	Description
FirstName	Text	Customer First Name
LastName	Text	Customer Last Name
CustomerNumber	Number	

Field Properties

General | Lookup

Field Size	50
Format	
Input Mask	
Caption	
Default Value	
Validation Rule	
Validation Text	
Required	No
Allow Zero Length	No
Indexed	Yes (Duplicates OK)

An index speeds up searches and sorting on the field, but may slow updates. Selecting "Yes - No Duplicates" prohibits duplicate values in the field. Press F1 for help on indexed fields.

Creating a Clustered Index

Clustered indexes use more than one column to create the key value. You create a clustered index using practically the same method as you use to create a secondary index, but you place multiple column names within the parentheses of the SQL expression.

You can use several columns to create the key value for the clustered index. The DBMS concatenates values of each column to form the key value (see Chapter 4). This means that although the value of two columns may make up the key value of the index, there is only one key value.

For example, Listing 11-3 creates a clustered index using LastName and FirstName columns. If the last name is Keogh and the first name Jim, the key value for that row is KeoghJim.

Writing the code

Listing 11-3 contains an example of an SQL expression that creates a clustered index. The index custLFname is built using the LastName and FirstName columns from the customername table.

You must place the names of columns within parentheses and separate them by a comma; otherwise, the DBMS will return an error.

Listing 11-3:   Creating a Clustered Index

```
try {
    String query = "CREATE INDEX custLFname " +
                        " ON customername (LastName,
    FirstName) ";
    DataRequest = Database.createStatement();
    DataRequest.executeQuery (query);
    DataRequest.close();
    Database.close();
}
```

Converting data types

A clustered index can use columns of unlike data types to create the index. However, you must temporarily convert the data type of the columns to a common data type. If you don't, an error will occur and the index won't be created.

You can temporarily convert a data type using the CAST keyword. CAST tells the DBMS to convert the value in the column to another data type and then concatenate the value to the key value. The data type of the column remains unchanged.

Listing 11-4 illustrates how this works. The SQL expression creates a new index using the LastName, FirstName, and CustomerNumber columns.

LastName and FirstName columns are Character data types. CustomerNumber is a Numeric data type. The program needs to convert the CustomerNumber to a Character data type before you can use it as part of the key value of the index.

The column name CustomerNumber and other data type VARCHAR follow CAST. VARCHAR is a variable character data type, which is compatible with the Character data type of the LastName and FirstName columns. See Table 10-1 in Chapter 10 for a listing of the data types.

Make sure that you modify the table to include the CustomerNumber column and then enter dates in the CustomerNumber column.

Microsoft Access doesn't support the CAST syntax. In this example, you don't need to convert the value in the CustomerNumber column. Microsoft Access does this for you. Replace CAST CustomerNumber AS VARCHAR) with CustomerNumber if you are using Microsoft Access.

Listing 11-4: Converting a Data Type

```
try {
    String query = "CREATE INDEX custmix " +
                   "ON customername (LastName,
FirstName, " +
                   " CAST CustomerNumber AS VARCHAR)
";
    DataRequest = Database.createStatement();
    DataRequest.executeQuery (query );
    DataRequest.close();
    Database.close();
}
```

You Don't Need Slippery Hands to Drop an Index

A program can use an SQL expression to drop an index from the database only if the database administrator authorizes the program to do so. You'll find that the database administrator gives the user ID used by the program certain rights to access the database.

The user ID used by your program needs rights to

✔ Create a table

✔ Drop a table

✔ Create an index

✔ Drop an index

It's common that a database administrator gives the user ID limited rights to a database. In security-tight companies, only a database administrator may have the right to drop a table or drop an index to ensure control over any event that can lose data.

Ask your database administrator for create and drop rights to tables and indexes. Sometimes a database administrator will grant those rights in the development environment. A *development environment* is a database server and other servers, such as an application server, that are used by programmers to develop applications. You can't conduct business using applications from the development environment. Applications that run business operations operate in a production environment.

One, two, three, drop!

You can drop an index from the database by using the DROP INDEX statement in the SQL expression and by specifying the name of the index and the name of the table. Listing 11-5 shows the try{} block that you can substitute for the second try{} in the Listing 11-4 example.

This code segment drops the custlname index associated with the customername table. You don't have to specify the column names used to create the key value for the index that you're dropping.

Listing 11-5:   Dropping an Index

```
try {
    String query = "DROP INDEX custlname ON
customername ";
    DataRequest = Database.createStatement();
    DataRequest.executeQuery (query );
    DataRequest.close();
    Database.close();
}
```

Drop the index? Let's check!

When you run Listing 11-5 as part of the program, the DBMS drops the index from the database. If you use Microsoft Access as your DBMS, you can verify that the index is gone by using the graphical user interface. Here are the steps.

Open the database in Microsoft Access, and view the customername table in Design mode (see "Verifying that you have a primary index"). Notice that the Indexed property is set to No in the column used for the key value (see Figure 11-3). Sure enough — the index is gone!

If you are using a remote DBMS, ask your database administrator to verify that your program actually dropped the index.

Dropping an index might decrease the performance of your Java database application.

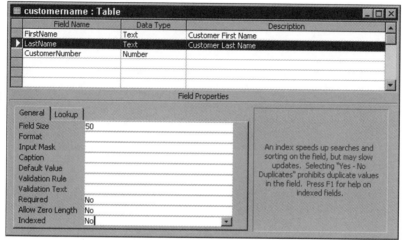

Figure 11-3:
Point to the
LastName
column and
you'll notice
the column
is no longer
indexed.

Chapter 12

Stuffing Data into a Table

. . . .

In This Chapter

▶ Inserting a row into a table

▶ Inserting data into a column

▶ Validating data

▶ Inserting system values

. . . .

*Y*our wish is the DBMS's command — that is, as long as the DBMS has the data that you're wishing to see. A database is useless if it doesn't contain the data that you need to retrieve.

However, you can be assured that all the data you want is at your fingertips by developing a Java database application that places data into tables of the database. The process of storing data into a database is called *inserting*, which is the topic of this chapter.

Here is what your application needs to do to insert data into a table in a database:

- ✔ Find data to insert into the table.
- ✔ Validate the data before inserting it into the table.
- ✔ Determine the columns of the table.
- ✔ Insert the data into the appropriate columns.
- ✔ Verify that the data was successfully inserted into the table.

Some of these things you might have anticipated such as finding data, but others are tasks that you probably aren't familiar with — and that's why you're reading this chapter. Inserting data will be old hat to you once you build the sample Java database applications that I show you in this chapter.

Before Inserting Data

There is more to inserting data into a database than simply using the insertion statement within your program. Before you get to that point, though, you need to make sure that the data is available and accurate.

Your application can run aground if you fail to take steps to ensure the integrity of the data prior to using the data in your application. Otherwise, you might be requesting erroneous data from the database.

Whenever anyone runs your Java database application, they are assuming that

✔ The database contains the data that they are requesting.

✔ The data is accurate.

✔ Your program operates without errors.

It's your job to ensure that your application meets the user's expectations. This is not an easy job, as you'll learn in this chapter. Developing a reliable Java application requires you to carefully plan the moves you make to create the application.

Finding data to insert

You might think that finding the data to insert into a database is a "no brainer" because you and I tend to assume that the data is always available. Yet, there are times when we can be mistaken.

Data that is placed into a database can come from a variety of sources, and each source requires you to build certain error-trapping routines into your program should the source become unavailable.

Your program can receive data to store into a database from

✔ Someone entering data into your program from the keyboard

✔ Another table

✔ A file

✔ Data written into your program

The examples in this chapter have the data to insert into the table written directly into the program. This is the most secure — and least desirable — way of collecting data. It's secure in the sense that the data will always exist when I run the program because I wrote it into the program. However, this approach is the least desirable because I cannot readily change the data. A programmer must change the data.

Getting the data from the other sources enables you to change the data easily, but also requires you to verify that the data source is available before having your program try to insert the data into the table. You can determine whether the source is available by using the Java language if statement.

Pick up a copy of *Java For Dummies,* 3rd Edition, by Aaron Walsh (Hungry Minds, Inc.) if you're unsure how to test whether data sources are available.

Validating before inserting data

You're not out of the woods yet. Even if your program determines that the source of the data is available, you must verify that the data coming from the source is valid; otherwise, you'll be entering erroneous data into the table.

The validation process consists of Java statements written into your program that test the data to make sure that it's correct. Many times, you won't be 100 percent sure of the data's validity because your program doesn't have sufficient data to make that determination.

Let's say that your program received a customer's last name from someone entering data about a new customer into your program. Your program isn't capable of knowing whether the last name is truly the last name of a customer.

However, your program can test the data to be assured it seems reasonable. Here is what your program should do:

- ✔ **Verify that the data submitted contains data and is not empty:** Some columns of a table don't permit NULL data, which is the term used to refer to data that doesn't contain a value.

- ✔ **Verify that the data is the correct kind of data:** For example, you won't expect a customer's last name to contain numbers. If your program finds numbers in a last name, it won't enter the last name into the table because it would be suspected of containing erroneous data.

- ✔ **Verify that the data is the correct data type:** Your program cannot place a number in a column that has a Character data type. Therefore, your program must make sure the source data and the column are compatible data types.

- ✔ **Verify that the data makes sense:** I call this the reasonableness test, whereby you write logic into your program that simulates the logic you use when looking at the data. For example, you probably would be suspicious of a salary that is $500,000 or more for an employee who isn't one of the top executives of the company. Therefore, you can write Java statements, such as the if statement, to trap suspicious data before inserting it into the table.

The program should place source data that doesn't pass the validation test into an error table. Then it should display a message telling the user about the potential errors. The user can then correct and resubmit the data.

Creating a table

It should go without saying that you must create the database and tables before your program tries to insert data. Figure 12-1 contains the table that I use for all the examples in this chapter.

customername : Table		_ □ ×

Field Name	Data Type	Description
FirstName	Text	Customer First Name
LastName	Text	Customer Last Name
CustomerNumber	Number	
StartDate	Date/Time	

Field Properties

General | Lookup

Field Size	50
Format	
Input Mask	
Caption	
Default Value	
Validation Rule	
Validation Text	
Required	No
Allow Zero Length	No
Indexed	No

The field description is optional. It helps you describe the field and is also displayed in the status bar when you select this field on a form. Press F1 for help on descriptions.

Figure 12-1: Create this table for use with the examples in this chapter.

Be sure to create this table before you try any of the examples that insert data into the table. I call the table customername because it contains data about the customer. You can call the table whatever you wish as long as you also substitute that name for customername in these examples.

Likewise, I call the database customers, which you can change. You'll need to change the name of the database in these examples to the name that you'll be using for the examples.

Don't Be Shy. Be Insertive!

Your Java database application can insert data into a table using the SQL `INSERT` statement, specifying the names of columns where the data should go, and specifying the data that is to be inserted into the columns.

All data that is inserted into a table is placed in a new row at the end of the table by the DBMS. This means that if you select all the rows from the table without previously sorting the rows, you'll find the new row that you inserted at the bottom of the rows of data.

You have several ways to insert your data:

- Insert data into all the columns without specifying the column name
- Insert data into specific columns by specifying the column name
- Insert data by referencing system data, such as the current date, rather than specifying data to insert into the column

Don't confuse inserting data into a table with updating data. Updating data refers to replacing data that was previously inserted into the table, which I show you how to do in Chapter 15.

Inserting your first row of data

Listing 12-1 illustrates the technique for inserting a full row of data into a table. I call the application inserttst, which is short for "insert test." It inserts data about the customer Mary Smith into the customername table.

You'll notice in this example that I don't have to specify the names of the columns in the table. This is because the DBMS assumes that the first piece of data belongs in the first column, the second piece of data belongs to the second column, and so on.

Data is identified by the VALUES SQL modifier, followed by the data. You must enter all Character data within single quotations. Don't place numbers within single quotations. You must separate each piece of data by a comma, except for the last piece of data.

If you populated the CustomerNumber column in Chapter 11 with the number 1 for any row, you need to change the number in this code to a Customer Number that hasn't been used.

When running this problem you'll see a message displayed onscreen, telling you that no ResultSet is found. Whenever you insert, update, or delete data in a table, you don't request data to be returned; therefore, there isn't a ResultSet. You can verify that data was inserted, updated, or deleted from a table by looking at the table in Microsoft Access or asking the DBMS to display the data, which I show you how to do in Chapter 13.

Listing 12-1:   Inserttst

```java
import java.sql.*;

public class inserttst
{
    private Connection Database;

    public inserttst()
    {
        String url = "jdbc:odbc:customers";
        String userID = "jim";
        String password = "keogh";

        try {
            Class.forName( "sun.jdbc.odbc.JdbcOdbcDriver");

            Database =
            DriverManager.getConnection(url,userID,password);
        }
        catch (ClassNotFoundException error) {
            System.err.println("Unable to load the JDBC/ODBC
            bridge." + error);
            System.exit(1);
        }
        catch (SQLException error) {
            System.err.println("Cannot connect to the
            database.");
            System.exit(2);
        }

        Statement DataRequest;
        try {
            String query = "INSERT INTO customername  " +
                                " VALUES
            ('Mary','Smith',1,'10/10/2002') ";
            DataRequest = Database.createStatement();
            DataRequest.executeQuery (query);
            DataRequest.close();
        }
        catch ( SQLException error ){
            System.err.println("SQL error." + error);
        }
    }

    public static void main ( String args [] )
    {
        final inserttst link = new inserttst();
            System.exit ( 0 ) ;
    }
}
```

Insert Data walk-about

Let's begin the walk-about in the `main()` method since this is the program's starting point. The program starts by creating an object of the `inserttst` class, which I call `link`. This statement runs the constructor of the `inserttst` object that is defined at the beginning of the example.

You'll notice that the constructor is the workhorse of the application because this is where most of the action takes place. The program assigns the `url`, `userID`, and `password` to Strings that are used by the `getConnection()` method to connect to and open the database in the `try{}` block.

Next, `forName()` loads the JDBC/ODBC bridge (see Chapter 8). If either `forName()` or `getConnection()` create an error, the program throws an exception and one of the two `catch{}` blocks that follow trap the problem.

Notice that the first `catch{}` block displays an error message and then exits the program if the JDBC/ODBC bridge doesn't load. The second `catch{}` block displays an error message if the program is unable to connect to the database. The program then exits.

A successful loading of the JDBC/ODBC bridge and the connection to the database cause the second `try{}` block to execute the SQL expression needed to insert data. The program assigns the SQL expression to a String variable called `query` and then places the expression into an SQL statement. The `executeQuery()` method sends the SQL statement to the DBMS for execution. The SQL statement and the database then close.

When the `catch{}` block detects a problem, it throws an error. The `catch{}` block displays the SQL error. You'll notice a message saying that the DBMS didn't return a ResultSet. Since we didn't expect a ResultSet (because we didn't request any data), you can ignore the error message.

The program returns to the statement in the `main()` method that is below the statement that created the `createix` object after the constructor finishes execution. This exits the program.

A closer look at Insert Data code

The `INSERT INTO` statement tells the DBMS that you want to insert a new row into a table. The program places the name of the table that will receive the data in the SQL expression immediately to the right of the `INTO` keyword.

The `VALUES` modifier tells the DBMS that what follows is the data to be inserted into the row. Parentheses contain the data, and the data appears in the same order as the columns appear in the table. Single quotations contain the character data, such as the customer's name and start date. You place numbers, such as the Customer Number, in the SQL expression without quotations. A comma must separate data values.

The order of columns in a table might differ from the order of the columns that appear as a result of your data request. All of the columns may not be selected when you request to see data. Therefore, always refer to the order of columns in the table structure (refer to Figure 12-1).

Verifying that data was inserted

If you're using Microsoft Access, you can verify that the program inserted data into the table by using the Access graphical user interface. Here's what you need to do:

1. **Start Microsoft Access.**

2. **Open the customer database.**

3. **Double-click the customername table.**

4. **Look at the last row in the table, and you should see the data the program entered into the table (see Figure 12-2).**

customername : Table			
FirstName	**LastName**	**CustomerNum**	**StartDate**
Mary	Smith	1	10/10/02
		0	

Record: ◄◄ ◄ 2 ► ►◄ ►✳ of 2

Figure 12-2: Open the customer-name table to verify that the new row has been inserted into the table.

5. **If you don't see the data, rerun the program and keep an eye peeled for any error messages generated by your program. The error message will tell you what went wrong with your program.**

Alternatively, you can use the SELECT SQL statement to request the data that your program inserted into the table (see Chapter 13). If the DBMS returns the data, you know that it was inserted into the table.

Inserting data into specific columns

You may have occasions when you have data to fill some, but not all, of the columns in the table. This isn't a problem because you can write an SQL expression to insert data into columns that you specify in your program.

For example, suppose you create a Java database application that tracks employee data for your company. The application inserts data about an employee when he or she joins the firm, but you probably don't have all the data about the employee at that time. You may not know the employee's work telephone number until the employee begins working. In this case, your application will insert employee data into the table and leave the work telephone number blank. Another portion of your application can update the table once you find out the missing data.

Listing 12-2 shows how to specify the columns and the data for those columns. You can substitute this code segment for the first `try{}` block in Listing 12-1. Once you make the substitution, recompile and run the application to insert the new row into the table.

Listing 12-2:   Insert Data into Specific Columns

```
try {
    String query = "INSERT INTO customername
    (FirstName, LastName,CustomerNumber,StartDate )
    VALUES ( 'Bob','Jones',2,'10/11/2001') ";
    DataRequest = Database.createStatement();
    DataRequest.executeQuery (query );
    DataRequest.close();
}
```

The SQL expression in Listing 12-2 is similar to the SQL expression in Listing 12-1. Both use the `INSERT INTO` statement to tell the DBMS to insert a new row into the customername table.

However, that's where the similarities stop. Following the name of the table in the SQL expression are the names of the columns that will receive the data. You must enclose column names within parentheses, and you must separate each column name with a comma.

The `VALUES` keyword precedes the data that will be stored in each column. This is similar to the data that you inserted into the previous program. The position of the data within the parenthesis determines in which column the data will be inserted. That is, the first piece of data goes into the first column listed in the SQL expression, the second piece of data goes into the second column, and so on.

Make sure that the data and column names appear in the correct order, otherwise you might discover that the DBMS places the data in the wrong column when you retrieve the data. You might also receive an error message if an attempt is made to place data with the wrong data type into the wrong column.

Preventing errors by making your code easy to read

Sometimes I inadvertently make errors by not properly matching the column names with the appropriate data. I found a way to reduce the chance of errors and I thought that I'd pass this along to you.

Listing 12-3 has two Strings: col, which has column names, and dat, which contains the data. I can easily match the data to column names because the data are positioned nearly below the correct column name.

Next, I concatenate the String names to the SQL expression. I'm sure that you'll agree that the SQL expression is easier to read than Listing 12-2.

Listing 12-3: Making Code Easier to Read

```
try {
    String col = "FirstName, LastName,
CustomerNumber, StartDate";
    String dat = "'Bob', 'Jones', 2 , '10/11/2001'";
    String query = "INSERT INTO customername ( " +
col + ") VALUES (" + dat +");
    DataRequest = Database.createStatement();
    DataRequest.executeQuery (query );
    DataRequest.close();
}
```

Let the DBMS Insert Values for You

Some DBMSs recognize SQL2 functions that automatically insert certain kinds of data into a column. SQL2 is a revision of the original SQL. An SQL function is similar to a Java method but isn't associated with a Java class.

You can use these functions within the SQL expression of your Java database application in place of actual data. The DBMS executes the function before inserting data into the table. The function returns the actual data, which is then inserted into the table along with all the other data that you submitted as part of the SQL expression.

You can learn more about SQL functions by reading *SQL For Dummies,* 4th Edition, by Allen Taylor (Hungry Minds, Inc.). Keep in mind that not all DBMSs recognize these functions. Therefore, you should be alert for error messages the first time you run a Java database program that uses an SQL function or when you change databases.

The DBMS has a date for you

You can have the DBMS insert the current date into a column by using the CURRENT_DATE() function in your SQL expression (see Listing 12-4). The DBMS replaces the name of the function (CURRENT_DATE()) with the date found on the database server where the DBMS is running.

Microsoft Access doesn't recognize the CURRENT_DATE() function. Therefore, you'll need to substitute month(now)+day(now)+year(now) for CURRENT_DATE().

Listing 12-4:   Using CURRENT_DATE

```
try {
    String query = "INSERT INTO customername
    (FirstName, LastName,CustomerNumber,StartDate )
    VALUES ( 'Bob','Jones',2,CURRENT_DATE()) ";
    DataRequest = Database.createStatement();
    DataRequest.executeQuery (query );
    DataRequest.close();
}
```

The DBMS has time for you

For Java database applications that are time dependent, such as an order-entry system, you can use the CURRENT_TIME SQL function. This is a valuable feature to include in your application since the DBMS records the exact time the data enters the table. Listing 12-5 has the DBMS insert both the current date and the current time.

Microsoft Access doesn't recognize the CURRENT_DATE() function or the CURRENT_TIME() function. Therefore, you'll need to substitute month(now)+day(now)+year(now) for CURRENT_DATE() and Time() for CURRENT_TIME().

Listing 12-5:   Using CURRENT_TIME

```
try {
    String query = "INSERT INTO customername
(FirstName, LastName,CustomerNumber,StartDate,
StartTime ) VALUES (
'Bob','Jones',2,CURRENT_DATE(), CURRENT_TIME()) ";
    DataRequest = Database.createStatement();
    DataRequest.executeQuery (query );
    DataRequest.close();
}
```

Hold out your wrist for a TIMESTAMP

For some applications, it's critical that you insert both the date and time into a new row of data the moment you place the data into the database. This is a very common practice in applications that are used to track orders for buying and selling stocks.

Instead of using two columns and two SQL functions to capture the system's date and time, you can use one column and the CURRENT_TIMESTAMP() function (see Listing 12-6). The DBMS replaces the CURRENT_TIMESTAMP() function call in your SQL expression with the current date and time on the database server running the DBMS.

Microsoft Access doesn't recognize the CURRENT_TIMESTAMP() function. Therefore, you'll need to substitute now for CURRENT_TIMESTAMP().

Listing 12-6:   Using CURRENT_TIMESTAMP

```
try {
    String query = "INSERT INTO customername
(FirstName,
LastName,CustomerNumber,StartDateAndTime ) VALUES
( 'Bob','Jones',2,CURRENT_TIMESTAMP()) ";
    DataRequest = Database.createStatement();
    DataRequest.executeQuery (query );
    DataRequest.close();
}
```

Test your newfound knowledge

1. What does INSERT do in an SQL expression?

a. It inserts the current date into the SQL expression.

b. It tells the DBMS to insert a new row in the table.

c. It tells the DBMS to insert a new table in a database.

d. It inserts a new database into a table.

2. Why must your application validate data before placing it into a table?

a. So you don't have to pay for parking.

b. To prevent erroneous data from entering the database.

c. To make sure the DBMS places the current date in the row.

d. So the correct SQL expression can be created.

Answers: (1) b. (2) b.

Chapter 13

I'll Just Pick: Selecting Data from a Table

. . . .

In This Chapter

▶ Selecting only columns you need

▶ Selecting rows that are within a range of data

▶ Selecting rows where data is missing

▶ Selecting rows that match a set of criteria

. . . .

*T*he purpose of designing, creating, and storing data into a database is to be able to retrieve that data quickly and easily. Database management systems (DBMSs) can efficiently serve up any data contained in the database as long as you tell it what you want.

Your job is to create a Java database application that clearly and specifically provides instructions to the DBMS to locate the data in the database. You write your instructions as an SQL expression, which you place into an SQL statement and send to the DBMS.

This chapter shows you how to create a Java database application that executes an SQL statement to retrieve data that

✔ Matches your search criteria

✔ Doesn't match your search criteria

✔ Matches a portion of your search criteria

I'll also show you how to pick and choose the columns of data from rows that match your search criteria.

Getting Ready: Before You Select Data

Search engines on the Internet have spoiled us to a point where we expect to enter data that we're searching for, click a button on the browser, and have the matching data appear onscreen almost instantly.

Sometimes we are happy with the results of our search because the search engine is able to find the exact data that we need. Other times, the volume of data the search engine returns overwhelms us. We have to sift through lines of irrelevant data before finding what we're looking for — assuming the search engine found the needed data. I've found myself having to refine my request several times before the search engine located the data I needed.

A DBMS is not a search engine. You can't simply enter the search criteria into your program and have the DBMS retrieve the data. Unlike working with a search engine, you must carefully create your request for data.

The database schema contains most of the data that you need to create a request for data (see Chapter 6). Here is the data that you need to include in your request:

- The name of the table that contains the data
- The name of the columns of the table that you want to see
- The name of the column that contains the search criteria
- The data type of the column that contains the search criteria
- The search criteria
- The search expression

The search expression determines how you want the DBMS to decide which rows of data to return to your application.

Finding data

The data dictionary tells you the kind of data that each table contains. If you designed and created the table, you probably already know this data.

However, this may not be the case if you are building a Java database application for a company, since companies tend to hire specialists to design and create a database and all associated tables. Therefore, you'll need to do a little searching to figure out which tables and columns you need for your application.

You can locate the data dictionary with two commonly used methods:

✔ **Contact your database administrator and ask if he or she can provide you with the necessary data:** Typically the database administrator can query the DBMS and send you the data dictionary for the tables in the database.

✔ **Create a program that retrieves metadata from the database:** *Metadata* is data that describes the real data, such as the column name and column data types (see Chapter 14 for instructions on how to do this).

For now, create a new table called customers using the following specifications:

Column	Data Type	Size
FirstName	Text	50
LastName	Text	50
Street	Text	50
City	Text	50
State	Text	2
ZipCode	Text	12

I am using a similar table in the examples throughout this chapter. Figure 13-1 contains the customer data that I've entered in my tables. You can enter the same data so you can duplicate the examples in this chapter. You can also enter your own customer data into the table, but remember that the results of your selection will be different from those that I show you in this chapter.

Customer Names

FirstName	LastName	Street	City	State	ZipCode
Mary	Smith	24 Oak Street	San Jose	CA	77777
Bob	Jones	121 Spruce ...	New York City	NY	55555
Mark	Jones	15 Maple Str...	Dallas	TX	66666
Mary	Smith	56 Pine Street	Trenton	NJ	88888

Figure 13-1: Enter these rows into your table.

Getting to know the data type

You need to know the data type of the columns containing the data that you'll be searching for because you must make sure that your search value is of the same data type.

For example, imagine that you are looking for data about Employee Number 5555. The column that contains Employee Numbers in a table is a Character data type. This means that the number 5555 is a series of four characters rather than the number 5,555.

The search value must be the same data type as the column that is going to be searched by the DBMS. In this example, the search value is '5555'. Notice that the Employee Number has single quotation marks surrounding it. This tells the DBMS that the search value is a character — actually a series of four characters.

The DBMS won't return an error because the data type of the search value is the same as the data type of the column. However, by removing the single quotations, the data type of the search value suddenly changes to a NUMERIC data type. This change causes the DBMS to return an error because the search value's data type is different from the column's data type.

Starting with a Simple Request

Let's begin by requesting all the rows and all the columns of each row from a table. You'll find this request useful whenever you're unsure of the kind of data in a table. The database administrator might provide the data dictionary for the table, but the data dictionary may not necessarily provide a clue as to the kind of data that's in the table.

For example, a column name in the data dictionary may say Social Security number, which probably seems explicit because you know what a Social Security number looks like. However, are Social Security numbers in the column displayed with or without hyphens embedded within the number?

The data dictionary doesn't answer this question, although some DBMSs enable the database designer to include a data format as part of the table's design. A data format defines whether the data uses hyphens and other formatting characters. If so, the data format tells you the position of the formatting characters in the data.

By selecting all the rows from a table, you can see the format of data in all the columns. You can then use this data to determine whether the search values should be formatted a particular way.

You select data from a table using the SELECT SQL statement followed by the names of the columns you want to see. Listing 13-1 shows you how to select all the rows and all the columns from the customers table (refer to Figure 13-1).

The DBMS won't become confused if you call the table by the same name as the database. It knows which one you are referring to in your Java database program.

In this example, I use an asterisk (*) instead of column names. The asterisk is a wild card character that represents any value. Since the asterisk appears in the SQL expression where the DBMS expects to see column names, it implies that we want to see all the columns from the table.

I use the WHERE clause to describe the search criteria for the query. I didn't include a WHERE clause since I wanted to see all the data contained in the table. I'll show you how to use the WHERE clause in "Picking the Rows You Want to See with WHERE Clause."

The program inserts and displays onscreen the rows that the DBMS returned. However, your program doesn't have to display data from a database. It can manipulate the data or transmit it to another computer.

I show you how to save the results of a query to variables in your Java application in Chapter 14. Once data is assigned to variables, you can use the data just as you would use a variable in your program.

Listing 13-1: Selecting All the Rows and Columns

```java
        import java.sql.*;
import javax.swing.*;
import java.awt.event.*;
import java.awt.*;
import java.util.*;
import java.lang.*;

    public class selecttst extends JFrame
    {
        private JTable DataTable;
        private Connection Database;

        public selecttst()
        {
            String url = "jdbc:odbc:customers";
            String userID = "jim";
            String password = "keogh";
            Statement DataRequest;
            ResultSet Results;

            try {
                Class.forName( "sun.jdbc.odbc.JdbcOdbcDriver");
                Database =
                DriverManager.getConnection(url,userID,password);
            }
            catch (ClassNotFoundException error) {
```

(continued)

Listing 13-1 *(continued)*

```
            System.err.println("Unable to load the JDBC/ODBC
        bridge." + error);
            System.exit(1);
    }
    catch (SQLException error) {
        System.err.println("Cannot connect to the
        database." + error);
        System.exit(2);
    }

    try {
        String query = "SELECT * FROM customers";
        DataRequest = Database.createStatement();
        Results = DataRequest.executeQuery (query);
        DisplayResults (Results);
        DataRequest.close();
    }
    catch ( SQLException error ){
        System.err.println("SQL error." + error);
        System.exit(3);
    }

    setSize (500, 200);
    show();
}

private void DisplayResults (ResultSet
        DisplayResults)throws SQLException
{
    boolean Records = DisplayResults.next();

    if (!Records ) {
      JOptionPane.showMessageDialog(this, "End of data.");
    setTitle( "Process Completed");
    return;
    }
    setTitle ("Customer Names");
    Vector ColumnNames = new Vector();
    Vector rows = new Vector();

    try {
        ResultSetMetaData MetaData =
          DisplayResults.getMetaData();

        for ( int x = 1; x <= MetaData.getColumnCount();
          ++x)
          ColumnNames.addElement (MetaData.getColumnName (
          x ) );

        do {
            rows.addElement (DownRow( DisplayResults,
          MetaData ) );
```

```
        } while ( DisplayResults.next() );


        DataTable = new JTable (rows, ColumnNames ) ;
        JScrollPane scroller = new JScrollPane ( DataTable
          ) ;
        getContentPane(). add ( scroller,
          BorderLayout.CENTER );
        validate();
      }
    catch (SQLException error ) {
        System.err.println("Data display error." + error);
        System.exit(4);
      }
  }

  private Vector DownRow ( ResultSet DisplayResults,
        ResultSetMetaData MetaData )
      throws SQLException
  {
    Vector currentRow = new Vector();
    for ( int x = 1; x <= MetaData.getColumnCount(); ++x )
      switch ( MetaData.getColumnType ( x ) ) {
      case Types.VARCHAR :
        currentRow.addElement( DisplayResults.getString
      ( x ) ) ;
        break;
      }
    return currentRow;
  }

  public static void main ( String args [] )
  {
    final selecttst link = new selecttst();

    link.addWindowListener (
        new WindowAdapter() {
        public void windowClosing(WindowEvent WinEvent )
        {
          System.exit (0) ;
        }
      }

  );
  }
}
```

Simple Selection walk-about

The program begins with the first statement in the main() method, which creates an object of the selecttst class. The selecttst class is defined at the top of the listing.

The `selecttst()` constructor automatically executes when the `selecttst` object is created in your program. The first three statements in the constructor assign data you need to access the database to String variables. You use the String variables later to connect to the database. The `url` String contains a reference to the data source (`jdbc:odbc:customers`).

The constructor also creates a `Statement` object and a `ResultSet` object. The program later uses the `Statement` object to create an SQL statement from the SQL expression, which contains the query to request data from the DBMS.

The `try{}` block loads the JDBC/ODBC bridge (see Chapter 7) and then connects and opens the database using the `getConnection()` method. The program passes the `url` of the database, `userID`, and `password` to the `getConnection()` method.

One of the `catch{}` blocks captures errors that occur within the `try{}` block. The first `catch{}` block displays an error and exits the program if the JDBC/ODBC bridge can't load. The second `catch{}` block displays an error and exits the program if a connection cannot be made to the database. The program returns the values 1 and 2, respectively, which are error codes, to the operating system, indicating that it found an error.

If the program is able to load the JDBC/ODBC bridge and connect to the database, it then constructs an SQL expression within the second `try{}` block. The SQL expression selects all the columns from the customers table and is assigned to the `query` String. The asterisk (*) is a wild card that represents any column name.

Next, the program creates a new SQL statement (`createStatement()`), which returns a reference to the SQL `Statement` object. The program calls the `executeQuery()` method of the `Statement` object and passes the `query` String. The `executeQuery()` object sends the query to the DBMS. The `Results` object references `Rows` from the table, which is an object of the `ResultSet` class.

The program then passes the `Results` object to the `DisplayResults()` method, which is the next method defined in the program. The database connection then closes, and the program creates and shows a graphical user interface window (`show()`). The size of the window is measured in pixels and set by the `setSize()` method.

The `catch{}` block captures SQL errors that occur in the second `try{}` block. The `catch{}` block then displays the SQL error onscreen and exits the program.

Once all the data displays onscreen, the `selecttst` constructor completes execution and returns control to the `main()` method. The program creates a

WindowListener (addWindowListener()), which monitors messages sent to the program by the operating system and passes those messages to the WindowAdapter (WindowAdapter()).

Programs running in the operating system generate events. The operating system detects an event when someone uses the mouse or keyboard and sends a message containing the event to the program.

In this example, the WindowAdapter contains one method called windowClosing() that is called whenever someone closes the window that contains the data. The program then ends.

DisplayResults () walk-about: The query

The DisplayResults() method takes the column names from the table and values of each column and displays them in a table within a graphical user interface window (refer to Figure 13-1). First, the program calls the next() method to move the virtual cursor to the first row in the rows that were returned by the DBMS.

The next() method returns a true value, which is assigned the Records variable if the row contains data. If not, the next() method returns a false, and a dialog box displays onscreen stating that the program is at the end of the data. The program returns to the selecttst constructor and executes the statement (DataRequest.close()) following the call to DisplayResults(), which closes the connection to the database.

As long as there is data in the row, the program creates two Vectors: one for column names and the other for data contained in the columns. The try{} block retrieves the medadata from the data returned by the DBMS and loads the column names into the Vector.

Also, the try{} block contains a do...while loop that calls the DownRow() method and loads the data for each row in the Vector. The DownRow() method is the next method defined in the program.

The program loads both column names and data into a table and displays them onscreen. However, before you see the column names and data displayed, the program calls the validate() method to make sure that there aren't any GUI errors. Then the catch{} block captures errors and displays them onscreen.

DownRow () walk-about: The query

The purpose of the DownRow() method is to provide an orderly way to move the virtual cursor to the next row in data returned by the DBMS and then position the data into a Vector so that the data can appear onscreen.

First, the program creates a Vector that will hold data collected from the row. This Vector returns to the DisplayResults() method for display. The program uses the getColumnCount() method to determine the number of columns in the return data. This value is the maximum value for the for loop.

For each column, the program determines the data type of the column (get.ColumnType()) using the switch() statement. Since I know the table only has columns of the String data type, I use only one case statement. You can easily expand the switch() statement to include other case statements (see Chapter 14).

The get.String() method uses the column number passed to getString() by the program. The getString() method returns the String object that contains data in the column associated with the column number. The data is placed into the Vector (addElement()). Once data has been collected from all the columns, the DownRow() method returns the Vector containing the data to the DisplayResults() method, and the data displays onscreen.

Selecting the Columns You Want to See

You probably will want to pick and choose the columns of data to use in your program rather than use all the columns of a table. This is because some columns may not be useful to your program.

For example, you might want to retrieve a customer's telephone number. The table is likely to have other data about the customer. It doesn't make sense to ask the DBMS for all the columns when you only need data contained in one column.

You can choose the column you want to retrieve by placing the name of the column in the SQL expression following the SELECT statement.

Selecting a single column

Listing 13-2 shows you how to specify a column when you're requesting data from a database. In this example, I ask the DBMS to return the LastName column of all the rows from the customers table.

You can replace the second try{} block in the constructor of Listing 13-1 with the try{} block in this code segment, recompile, and run the program. The program sends the SQL statement to the DBMS and displays the data in a table onscreen (see Figure 13-2).

Figure 13-2:
Select
values in the
LastName
column of
all the rows
in the
customers
table.

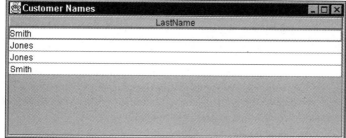

 Listing 13-2:   Selecting a Specific Column

```
try {
    String query = "SELECT LastName FROM customers";
    DataRequest = Database.createStatement();
    Results = DataRequest.executeQuery (query);
    DisplayResults (Results);
    DataRequest.close();
}
```

Selecting multiple columns

You can ask the DBMS to return more than one column from the table by modifying the SQL expression in Listing 13-2. Listing 13-3 shows you how to select both the customer's first name and last name for each row in the table.

In Listing 13-3, I place the name of the columns that contain the first name and last name in the SQL expression following the SELECT statement. Notice that a comma separates the column names.

You can include multiple column names in your Java database application by placing the names of the columns in the SQL expression. Substitute the following code segment for the second try{} block in the program. You should see the customers' first names and last names appear onscreen when you run the program.

 Listing 13-3:   Selecting More Than One Column

```
try {
    String query = "SELECT FirstName, LastName FROM
customers";
    DataRequest = Database.createStatement();
    Results = DataRequest.executeQuery (query);
    DisplayResults (Results);
    DataRequest.close();
}
```

Picking the Rows You Want to See with WHERE

You can have your Java database application filter those rows of data that your application doesn't need by using the WHERE clause. The WHERE clause is like having your own assistant who will screen your calls, so you need to deal only with people who are important to you.

Imagine that someone who is using your application receives a telephone call from a customer. Her assistant took the message since she was busy on another call, but she can't read her assistant's handwriting and her assistant is out to lunch. She can make out the customer's name; however, the telephone number is illegible.

She has nothing to worry about because your Java database application can come to the rescue. She enters the customer's name into a data-entry screen that you built for your application and then clicks the OK button.

Your application uses the customer's name as the search value in the SQL expression and has the DBMS retrieve data about the customer, which includes the customer's telephone number. Your application then displays the customer's data onscreen (see Chapter 14).

You become the hero because your application uses the WHERE clause in the SQL expression to filter all data except for the requested customer. This section shows you the effective ways of using the WHERE clause.

The WHERE clause contains an expression that tells the DBMS characteristics of rows of data that you need from the database. Listing 13-4 illustrates where to place the WHERE clause in an SQL expression.

The expression used in the WHERE clause must specify three factors:

- The name of the column that contains the search value
- An operator that indicates the type of comparison that is used to filter rows
- The search value

In Listing 13-4, I tell the DBMS to return all the columns of rows in the customers table where the LastName column contains the value Jones. The column name in this expression is LastName.

I use the equal operator, which tells the DBMS that I'm looking for rows where the value of the LastName column is equal to Jones. I show you how to use the other operators later in this section.

Jones is the search value. Notice that I place Jones within single quotations, which means that Jones is a String. If I were to leave out the single quotes, I'd get an error from the DBMS. When I run this program, I get only the rows that have the last name Jones.

Replace the second `try{}` block in the constructor of Listing 13-1 with the following code segment.

Listing 13-4:   Selecting Rows

```
try {
    String query = "SELECT * " +
                   "FROM customers " +
                   "WHERE LastName = 'Jones' ";
    DataRequest = Database.createStatement();
    Results = DataRequest.executeQuery (query);
    DisplayResults (Results);
    DataRequest.close();
}
```

When you recompile and run the program, the results will look like Figure 13-3, unless you use different customer data in your tables.

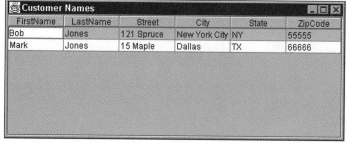

Figure 13-3: Select rows with a LastName of Jones.

FirstName	LastName	Street	City	State	ZipCode
Bob	Jones	121 Spruce	New York City	NY	55555
Mark	Jones	15 Maple	Dallas	TX	66666

Selecting Rows and Columns

You may find that many Java database applications that you build require you to search for particular rows and use only a few of the columns of those rows. Tables are often chock-full of data that the company can use to address any of its needs. Luckily, each application typically addresses one of those needs.

By using the WHERE clause and carefully specifying the columns you want the database to retrieve, you can narrow the amount of data that your Java database application receives.

Listing 13-5 illustrates how you can choose rows and columns that are important to your application. In this example, I request the first name and last name of any row in the customers table that contains the last name of Jones.

Notice that I specify the column names in the SELECT statement with a comma separating each column name. You can use as many column names as your application needs.

I also use the LastName column name in the search expression. It just so happens that I'm searching the LastName column and I also want to retrieve the LastName column. You don't have to retrieve the column that contains the search value.

For example, I could have used the Telephone column as the SELECT criteria and used LastName as the column to search. This would result in the DBMS returning the telephone number of everyone who had the last name Jones in the customers table. Of course, this wouldn't make sense since I wouldn't have any way of knowing which telephone number is associated with the Jones that I want to call.

Of course, you need to substitute this code segment with the second try{} block in the constructor of Listing 13-1.

Listing 13-5:   Selecting Specific Rows and Columns

```
try {
    String query = "SELECT FirstName, LastName " +
                   "FROM customers " +
                   "WHERE LastName = 'Jones' ";
    DataRequest = Database.createStatement();
    Results = DataRequest.executeQuery (query);
    DisplayResults (Results);
    DataRequest.close();
}
```

Figure 13-4 shows you the results of running Listing 13-5.

Customer Names		_ □ ✕
FirstName		LastName
Bob		Jones
Mark		Jones

Figure 13-4:
Select
LastName
equal to
Jones.

Getting to Know AND, OR, and NOT

I've discovered that many of my Java database applications require multiple search criteria, so you should expect a similar experience. Therefore, you need to be able to include more than one search criterion in your SQL expression.

You have three ways to use multiple search criteria. These are by using

- AND
- OR
- NOT

The AND keyword joins together two search expressions to form the search criteria for your SQL expression. For example, you may want rows of data about customers who reside in a particular Zip Code and who have a certain last name.

Your search criteria must say, "get me customers who live in 07660 *and* who have the last name Jones." The DBMS returns rows of data that meet both criteria and ignores all other rows.

Likewise, your application may need data that meets either search criterion. For example, you might say, "get me customers who live in 07660 *or* who have the last name Jones." In this example, the DBMS returns all rows that have Jones in the LastName column and all rows that have 07660 in the ZipCode column.

You can ask for rows that don't contain the value of the search expression by using the NOT keyword. For example, you may want to retrieve customer data for customers that don't reside in a particular Zip Code.

This means that you'll tell the DBMS, "send me all rows where the Zip Code is *not* equal to 07660." Of course, you'd use the proper SQL words, which I'll show you in the following sections.

Combining conditions with AND

You can use the AND keyword to join together two search expressions, as you'll see in Listing 13-6. In this example, I'm looking for my customer Bob Jones, so I tell the DBMS to search the LastName column for the name Jones and the FirstName column for the name Bob.

Using the equal operator, the DBMS returns only rows that contain Bob and Jones in the FirstName and LastName columns. The DBMS ignores the other rows.

Listing 13-6:   Using the AND Keyword

```
try {
    String query = "SELECT FirstName, LastName " +
                   "FROM customers " +
                   "WHERE LastName = 'Jones' " +
                   "AND FirstName = 'Bob' ";
    DataRequest = Database.createStatement();
    Results = DataRequest.executeQuery (query);
    DisplayResults (Results);
    DataRequest.close();
}
```

Using OR whenever you're not sure

Suppose someone left you a note to call Mary, but he scribbled the note in his worst handwriting and you're not sure if the last letter is a *y* or *k*. Don't fret because you can ask the DBMS for help.

You can use the OR keyword in your application's SQL expression to request rows that contain either Mary or Mark as the customer's first name. Listing 13-7 contains this SQL expression.

Listing 13-7:   Using the OR Keyword

```
try { .
    String query = "SELECT FirstName, LastName " +
                   "FROM customers " +
                   "WHERE FirstName = 'Mary' " +
                   "OR FirstName = 'Mark' ";
    DataRequest = Database.createStatement();
    Results = DataRequest.executeQuery (query);
    DisplayResults (Results);
    DataRequest.close();
}
```

Using NOT when you know what you don't want

"I love you — *not!*" Remember the fad of saying something positive and then using the word "not" at the end?

You and I don't normally speak that way unless we're joking, but we need to speak that way when telling the DBMS to return data that doesn't match a search value. Listing 13-8 illustrates this.

First, I write the expression using the equal operator, which tells the DBMS to give me rows that contain Mary in the FirstName column. However, preceding the expression with the word NOT reverses the logic of this expression.

I'm actually telling the DBMS to send me rows where the value of the FirstName column does not equal Mary. Figure 13-5 shows the result of this request.

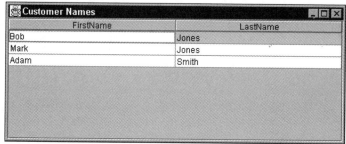

Figure 13-5:
Using NOT reverses the logic of the expression.

NOT reverses the logic of the expression that follows it. Therefore, write the expression that includes the search value and then run the program. If you receive rows that contain only the search value, you know that you've written the search expression correctly. You can then insert the word NOT to exclude the original search value from the returning data when you run the program again.

Listing 13-8: Using the NOT Keyword

```
try {
    String query = "SELECT FirstName, LastName " +
                   "FROM customers " +
                   "WHERE NOT FirstName = 'Mary'";
    DataRequest = Database.createStatement();
    Results = DataRequest.executeQuery (query);
    DisplayResults (Results);
    DataRequest.close();
}
```

Test your newfound knowledge

1. How do you instruct the DBMS to give your application rows that don't match your search criteria?

   a. Use AND.

   b. Use OR.

   c. Use NOT.

   d. Use NEITHER.

2. How do you set the search criteria for the DBMS?

   a. Use SELECT.

   b. Use WHERE.

   c. Use FROM.

   d. Use SELECT *.

   Answers: (1) c. (2) b.

Making Sure Data Passes Your Test

Another way to get the rows that you need is to ask the DBMS to compare the value in a particular column against a search value that you enter into the SQL expression in your program.

For example, you might want to retrieve customers whose sales are above $10,000. So, you need to tell the DBMS, "Give me all the columns of data for customers whose sales are greater than $10,000." Of course, you need to write your request in a language the DBMS understands, which is SQL. I'll show you how to do this in this section.

The DBMS can make seven common comparisons, depending on the operator that you use in the SQL expression. (The *operator* is the symbol in the SQL expression that defines the type of comparison you need.) The comparisons are

- Equal (=)
- Not equal (<>)
- Less than (<)
- Greater than (>)
- Less than equal (<=)
- Greater than equal (>=)
- Between (BETWEEN)

I'll show you how to use each of these comparisons. However, before doing so, you need to modify the customers table that you built at the beginning of the chapter. These changes enable you to experiment with the programs I use to demonstrate comparisons. Here are the changes:

✔ Insert two new columns in the table, and call them Profit and Sales. Your customers table should look like this:

Column	Data Type	Size
FirstName	Text	50
LastName	Text	50
Street	Text	50
City	Text	50
State	Text	2
ZipCode	Text	12
Sales	Number	
Profit	Number	

✔ Open the table, and enter profit and sales numbers for each row in the table. See my example:

Name	Sales	Profit
Bob Jones	10000	2000
Mark Jones	20000	4000
Adam Smith	30000	6000
Mary Smith	40000	10000

You can use the profit and sales numbers that I use or you can insert your own values into those columns. However, if you choose to use your own numbers, remember that the data the DBMS returns to you will be different from my data.

Equal

If you've been trying the sample programs in this chapter, you have already used the equal operator. You're welcome to skip this section and move on to the "Not equal" section.

Here I'll formally introduce you to the equal operator if you haven't tried those programs. The equal operator (=) tells the DBMS that you want rows of data where the value of a particular column is equal to the search value in your SQL expression.

You can see how this works in Listing 13-9. I ask the DBMS to show me all the columns of rows from the customers table where the value of the Sales column is 30000. When you run this program, you'll see the data shown in Figure 13-6.

Listing 13-9:   Using the Equal Operator

```java
        import java.sql.*;
import javax.swing.*;
import java.awt.event.*;
import java.awt.*;
import java.util.*;
import java.lang.*;

   public class selecttst extends JFrame
   {
       private JTable DataTable;
       private Connection Database;

       public selecttst()
       {
           String url = "jdbc:odbc:customers";
           String userID = "jim";
           String password = "keogh";
           Statement DataRequest;
           ResultSet Results;

           try {
               Class.forName( "sun.jdbc.odbc.JdbcOdbcDriver");

               Database =
             DriverManager.getConnection(url,userID,password);
           }
           catch (ClassNotFoundException error) {
               System.err.println("Unable to load the JDBC/ODBC
           bridge." + error);
               System.exit(1);
           }
           catch (SQLException error) {
               System.err.println("Cannot connect to the
           database." + error);
               System.exit(2);
           }

           try {
               String query = "SELECT * " +
                              "FROM customers " +
                              "WHERE Sales = 30000 ";
               DataRequest = Database.createStatement();
               Results = DataRequest.executeQuery (query);
               DisplayResults (Results);
               DataRequest.close();
           }
```

```
        catch ( SQLException error ){
            System.err.println("SQL error.");
            System.exit(3);
        }

        setSize (500, 200);
        show();
    }

private void DisplayResults (ResultSet
        DisplayResults)throws SQLException
{
    boolean Records = DisplayResults.next();

    if (!Records ) {
        JOptionPane.showMessageDialog( this, "End of
            data.");
    setTitle( "Process Completed");
    return;
    }
    setTitle ("Customer Names");
    Vector ColumnNames = new Vector();
    Vector rows = new Vector();

    try {
        ResultSetMetaData MetaData =
          DisplayResults.getMetaData();

        for ( int x = 1; x <= MetaData.getColumnCount();
        ++x)
            ColumnNames.addElement (MetaData.getColumnName
        ( x ) );

        do {
           rows.addElement (DownRow( DisplayResults,
        MetaData ) );
        } while ( DisplayResults.next() );


        DataTable = new JTable ( rows, ColumnNames ) ;
        JScrollPane scroller = new JScrollPane ( DataTable
          ) ;
        getContentPane(). add ( scroller,
          BorderLayout.CENTER );
        validate();
    }
    catch (SQLException error ) {
        System.err.println("Data display error." + error);
        System.exit(4);
    }
}
```

(continued)

Listing 13-9 *(continued)*

```
private Vector DownRow ( ResultSet DisplayResults,
        ResultSetMetaData MetaData )
    throws SQLException
{
    Vector currentRow = new Vector();
    for ( int x = 1; x <= MetaData.getColumnCount(); ++x )
        switch ( MetaData.getColumnType ( x ) ) {
        case Types.VARCHAR :
            currentRow.addElement( DisplayResults.getString
            ( x ) ) ;
            break;
        case Types.INTEGER :
            currentRow.addElement( new Long(
            DisplayResults.getLong( x )) ) ;
            break;
        }
    return currentRow;
}

public static void main ( String args [] )
{
    final selecttst link = new selecttst();

    link.addWindowListener (
            new WindowAdapter() {
        public void windowClosing(WindowEvent WinEvent )
        {

            System.exit ( 0 ) ;
        }
    }

    );
}
}
```

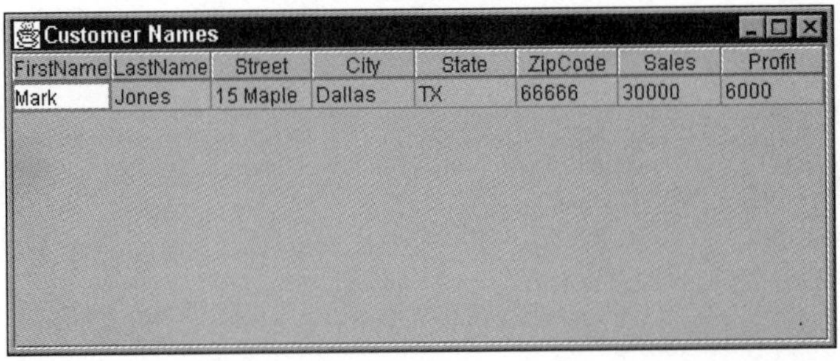

Figure 13-6:
Looking for
values equal
to the
search
criteria.

FirstName	LastName	Street	City	State	ZipCode	Sales	Profit
Mark	Jones	15 Maple	Dallas	TX	66666	30000	6000

Customer Names

Not equal

The not equal operator ($<>$) simply tells the DBMS that you want all the rows except the rows that contain the search value that you specify in the SQL expression in your program. You'll find that using the not equal operator is a handy way to exclude data that you know your Java database application doesn't need.

Listing 13-10 illustrates how to use the not equal operator in your application. In this example, I ask for all the columns in rows where the value of the Sales column doesn't equal 30000. Figure 13-7 shows the result of this program. You can test this yourself by substituting this code segment for the second try{} block in the constructor of Listing 13-9.

Listing 13-10:   Using the Not Equal Operator

```
try {
    String query = "SELECT * " +
                   "FROM customers " +
                   "WHERE Sales <> 30000 ";
    DataRequest = Database.createStatement();
    Results = DataRequest.executeQuery (query);
    DisplayResults (Results);
    DataRequest.close();
}
```

Customer Names

FirstName	LastName	Street	City	State	ZipCode	Sales	Profit
Mary	Smith	24 Oak ...	San Jose	CA	77777	10000	2000
Bob	Jones	121 Spr...	New Yor...	NY	55555	20000	4000
Adam	Smith	56 Pine	Trenton	NJ	88888	40000	10000

Figure 13-7: Values where sales don't equal 30000.

Less than

You can use the less than operator ($<$) whenever you want rows where the value of the column that you specify in the SQL expression is less than the value of the search value. In Listing 13-11, I use the less than operator to retrieve rows of customer data that have sales of less than 30000.

Keep in mind that the DBMS returns only values that are less than the search value. It doesn't return the values equal to or greater than the search value. This means that if you want rows that contain sales of 30000 or less, you need to change the search value to 30001. You can also combine operators and use the less than equal operator (<=), which I'll explain later in this chapter.

Listing 13-11:   Using the Less Than Operator

```
try {
    String query = "SELECT * " +
                   "FROM customers " +
                   "WHERE Sales < 30000 ";
    DataRequest = Database.createStatement();
    Results = DataRequest.executeQuery (query);
    DisplayResults (Results);
    DataRequest.close();
}
```

Greater than

Use the greater than operator (>) to retrieve rows of data where the value of the column that you specify in the SQL expression is greater than the value of the search value. In Listing 13-12, I use the greater than operator to direct the DMBS to return rows from the customers table that have sales greater than 30000.

The DBMS doesn't return rows that have sales of 30000. If you want to include rows that have sales of 30000, you need to modify the comparison portion of the SQL expression. You can do this two different ways: Change the search value of 30000 to 29999 or use the greater than equal (>=) operator, which I'll show you later in this chapter.

Listing 13-12:   Using the Greater Than Operator

```
try {
    String query = "SELECT * " +
                   "FROM customers " +
                   "WHERE Sales > 30000 ";
    DataRequest = Database.createStatement();
    Results = DataRequest.executeQuery (query);
    DisplayResults (Results);
    DataRequest.close();
}
```

Less than equal

The less than equal operator (<=) functions like the less than operator and the equal operator in an SQL expression. Use the less than equal operator whenever you want the DBMS to return rows that are less than and rows that are equal to the search value.

Listing 13-13 shows how to use the less than equal operator. In this example, I ask the DBMS to return rows where sales are less than 30000 and rows that have sales equal to 30000. Figure 13-8 shows the results of this program.

Listing 13-13:   Using the Less Than Equal Operator

```
try {
    String query = "SELECT * " +
                   "FROM customers " +
                   "WHERE Sales <= 30000 ";
    DataRequest = Database.createStatement();
    Results = DataRequest.executeQuery (query);
    DisplayResults (Results);
    DataRequest.close();
}
```

Figure 13-8:
Values
where sales
are less
than or
equal to
30000.

FirstName	LastName	Street	City	State	ZipCode	Sales	Profit
Mary	Smith	24 Oak ...	San Jose	CA	77777	10000	2000
Bob	Jones	121 Spr...	New Yor...	NY	55555	20000	4000
Mark	Jones	15 Maple	Dallas	TX	66666	30000	6000

Customer Names

Greater than equal

The greater than equal operator (>=) functions like the greater than and the equal operators, which means the DBMS returns rows with values greater than or equal to your search value. I use the greater than equal operator in Listing 13-14 to retrieve rows of customer data where sales are greater than or equal to 30000.

Listing 13-14: **Using the Greater Than Equal Operator**

```
try {
    String query = "SELECT * " +
                   "FROM customers " +
                   "WHERE Sales >= 30000 ";
    DataRequest = Database.createStatement();
    Results = DataRequest.executeQuery (query);
    DisplayResults (Results);
    DataRequest.close();
}
```

Between

Sometimes you need your Java application to use data that falls within a range of values. For example, you may want to see all the customers who placed an order within the past ten days. Another way to say this is to retrieve all rows where the order date is between April 1 and April 10, assuming today is April 11.

You request data that falls within a range of values by using the BETWEEN operator and inserting the beginning and ending search values of the range. In Listing 13-15, the Java database application asks the DBMS for the data of customers that have sales within the range of 20000 and 39999. Figure 13-9 shows you the data this program generates.

The BETWEEN operator follows the column name in the SQL expression, and the lower value of the search value follows it. The AND keyword precedes the higher value of the search value.

Listing 13-15: **Using the BETWEEN Operator**

```
try {
    String query = "SELECT * " +
                   "FROM customers " +
                   "WHERE Sales BETWEEN 20000 AND
    39999";
    DataRequest = Database.createStatement();
    Results = DataRequest.executeQuery (query);
    DisplayResults (Results);
    DataRequest.close();
}
```

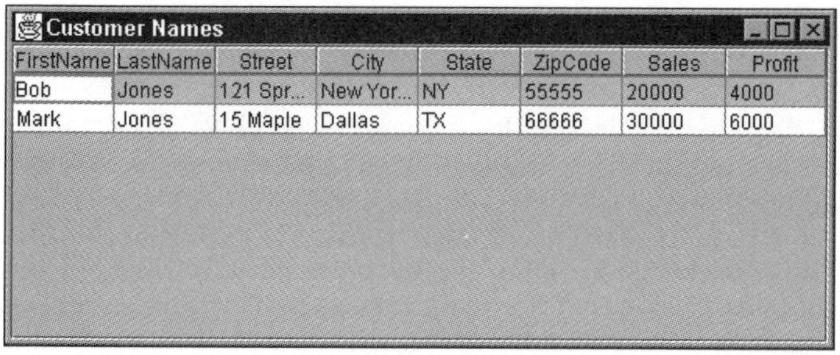

Figure 13-9:
Values
where
sales are
between
20000 and
39999.

Finding Almost the Perfect Match with LIKE

One of the most useful features that you can build into your Java database application is the capability to find data even when the user isn't sure of the search criteria.

Someone might be looking for data about a client, for example, but doesn't remember the correct spelling of the client's name. The person could enter all the possible spellings of the client's name into your application, but that would take forever to find the right data because of all the possible spellings.

However, the person could enter a partial name. Your application could then insert a wild card character into the partial name and ask the DBMS to retrieve all the partial names that are similar to the name he entered.

You need to know three things about using a wild card in your application:

- ✔ The LIKE operator
- ✔ The single character wild card
- ✔ The multicharacter wild card

The DBMS uses pattern matching to find partial search values. *Pattern matching* is where the DBMS compares the non-wild card values in the search value to the value in the designated column. The DBMS returns the row to your application only if the non-wild cards match in the same sequence as the value in the column.

Here is an example to illustrate this. Suppose that the search value is "ABC%" where "ABC" is non-wild card characters and the % is the multicharacter wild card, which I explain in the next section. The DBMS returns rows that have the first three letters of the column value as "ABC". The column value might have other characters after "ABC" or no other characters after "ABC". In either case, the DBMS considers the value of the column a match to the search criteria.

The LIKE operator tells the DBMS that the search value contains one or more wild cards and that you want rows that have the value of the column equal to the non-wild card characters. There are two wild cards:

- ✔ **The underscore (_) is the single-character wild card:** Any column that contains a value that is equal to the search criteria, except for the single-character wild card, is considered a match. If the search value is "A_C", for example, a column with a value of "ABC" will match the search value. However, "ABBC" won't be a match.

- ✔ **The percent (%) is the multicharacter wild card:** The multicharacter wild card matches any sequence of zero or more characters. If the search value is "A%C", a column with a value of "ABC" matches the search value as does a column with a value of "ABBC".

Listing 13-16 shows you how to use the multicharacter wild card in your program. In this example, the application asks the DBMS to look at the value in the LastName column and determine if the first three letters are equal to Smi. The value in the column could be Smit, Smith, or other characters combined with Smi.

Listing 13-16:   Using the LIKE Operator

```
try {
    String query = "SELECT * " +
                   "FROM customers " +
                   "WHERE LastName LIKE 'Smi%'";
    DataRequest = Database.createStatement();
    Results = DataRequest.executeQuery (query);
    DisplayResults (Results);
    DataRequest.close();
}
```

Looking for Nothing with NULL

NULL is term that means nothing. You can say that the definition of NULL is nothing, but that is confusing to understand. A better way to say it is that a column that has no data has a NULL value or simply say the column is empty of data.

Suppose that your sales representative needs a list of customers within the state she is going to visit so she can make some sales calls. Your job is to write a program that determines whether the state for each customer is present in your table. You don't want to include those customers with incomplete data in your table. Therefore, you need the DBMS to determine whether the State column is empty before it sends you the row of data. To do this, you include IS NULL in the SQL expression in your program.

Your SQL expression is asking the DBMS whether the column is empty — is the column NULL. Listing 13-17 shows you how to use the IS NULL phrase in your program. This example asks for rows where the State column is NULL or empty.

Before you run this program, insert a row in the customers table. Make sure that you include a value in the FirstName column and LastName column, but leave the other columns empty. When you run this program, the DBMS will return this row.

Listing 13-17:   Using IS NULL

```
try {
    String query = "SELECT * " +
                   "FROM customers " +
                   "WHERE State IS NULL";
    DataRequest = Database.createStatement();
    Results = DataRequest.executeQuery (query);
    DisplayResults (Results);
    DataRequest.close();
}
```

Weeding Out Duplicates with DISTINCT

A table can contain rows that have some identical data if the table isn't associated with a primary index (see Chapter 4). A primary index uses unique values to identify each row in the table. Many tables that you'll encounter when developing a Java database application work with a primary index and therefore won't have duplicate rows.

However, those tables without a primary index could have rows containing the same data. Sometimes you need to retrieve non-duplicate rows. For example, someone might have inadvertently entered data about a customer more than once into the table.

Therefore, whenever your program needs customer data, the DBMS returns more rows than there are customers because some rows are duplicates. You can ask the DBMS to remove duplicate rows by using the DISTINCT keyword.

You place the DISTINCT keyword between the SELECT statement and the column names in the SQL expression. Listing 13-18 uses the DISTINCT modifier to return all the rows that are not duplicated and only one copy of any duplicated row.

Before running this program, insert one or more duplicate rows in the table. Run the program and your screen should look similar to Figure 13-10. Your results might be different than Figure 13-10 because you might have duplicated a different row of data than I did in my program, but that's fine.

Make sure that you insert at least one duplicate row in the table before running this program, otherwise all the rows in the table are distinct.

Figure 13-10:
Don't show
duplicate
rows.

FirstName	LastName	Street	City	State	ZipCode	Sales	Profit
Adam	Smith	56 Pine	Trenton	NJ	88888	40000	10000
Bob	Jones	121 Spr...	New Yor...	NY	55555	20000	4000
Mark	Jones	15 Maple	Dallas	TX	66666	30000	6000
Mary	Smith	24 Oak ...	San Jose	CA	77777	10000	2000
Tom	Jones					0	0

Customer Names

Remove the keyword `DISTINCT` from the program and rerun the program. You'll see all the rows in the table, including the rows that contain duplicate data.

Listing 13-18: Using the DISTINCT Keyword

```
try {
    String query = "SELECT DISTINCT * " +
                   "FROM customers ";
    DataRequest = Database.createStatement();
    Results = DataRequest.executeQuery (query);
    DisplayResults (Results);
    DataRequest.close();
}
```

Searching for One of Many with IN

You'll come across times when your application requires rows that have one of multiple values in the search criteria. For example, the application needs data about customers who are located in three different Zip Codes. You have three ways to do this:

✔ Use three SQL expressions, each using the equal operator to match a Zip Code (see the "Equal" section).

✔ Use one SQL expression that contains three search conditions that are joined together with the AND keyword (see "Combining Conditions with AND").

✔ Use the IN keyword.

The IN keyword tests the value in the specified column with each of the search values you specify in the IN expression. Any match causes the DBMS to return the row to the application. I find the IN test a more convenient way to have the DBMS search for multiple search values.

You're IN the group

Listing 13-19 shows how you can use the IN test as part of your Java database application. You place the IN keyword in the SQL expression following the name of the column that you want the DBMS to search.

Place search values within parentheses and separate values with a comma. Although this example uses numbers as the search value, you can also use other data types, such as CHARACTER.

The data types of the search value used in the IN test must be the same data type as the column specified in the SQL expression.

In this example, I ask the DBMS to return rows that have the value of the Sales column as either 10000, 20000, or 30000.

Duplicate rows that you inserted into the database earlier may show up as a result of this listing.

Listing 13-19: Using the IN Keyword

```
try {
    String query = "SELECT * " +
                   "FROM customers " +
                   "WHERE Sales IN (10000, 20000,
    30000)";
    DataRequest = Database.createStatement();
    Results = DataRequest.executeQuery (query);
    DisplayResults (Results);
    DataRequest.close();
}
```

You're NOT IN one of the group

You can also use the IN test to request rows of data where the contents of the column being searched don't match any of the search values contained in the IN test. You can do this by placing the NOT keyword before IN.

Listing 13-20 illustrates how to use the NOT IN keywords in your program. In this example, I ask the DBMS to return rows where the value of the Sales column is not 10000, 20000, or 30000.

Listing 13-20: **Using the NOT IN Keywords**

```
try {
    String query = "SELECT * " +
                   "FROM customers " +
                   "WHERE Sales NOT IN (10000,
    20000, 30000)";
    DataRequest = Database.createStatement();
    Results = DataRequest.executeQuery (query);
    DisplayResults (Results);
    DataRequest.close();
}
```

Test your newfound knowledge

1. How do retrieve only one copy of duplicate rows?

   a. Use SELECT.

   b. Use SELECT *.

   c. Use DISTINCT.

   d. Use ONE COPY.

2. How do you retrieve rows that contain a column with a value that is similar but not exactly the same as your search criteria?

   a. Use ALMOST.

   b. Use LIKE.

   c. Use APPROXIMATE.

   d. Use ABOUT.

   Answers: (1) c. (2) b.

Chapter 14

Show Your Hand: Displaying Data from Tables

. . . .

In This Chapter

▶ Displaying data in a table

▶ Displaying data in a form

▶ Displaying data in a non-GUI display

▶ Using data in variables

. . . .

*A*fter your Java database application retrieves data from a database, it needs to do something with it. The way in which data is used in your application varies from application to application and is dependent on the nature of the application.

For example, you could write a Java application that records each time a representative of your company contacts a customer. The application enables employees to enter customer data into a database. Whenever an employee receives a call from the customer, the program retrieves and displays the data onscreen. The employee would then have the customer history in front of him and could effectively address the customer's needs.

In contrast, you could write an application that replicates data from one table into another table as a way to back up the data. A program could retrieve data from one table and insert it into another table. However, you'll never see the data onscreen because this isn't necessary to fulfill the objective of the application.

Here are the typical things that you do with data retrieved from a table:

✔ Display data in a table using a graphical user interface (GUI).

✔ Display data in a form using a GUI.

✔ Display data rows without using a GUI.

✔ Don't display data. Instead, assign the data retrieved from the DBMS to a variable, and then use the variable as necessary to fulfill the objectives of the application.

This chapter helps you decide how to handle your data once you retrieve it from the database. I show you how to write Java statements to use data from the database.

Non-GUI Versus GUI: Which Way Should I Go?

Business users generally work with GUI applications. A GUI typically contains buttons, edit boxes, list boxes, and other features that make it easy for the user to interact with the application.

You probably use a GUI whenever you write a memo using a word processor. You also use a GUI when you surf the Net with a browser. The Java Swing package contains the class definitions for building Java GUIs for your application.

An alternative to using a GUI is to use the console interface. The console interface displays an operating system prompt and uses characters instead of graphical images to form the database application.

You can see the console interface if you are using Windows by selecting Start⇨Programs and selecting MS-DOS Prompt. A DOS window appears, showing you the DOS prompt (c:>). You won't find list boxes, radio buttons, and other fancy graphical objects in a console interface.

Following the non-GUI approach

You would use a console interface for utility purposes, such as when displaying error messages. In fact, the applications in this book use the console interfaces to display error messages.

The two important advantages of using the console interface with your application are

✔ **Fewer lines of code:** A GUI requires appreciably more Java statements to build the graphical interface than an application that uses the console user interface.

✔ **Easier to read:** Typically your program executes one method and passes the data that is to be displayed onscreen to the method. You must execute several methods to display data using the GUI.

Two of the major disadvantages of using a console interface are

- ✔ **Unprofessional appearance:** Nearly all applications that interact with users do so using a GUI. Therefore, the console interface implies that the application isn't as well developed as a GUI application, although both might process data the same way.

- ✔ **More user training:** Many users know how to interact with a GUI application because most GUI applications have the same features as other applications, such as drop-down list boxes, list boxes, radio buttons, and other interface devices. On the other hand, people need much more training to get going with a console application.

The term *console application* comes from a time before personal computers when operators in a data center controlled computers from the console.

Getting all sticky and GUI

Scientists at the XEROX research lab in Palo Alto created GUI. Against the advice of their own scientists, the XEROX executives invited many up-and-coming developers to visit the lab. Among the visitors were folks from Apple Computer and Microsoft.

Until that time, all computer applications used a console interface. However, changes were in store following the fateful visit. You probably know what happened next. Apple Computer incorporated GUI into the Macintosh operating system and a few years later Microsoft follow suit with the Windows operating system. Since then, most applications use GUI.

Two major advantages of using GUI are

- ✔ **Standardized user interfaces across applications:** Until GUI took hold, each programmer created his or her own interface conventions. After GUI was widely adopted, programmers used the same conventions (that is, buttons, radio buttons, check boxes) to collect and display data in an application. This drastically reduced the need for extensive user training and allowed for code reusability.

- ✔ **Multiple windows:** A console application is limited to one display window at a time. In contrast, an application can show many GUI display windows. In addition, many applications can run and display windows at the same time.

The most important disadvantage of using GUI is that GUI requires much more coding than using non-GUI displays, which you'll see throughout this chapter.

Making your choice

Your choice of whether to use a graphical user interface or a console interface is an easy decision to make. Use a graphical user interface whenever your application needs to interact with its end users.

For example, a graphical user interface is necessary if you expect someone other than yourself or a technician to enter data into your application or to view retrieved data. This is because most people who use a computer application know how to use a graphical user interface and expect it.

However, consider using a console interface if your application displays data infrequently, such as displaying an error message onscreen or occasionally displaying data retrieved from the database. Applications that focus on processing data rather than interacting with users are prime candidates for the console interface.

Non-GUI Is for Me

Don't waste time developing a graphical user interface for your application unless it needs to dazzle its users. The other chapters of this book use a graphical user interface because I'm trying to impress you — and trying to show you how to impress your users.

However, I use the console interface to display error messages. I feel that by separating error messages from the data display, you can easily recognize when an error occurs and recognize the nature of the error.

You can create a console interface for your application by using the `System.out.println()` method, which displays a line of data onscreen in the console window rather than in a GUI window. I show you how to do this in this section.

Getting return data

Using the techniques I describe in Chapter 13, you must retrieve the data displayed in a console window from the database. Once the DBMS returns the data that your application needs, your application must extract the data from the columns of the ResultSet.

The ResultSet consists of rows and columns of data that match the search criteria from your SQL expression. Your application must copy the data from the rows and into the variables.

The program then concatenates the variables to form one String, which is then passed to the System.out.println() method and displayed in the console window. Listing 14-1 shows you how this is done. However, first you must create a table and insert a few rows of data. I use the same data from Chapter 13, as follows:

Column	Data Type	Size
FirstName	Text	50
LastName	Text	50
Street	Text	50
City	Text	50
State	Text	2
ZipCode	Text	12
Sales	Number	
Profit	Number	

Listing 14-1:   Getting Return Data from the Console Window

```
import java.sql.*;

public class plainselect
{
    private Connection Database;

    public plainselect()
    {
        String url = "jdbc:odbc:customers";
        String userID = "jim";
        String password = "keogh";
        Statement DataRequest;
        ResultSet Results;

        try {
            Class.forName( "sun.jdbc.odbc.JdbcOdbcDriver");

            Database =
            DriverManager.getConnection(url,userID,password);
        }
        catch (ClassNotFoundException error) {
            System.err.println("Unable to load the JDBC/ODBC
            bridge." + error);
            System.exit(1);
        }
        catch (SQLException error) {
            System.err.println("Cannot connect to the
            database." + error);
```

(continued)

Listing 14-1 *(continued)*

```
            System.exit(2);
        }

        try {
            String query = "Select DISTINCT * " +
                            "FROM customers " +
                            "WHERE Sales IN (10000, 20000,
        30000)";
            DataRequest = Database.createStatement();
            Results = DataRequest.executeQuery (query);
            DisplayResults (Results);
            DataRequest.close();
        }
        catch ( SQLException error ){
            System.err.println("SQL error.");
            System.exit(3);
        }
        shutDown();
    }

private void DisplayResults (ResultSet
        DisplayResults)throws SQLException
{

    boolean Records = DisplayResults.next();

    if (!Records ) {
        System.out.println( "End of data.");
    return;
    }

    try {
        do {
            DownRow( DisplayResults) ;
        } while ( DisplayResults.next() );


    }
    catch (SQLException error ) {
        System.err.println("Data display error." + error);
        System.exit(4);
    }
}

private  void DownRow ( ResultSet DisplayResults )
        throws SQLException
{
    String FirstName= new String();
    String LastName= new String();
    String Street= new String();
    String City = new String();
```

```
        String State = new String();
        String ZipCode= new String();
        long Sales;
        long Profit;
        String printrow;

        FirstName = DisplayResults.getString ( 1 ) ;
        LastName = DisplayResults.getString ( 2 ) ;
        Street = DisplayResults.getString ( 3 ) ;
        City = DisplayResults.getString ( 4 ) ;
        State = DisplayResults.getString ( 5 ) ;
        ZipCode = DisplayResults.getString ( 6 ) ;
        Sales = DisplayResults.getLong ( 7 ) ;
        Profit = DisplayResults.getLong ( 8 ) ;
        printrow = FirstName + " " +
                LastName + " " +
                City + " " +
                  State +  " " +
                ZipCode + " " +
                Sales + " " +
                Profit;
        System.out.println(printrow);
    }

    public void shutDown()
    {
        try {
            Database.close();
        }
        catch (SQLException error) {
            System.err.println( "Cannot break connection." +
                error ) ;
        }
    }
    public static void main ( String args [] )
    {
        final plainselect link = new plainselect();
                System.exit ( 0 ) ;
    }
}
```

After running the program, the data displays in the console window (see Figure 14-1).

The program begins in the main() method, where an object from the plainselect class is created and the constructor is executed. The plainselect constructor is defined at the beginning of the program. The constructor assigns values to the url, userID, and password. It then loads the JDBC/ODBC bridge (Class.forName()) and opens a connection to the database (getConnection()).

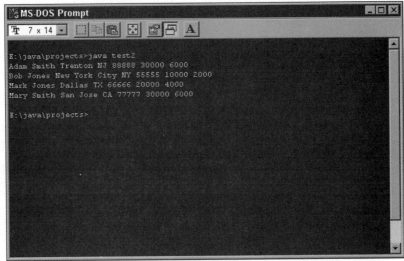

Figure 14-1:
Displaying
data without
using a GUI.

The two catch{} blocks trap any errors that occur when the JDBC/ODBC bridge loads and the connection to the database opens. The catch{} blocks display the appropriate error message onscreen.

If errors haven't been detected, statements in the second try{} block execute. The SQL expression directs the DBMS to return all the columns of rows that have 10000, 20000, or 30000 as the value in the Sales column. The DISTINCT keyword stops the DBMS from returning duplicate rows.

The program assigns the SQL expression to the query variable, which turns into an SQL statement by the executeQuery() method. The Results variable references the ResultSet returned by the DBMS. The ResultSet contains rows and columns that meet the search criteria.

The catch{} block catches any errors while the SQL statement executes and displays an error message onscreen. If errors aren't detected, the program passes the reference to the ResultSet to the DisplayResults() method.

The DisplayResults() method moves the virtual cursor to the first row in the ResultSet (DisplayResults.next()) and returns either a true or false value, depending upon whether the virtual cursor is pointing to a row (true) or to the end of the ResultSet (false).

If the return value is false (!Record), the program displays the "End of Data" message. Otherwise, the program calls the DownRow() method. The DownRow() method creates variables that are used to store values from the columns of the current row returned by the DBMS.

The data type of variables and columns must be compatible.

The program uses the getString() and getLong() methods to copy values from columns of the current row to the corresponding variable. The number passed to these methods represents the number of the column in the row. For example, the first getString(1) method retrieves the value of the FirstName column because that column is the first column in the rows returned by the DBMS.

Once all the values are copied to the variables from columns, the program concatenates the variables into one long string that is assigned to the printrow variable. The program then passes the printrow variable to the System.out.println() method, which displays the contents of all the variables onscreen (refer to Figure 14-1).

Next, the program returns to the while() statement in the DisplayResults() method, where the virtual cursor moves to the next row. As long as the virtual cursor doesn't point to the end of the ResultSet, the program calls the DownRow() method to display the data onscreen.

Once the last row is read, the program returns to the constructor below the statement that calls the DisplayResults() method. The program then closes the connection with the SQL statement (DataRequest.close()) and calls the shutDown() method. The shutDown() method closes the connection to the database.

The program returns to the main() method and exits the program (System.exit()).

Reading other types of data

You must use the correct method to copy the value of a column to a variable. The previous program uses two methods for this purpose: getString() and getLong(). Each of the SQL data types has similar methods available.

There is a difference between SQL data types and Java data types, so you must use a comparable Java data type to store an SQL data type. Table 14-1 contains a comparison of these data types. Refer to this table whenever you need to copy data from a column of a ResultSet to a Java variable.

Table 14-1	Comparing Java Data Types and SQL Data Types
Data Types in Java	*Comparable Data Types in SQL*
boolean	BOOLEAN
double	FLOAT()
float	REAL
int	INTEGER
	INT
java.sql.Array	ARRAY
java.sql.Blob	BLOB
java.sql.Clob	CLOB
java.sql.Date	DATE
java.sql.Numeric	NUMERIC()
	DECIMAL()
	DEC()
java.sql.Time	TIME
java.sql.Timestamp	TIMESTAMP
short	SMALLINT
String	CHARACTER
	CHAR()
String	VARCHAR()

If you're not sure of the SQL data type of a column, inquire about the data by reading the data type of the column (see "Reading the data type of a column"). You'll know which method to use to copy the value from the column to the Java variable once you identify the data type of the column.

Listing 14-2 reads five types of data from the ResultSet:

- ✔ String
- ✔ Double
- ✔ Date
- ✔ Time
- ✔ Boolean

You need to modify the customers table before you use this code segment. Here's what you need to do:

1. **Change the data type of the Sales and Profit column to Currency.**

2. **Insert a new column called StartDate (Date/Time in Microsoft Access).**

3. **Insert a new column called StartTime (Date/Time in Microsoft Access).**

4. **Insert a new column called New as a Boolean data type (Yes/No in Microsoft Access).**

5. **Enter values in the new columns for each row (see Figure 14-2 for my suggested values).**

Figure 14-2: My suggestions for the new values.

FirstN	LastNam	Street	City	State	ZipCod	Sales	Profit	StartDate	StartTime	New
Mary	Smith	24 Oak	San Jo	CA	77777	$10,000.00	$2,000.00	10/11/02	11:45:00 AM	☐
Bob	Jones	121 Sp	New Yo	NY	55555	$20,000.00	$4,000.00	10/12/02	11:45:00 AM	☑
Mark	Jones	15 Map	Dallas	TX	66666	$30,000.00	$6,000.00	10/13/02	11:45:00 AM	☐
Adam	Smith	56 Pine	Trentor	NJ	88888	$40,000.00	10,000.00	10/14/02	11:45:00 AM	☑
Tom	Jones					$0.00	$0.00	10/15/02	11:45:00 AM	☐
						$0.00	$0.00			☐

Once you've made the modifications to the table, substitute Listing 14-2 for the second `DownRow()` method in the constructor of Listing 14-1. Recompile and run the program.

Listing 14-2:   Using Other Types of Data

```java
private   void DownRow ( ResultSet DisplayResults )
       throws SQLException
{
   String FirstName= new String();
   String LastName= new String();
   String Street= new String();
   String City = new String();
   String State = new String();
   String ZipCode= new String();
   java.sql.Date StartDate ;
   java.sql.Time StartTime;
   double Sales;
   double Profit;
   boolean NewCustomer;
   String printrow;

   FirstName = DisplayResults.getString ( 1 ) ;
   LastName = DisplayResults.getString ( 2 ) ;
   Street = DisplayResults.getString ( 3 ) ;
   City = DisplayResults.getString ( 4 ) ;
   State = DisplayResults.getString ( 5 ) ;
```

(continued)

Listing 14-2 *(continued)*

```
        ZipCode = DisplayResults.getString ( 6 ) ;
        Sales = DisplayResults.getDouble ( 7 ) ;
        Profit = DisplayResults.getDouble ( 8 ) ;
        StartDate = DisplayResults.getDate ( 9 ) ;
        StartTime = DisplayResults.getTime ( 10 ) ;
        NewCustomer = DisplayResults.getBoolean ( 11 ) ;
        printrow = FirstName + " " +
                LastName + " " +
                City + " " +
                State +  " " +
                ZipCode + " " +
                Sales + " " +
                Profit + " " +
                StartDate + " " +
                StartTime + " " +
                NewCustomer;
        System.out.println(printrow);
    }
```

Your results should look like this:

DATETIME 11 StartDate 19

DATETIME 11 StartDate 19

DATETIME 11 StartDate 19

DATETIME 11 StartDate 19

DATETIME 11 StartDate 19

DATETIME 11 StartDate 19

DATETIME 11 StartDate 19

Of course, your program might display different data if you didn't enter the same data as I entered in my customers table.

Reading Metadata

Metadata is data that describes data. This is similar to how the name of a column describes the kind of data that that column contains. Sometimes when you write a Java database application you need to refer to the column name, the size of the column, the data type of the column, or other metadata. I show you how to use metadata in this section.

Fortunately, other metadata isn't arbitrarily created and will help you learn about the table used by your application. Here are the kinds of metadata that you'll find useful when writing your Java database application:

- Number of columns in the table
- Column name
- Column width
- Column data type

Your program can access a table's metadata by using the `getMetaData()` method to copy the metadata from the ResultSet. You can then use other methods for each type of metadata. Each of the following sections contains a code segment that reads a particular type of metadata.

Reading the number of columns in the table

You can use the following code segment to retrieve the number of columns that exists in a table. First, Listing 14-3 calls the `DisplayResults.getMetaData()` method. `DisplayResults` is a reference to a ResultSet that was returned previously from the execution of the SQL statements (see "Getting return data").

The program passes a reference to the `DisplayResults` set as an argument to the `DownRow()` method, and the reference retrieves metadata from the ResultSet. The `getMetaData()` method returns a reference to the `ResultSetMetaData`, which this code segment calls metadata.

The `ResultSetMetaData` is similar to the ResultSet except it references metadata associated with the ResultSet rather than the data contained in the ResultSet. Once the code segment retrieves the metadata, it then uses the `getColumnCount()` method to retrieve the number of columns in the `DisplayResults` ResultSet. The program then assigns a variable to the ResultSet and displays onscreen.

You can use the column count for other purposes besides displaying the column count. For example, you can use the column count in a `for` loop to access each column in sequence.

Listing 14-3:   Reading the Number of Columns

```
private  void DownRow ( ResultSet DisplayResults )
     throws SQLException
{
   ResultSetMetaData metadata = DisplayResults.getMetaData
        ();
   int NumberOfColumns;
   String printrow;
```

(continued)

Listing 14-2 *(continued)*

```
        NumberOfColumns = metadata.getColumnCount () ;

        System.out.println("Number Of Columns: " +
            NumberOfColumns);
    }
```

Reading the data type of a column

You can use the following code segment to determine the data type of a column. Listing 14-4 loads metadata and then uses the getColumnTypeName() method to retrieve the data type of the column.

The getColumnTypeName() method requires that you specify the number of the column that you want to access. I access column 9 in the example. You can place the getColumnTypeName() in a for loop to access all the columns in the ResultSet.

The program then copies the data type to a variable and displays it onscreen. You could use the data type in a switch() statement to determine the proper get method (for example, getString()) to use to copy data from the column to a variable (see "Data in a table" later in this chapter).

Listing 14-4: **Determining the Data Type of a Column**

```
    private  void DownRow ( ResultSet DisplayResults )
        throws SQLException
    {
        ResultSetMetaData metadata = DisplayResults.getMetaData
            ();
        String ColumnType = new String();
        String printrow;

        ColumnType = metadata.getColumnTypeName ( 9 ) ;

        System.out.println("Column Type: " + ColumnType );
    }
```

Reading the column name

The column name is the name you gave the column when you inserted it into the table. You can copy the name of a column to a variable for use in your program by using the getColumnLabel() method. *Column label* is another term used to refer to the column name.

You may find it handy to use the column name whenever your Java database application displays data in a table format onscreen. This way, you can use the name of the column retrieved from the database as a column heading for the data you display onscreen (see "Data in a table").

Listing 14-5 demonstrates how to copy the column name from the ResultSet's metadata. The code segment initially copies the metadata from the ResultSet and is passed to the DownRow() method by another part of the program (see "Getting return data").

The getMetaData() method returns a reference to the ResultSetMetaData. The metadata is data describing data contained in the ResultSet as a result of the SQL statement sent by the program.

The getColumnLabel() method requires that you specify the number of the column. In this example, I reference the ninth column of the ResultSet. The getColumnLabel() method returns the column name, which is assigned to a String. The String later displays onscreen.

Listing 14-5:   Copying the Column Name from the Metadata

```
private  void DownRow ( ResultSet DisplayResults )
      throws SQLException
{
   ResultSetMetaData metadata = DisplayResults.getMetaData
      ();
   String ColumnName = new String();
   String printrow;

   ColumnName = metadata.getColumnLabel (9) ;

   System.out.println("Column Name: " + ColumnName);
}
```

Reading the column width

The column width is important data for your application to know if it needs to display data from the column into a restricted area of the screen. For example, a screen design may set aside an area for a customer's first name.

However, the application may receive a customer's first name from the DBMS that is larger than the space allocated onscreen. If left unchecked, you may see the customer's name cut off.

If your application determines the size of the column before it creates the display, you can write your program to adjust the screen design based on the maximum column size. Listing 14-6 uses the `getColumnDisplaySize()` method to determine the column size.

The `getColumnDisplaySize()` method requires that your program specify the number of the column that you want to size. In this example, I determine the size of column 9 of the ResultSet.

Listing 14-6: Determining the Column Size

```
private void DownRow ( ResultSet DisplayResults )
    throws SQLException
{
    ResultSetMetaData metadata = DisplayResults.getMetaData
        ();
    int ColumnWidth;
    String printrow;

    ColumnWidth = metadata.getColumnDisplaySize ( 9 ) ;

    System.out.println("Column Width:" + ColumnWidth);
}
```

It's That GUI Kind of Thing

Many applications that directly interact with people require a graphical user interface. All of us have become familiar with GUI applications and expect all applications to use GUI.

You can write countless types of applications that use a graphical user interface, more than I have enough space to discuss in this book. However, all applications that display data onscreen typically use one of two GUI formats:

- ✔ **Table format:** A table format presents data in the form of rows and columns on the screen — very similar to a spreadsheet.

- ✔ **Form format:** A form format presents data in a less-structured display, where there are no columns and rows. Instead, you see the data in a similar form to what you'd see on paper.

Data in a table

Use a table whenever you need to display several rows on the screen at the same time. A table consists of rows and columns where the first row typically contains the name of the columns. The remaining rows contain data.

Column names for the display can be either the column label used to describe the column in the database table or a name you program yourself. Your application usually presents data unmodified.

Listing 14-7 — you may recognize most of it from Chapter 13 — retrieves the first name, last name, street, and city from all the rows in the customers table, and displays the column names and corresponding data in a table format. Figure 14-3 shows the results of running this program.

Data displayed onscreen may differ from data shown in Figure 14-3 because you might be using data different from mine.

Figure 14-3:
Data from
the table
displays in a
table format
on the
screen.

FirstName	LastName	Street	City
Mary	Smith	24 Oak Street	San Jose
Bob	Jones	121 Spruce Street	New York City
Mark	Jones	15 Maple Street	Dallas
Adam	Smith	56 Pine Street	Trenton

Customer Names

Listing 14-7:   Displaying Data in a Table Format

```java
import java.sql.*;
import javax.swing.*;
import java.awt.event.*;
import java.awt.*;
import java.util.*;
import java.lang.*;

    public class tabletst extends JFrame
        {
        private JTable DataTable;
        private Connection Database;

        public tabletst ()
            {
            String url = "jdbc:odbc:customers";
            String userID = "jim";
            String password = "keogh";
            Statement DataRequest;
            ResultSet Results;

            try {
                Class.forName( "sun.jdbc.odbc.JdbcOdbcDriver");
```

(continued)

Listing 14-7 *(continued)*

```
          Database =
          DriverManager.getConnection(url,userID,password);
       }
     catch (ClassNotFoundException error) {
         System.err.println("Unable to load the JDBC/ODBC
         bridge." + error);
         System.exit(1);
       }
     catch (SQLException error) {
         System.err.println("Cannot connect to the
         database." + error);
         System.exit(2);
       }

     try {
         String query = "SELECT FirstName, LastName,
         Street, City FROM customers";
         DataRequest = Database.createStatement();
         Results = DataRequest.executeQuery (query);
         DisplayResults (Results);
         DataRequest.close();
       }
     catch ( SQLException error ){
         System.err.println("SQL error." + error);
         System.exit(3);
       }

     setSize (500, 200);
     show();
    }

private void DisplayResults (ResultSet
        DisplayResults)throws SQLException
{
    boolean Records = DisplayResults.next();

    if (!Records ) {
       JOptionPane.showMessageDialog(this, "End of data.");
       setTitle( "Process Completed");
       return;
       }
    setTitle ("Customer Names");
    Vector ColumnNames = new Vector();
    Vector rows = new Vector();

    try {
        ResultSetMetaData MetaData =
         DisplayResults.getMetaData();

        for ( int x = 1; x <= MetaData.getColumnCount();
        ++x)
```

```
                ColumnNames.addElement (MetaData.getColumnName (
             x ) );

          do {
             rows.addElement (DownRow( DisplayResults,
          MetaData ) );
          } while ( DisplayResults.next() );


          DataTable = new JTable (rows, ColumnNames ) ;
          JScrollPane scroller = new JScrollPane ( DataTable
              ) ;
          getContentPane(). add ( scroller,
           BorderLayout.CENTER );
          validate();
       }
    catch (SQLException error ) {
       System.err.println("Data display error." + error);
       System.exit(4);
       }
    }

    private Vector DownRow ( ResultSet DisplayResults,
           ResultSetMetaData MetaData )
           throws SQLException
    {
       Vector currentRow = new Vector();
       for ( int x = 1; x <= MetaData.getColumnCount(); ++x )
          switch ( MetaData.getColumnType ( x ) ) {
          case Types.VARCHAR :
             currentRow.addElement( DisplayResults.getString
          ( x ) ) ;
             break;
          }
       return currentRow;
    }

    public static void main ( String args [] )
    {
       final tabletst link = new tabletst ();

       link.addWindowListener (
           new WindowAdapter() {
           public void windowClosing(WindowEvent WinEvent )
           {
             System.exit (0) ;
           }
       }
    );
  }
}
```

The Table Format walk-about

As with all Java applications, the program begins in the `main()` method and creates an object of `tabletst` class, which is defined at the top of the program. When the program creates the object, it automatically runs the `tabletst` constructor.

The `tabletst` constructor starts the JDBC/ODBC bridge (see Chapter 7) and then uses the `url`, `userID`, and `password` to open a connection with the database by calling the `getConnection()` method in the first `try{}` block of the constructor.

One of two `catch{}` blocks catch any errors that occur at this point. The first `catch{}` block reacts to errors caused by starting the JDBC/ODBC bridge, and the second `catch{}` block addresses errors that might occur when connecting to the database. The program terminates if either type of error occurs.

The second `try{}` block creates the SQL expression to request all the first names, last names, streets, and cities from the customers table. The SQL expression is then placed in an SQL statement. The `executeQuery()` method sends the SQL statement to the DBMS and returns a reference to the ResultSet. The ResultSet contains the rows the DBMS returned.

The `catch{}` block traps errors that occur during the execution of the SQL statement, displays the errors onscreen, and terminates the program.

If the SQL statement executes without errors, the program passes a reference to the ResultSet to the `DisplayResults()` method. The data then displays in a table format onscreen. Afterward, the program returns to the `main()` method and creates a WindowListener (`addWindowListener()`) that monitors messages that the operating system sent to the program. The program passes these messages along to the WindowAdapter (`WindowAdapter()`), which reacts to those messages. In this example, the WindowAdapter reacts to a "close window" message by exiting the program.

The DisplayResults() walk-about

The `DisplayResults()` method moves the virtual cursor to the first row in the table and returns either a true or false value. The program returns a true value if the virtual cursor isn't pointing to the end of the ResultSet. The program returns a false value if the virtual cursor is pointing to the end of the ResultSet and a message displays, telling the user that the end of the ResultSet has been reached. The program returns from the `DisplayResults()` to the constructor.

Two Vectors are created if rows of data exist in the ResultSet. The first Vector holds the names of columns in the ResultSet, and the second Vector holds the data. The `try{}` block loads metadata into the first Vector.

The try{} block also calls the DownRow() method in the do...while loop to copy data from each row into the second Vector. The DownRow() method loads one row at a time into a temporary Vector. That Vector returns to the DisplayResults() method where the data copies into the second Vector.

The DisplayResults() method then creates a table and loads the column names and data into the table. The program calls the validate() method to make sure the GUI is free from errors. The catch{} block traps any errors that occur and displays a message. The program then ends.

The DownRow() walk-about

The DownRow() method moves the virtual cursor through all the rows of the ResultSet one row at a time with each call to the DownRow() table. The program creates a Vector to hold data copied from the ResultSet. A reference to the Vector is returned to the DisplayResults() method. There the program copies the contents of the Vector to the second Vector that holds the data for display purposes.

A for loop addresses each column of the ResultSet and uses the number of columns returned by the getColumnCount() method as the maximum value. The getColumnCount() determines the number of columns in the ResultSet.

With each iteration of the for loop, the program retrieves the data type of the column using the getColumnType() method. Depending on the data type, the program executes the appropriate get statement in the switch...case statement. The get statement copies data from the specified column into the Vector using the addElement() method.

Data in a form

A GUI form is any GUI display that doesn't present data in rows and columns — for example, an online order form used to enter your name and address. Typically, data displays in a text box that is identified by a label inside of a column name. You can position the text box and label anywhere on the screen, rather than in rows and columns.

Programmers commonly use forms to display one row of data, which is efficient for many kinds of applications including those that retrieve data about one customer at a time. Programmers also use forms for data entry and data updates.

Listing 14-8 illustrates how to create a very simple GUI form and populate the form with data from a table. In this example, I request Mary Smith's first and last name from the table.

You might be scratching your head wondering why I'm asking for this information since I already have this data. The reason is that I'm not sure the name Mary Smith exists in the table. If it does, the value of the FirstName and LastName columns will display. If not, the form won't contain data. (Besides, this is an easy example to understand.)

Listing 14-8:   Displaying a GUI Form

```java
import java.sql.*;
import javax.swing.*;
import java.awt.event.*;
import java.awt.*;
import java.util.*;
import java.lang.*;

    public class guiform extends JFrame
    {
        private Connection Database;
        public static final int WIDTH = 300;
        public static final int HEIGHT = 200;

        public guiform()
        {
            String url = "jdbc:odbc:customers";
            String userID = "jim";
            String password = "keogh";
            Statement DataRequest;
            ResultSet Results;

            try {
                Class.forName( "sun.jdbc.odbc.JdbcOdbcDriver");

                Database =
                DriverManager.getConnection(url,userID,password);
            }
            catch (ClassNotFoundException error) {
                System.err.println("Unable to load the JDBC/ODBC
                bridge." + error);
                System.exit(1);
            }
            catch (SQLException error) {
                System.err.println("Cannot connect to the
                database." + error);
                System.exit(2);
            }

            try {
                String query = "SELECT DISTINCT FirstName,
                LastName " +
                                "FROM customers " +
                                "WHERE FirstName = 'Mary'" +
```

```
                        "AND LastName = 'Smith'";
        DataRequest = Database.createStatement();
        Results = DataRequest.executeQuery (query);
        DisplayResults (Results);
        DataRequest.close();
    }
    catch ( SQLException error ){
        System.err.println("SQL error.");
        System.exit(3);
    }
  }

private void DisplayResults (ResultSet
        DisplayResults)throws SQLException
{
  try{
    boolean Records = DisplayResults.next();

    if (!Records ) {
        JOptionPane.showMessageDialog( this, "End of
    data.");
        setTitle( "Process Completed");
    return;
    }

    String FirstName= new String();
    String LastName= new String();

    FirstName = DisplayResults.getString ( 1 ) ;
    LastName = DisplayResults.getString ( 2 ) ;

    setTitle("Customer");
    setSize(WIDTH,HEIGHT);
    JLabel label1= new JLabel("First Name:");
    JTextField textField1 = new JTextField(10);

        textField1.setMaximumSize(textField1.getPreferredS
        ize());
    textField1.setText(FirstName);

    Box hbox1 = Box.createHorizontalBox();
    hbox1.add(label1);
    hbox1.add(Box.createHorizontalStrut(10));
    hbox1.add(textField1);

    JLabel label2 = new JLabel("Last Name:");
    JTextField textField2 = new JTextField(10);

        textField2.setMaximumSize(textField2.getPreferredS
        ize());
    textField2.setText(LastName);
```

(continued)

Listing 14-8 *(continued)*

```
        Box hbox2 = Box.createHorizontalBox();
        hbox2.add(label2);
        hbox2.add(Box.createHorizontalStrut(10));
        hbox2.add(textField2);

        Box vbox = Box.createVerticalBox();
        vbox.add(hbox1);
        vbox.add(hbox2);
        vbox.add(Box.createGlue());

        Container contentPane = getContentPane();
        contentPane.add(vbox, BorderLayout.CENTER);
      }

    catch ( SQLException error ){
        System.err.println("SQL error." + error);
        System.exit(3);
      }
  }

public static void main ( String args [] )
{
    final guiform link = new guiform();

    link.addWindowListener(new
      WindowAdapter()
        {
        public void windowClosing(WindowEvent e)
          {
            System.exit(0);
          }
        }
      );
    link.show();

    }
  }
```

After you compile and run this program, the GUI form displays onscreen (see Figure 14-4).

Listing 14-8 has many of the same components as Listing 14-7. Therefore, I just mention them here; you can read the description in the "Data in a table" section.

The main() method and the constructor are basically the same in both this program and the last program, with a few exceptions. One of those exceptions is that guiform is the name of the class and the name of constructor instead of tabletst. The other exception is that I use different SQL expressions in the second try{} block of the constructor because I'm requesting different data from the DBMS.

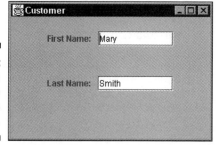

Figure 14-4:
Data from a
database
displayed in
a form.

However, the major difference between these two listings is in the
DisplayResults() method. The DisplayResults() method in Listing 14-8 creates several kinds of objects that are used to display text and
data onscreen.

The DisplayResults() method begins by moving the virtual cursor to the
first row in the ResultSet and then returns a true if the virtual cursor isn't
pointing to the end of the ResultSet. Otherwise, the method returns a false.

If the next() method returns a false, a dialog box displays, showing a message that the program has reached the end of the data. The program then
returns to the constructor.

If the next() method returns a true, the program creates two Strings and
uses the getString() methods to copy the data from columns in the
ResultSet to the Strings. Numbers 1 and 2 indicate the column numbers
in the ResultSet.

Next, the program sets the title and size of the window that will contain the
form. WIDTH and HEIGHT are defined at the top of the guiform class definition.

The program proceeds to create JLabel and JTextField objects. The
JLabel object is a label that describes data (similar to the column name).
The JTextField object is a placeholder for data. The text "First Name: "
passes to the JLabel constructor and the number of characters (10) of the
text field passes to the JTextField constructor.

The setMaximumSize() method sets the maximum number of characters that
you can enter into the JTextField. The preferred size set within the windowing environment, which is retrieved by calling the getPreferredSize()
method, determines the maximum size.

The program assigns data to the JTextField by calling the setText()
method and passing the name of the String that contains the data
(FirstName) to the setText() method. It then creates a horizontal
box as a container for the label and text.

The program creates a similar set of objects for the last name label and LastName data. However, the objects are called `label2`, `textField2`, and `hbox2` instead of `label1`, `textField1`, and `hbox1`.

The program creates a vertical box next. The vertical box is a container for the horizontal boxes that were previously created in the program. You'll notice that the `add()` method places the horizontal boxes into the vertical box. The `createGlue()` method adjusts the positions of the horizontal boxes within the vertical box.

The program then creates a pane and places the vertical box inside the pane. A *pane* is the portion of the window that contains labels, text, and other objects. In this example, the pane contains only labels and text.

The `add()` method has two arguments: the vertical object and the layout manager. The vertical object contains the horizontal boxes, each of which contains a label and data. The layout manager determines where the pane is going to appear in the window. In this example, the pane is centered within the window.

This program doesn't have a `DownRow()` method because I request only one row to be returned from the table.

Chapter 15

Did You Hear the Latest?: Updating Data in Tables

. . . .

In This Chapter
▶ Updating a single row
▶ Updating a single column
▶ Updating multiple columns
▶ Updating multiple rows

. . . .

*U*pdating has nothing to do with getting your date to get up and dance, as you probably surmised. But it does have a lot to do with keeping your database current. Every Java database application must provide a feature that enables the user to change data in the tables. Otherwise, you'll soon discover that the data in the table becomes outdated quickly.

You can easily build an update feature into your application by following the examples in this chapter. Here's what you'll learn how to do:

✔ Identify data that needs to be updated

✔ Verify the accuracy of the updated data

✔ Update a specific row or rows of data

✔ Update a specific column or columns of data

You can use many of the skills you already know to tell the database management system (DBMS) to select only the rows of data that need to be updated. I give a quick review of those skills in the appropriate places in this chapter and refer you to other chapters in this book if you need to jog your memory.

Finding Data to Update

Updating data in a table is very similar to inserting a new row of data into a table (see Chapter 12). In both cases, you must validate the data before you place it into the table. Validation is the process of ensuring that your data is reasonably correct.

However, updating data in a table is different than inserting a new row of data because the Java database application must specify the row that contains the column of data you want updated.

Here's what happens when your Java database application updates data in a table:

- It validates the data that is being placed into the table.
- It uses search criteria to find the row that contains the column to be updated.
- It replaces the existing data in the column with the new data.

Your application uses SQL statements to direct the DBMS to update data in a table. The DBMS updates only those rows that match the search criteria. Data in all other rows remain unchanged.

Making changes one row at a time

Updates are made to a single row in a table whenever the search criteria match only one row. For example, your application may want to update the salary of an employee. The application provides the DBMS with the Employee Number and the new salary.

The DBMS searches the table for the Employee Number and replaces the existing salary with the salary provided by your application. Each employee has a unique Employee Number; therefore, only one row is updated in this example.

You can have your application update multiple columns of a row by specifying the column names and the corresponding new values for the columns in the SQL statement of your application. I'll show you how to do this later in this chapter.

Making changes in multiple rows

Your Java database application can update more than one row in a table if your application specifies search criteria that match more than one row in the table. Suppose you want to give employees who have a salary less than $20,000 an increase of 5 percent. Here's the search criterion: salary < $20,000 (see Chapter 13).

The DBMS looks for all rows that have a salary value that is less than $20,000. It then calculates the new salary and replaces the existing salary in the column. There can be more than one row in the Employee table that has a salary of less than $20,000. Therefore, a single SQL expression updates multiple rows.

 Make sure that you want your application to update multiple rows before updating the table. Sometimes you write the application thinking only a single row will be updated when in reality multiple rows meet the search criteria and therefore are updated.

Here's how to determine the number of rows that will update:

1. **Create a** SELECT **SQL statement that displays the column or columns of rows that meet your search criteria (see Chapter 13).**

2. **Run the SQL statement.**

3. **Review the ResultSet.**

   If you receive multiple rows back, those rows will be updated when your Java database application runs the UPDATE SQL statement.

Rewrite the search criteria if the ResultSet contains rows that shouldn't be updated. Make sure that you retest your rewritten search criteria before running the UPDATE SQL statement.

Fight for your right to update

You must acquire special rights before your Java database application can update data in a table. The database administrator restricts the rights of users based on their need to interact with the data stored in the database. For example, many users can select data from the table, but they cannot insert new rows or update existing rows.

The reason for these restrictions is *data integrity*. The database administrator needs to be sure that the database doesn't include any erroneous data. Therefore, your Java database application's user ID must have permission to update data before you're able to make changes.

You typically have full rights to databases that are local to your computer, such as Microsoft Access.

Updating an Entire Table

You can have your Java database application update a table by placing an SQL expression in your application that uses the UPDATE statement. The UPDATE statement precedes the name of the table that is being updated.

You also need to include the SET clause, which specifies the column names that are being updated and the new values that are to be placed in those columns. For example, if you want to update the salary to $30,000, you would need to include SET salary = 30000 in your application's SQL expression.

This example tells the DBMS to replace the current value of the Salary column with the value of 30000. The new value overwrites the current value once your application executes the SQL expression.

The WHERE clause, an optional feature, uses a search expression to tell the DBMS which rows to update. All rows update if you don't use a WHERE clause in your application.

Updating your first table

Before you write your first Java database application to update a table, you need to create the table and enter rows. Here are the table's values I use for my examples:

Column	Data Type	Size
FirstName	Text	50
LastName	Text	50
Street	Text	50
City	Text	50
State	Text	2
ZipCode	Text	12
Discount	Number	

You should create the same table so you can try the programs in this chapter for yourself.

Here is the data I entered into the table:

Name	Address	Discount
		10
Bob Jones	121 Spruce Street New York City NY 55555	12
Mark Jones	15 Maple Street Dallas TX 66666	20
Adam Smith	56 Pine Street Trenton NJ 88888	11
Mary Smith	24 Oak Street San Jose CA 77777	16
Tom Jones	15 Maple Street Dallas TX 66666	15
Tom Jones	15 Maple Street Dallas TX 66666	15

You can enter the same data into your table or enter your own data. Just remember that you'll see different results if you create your own data.

Once you create the table and enter data into it, you're all set to create your first Java database application that will update data. Listing 15-1 changes the street address for any customer whose first name is Bob.

Before running this program, notice that the street address for Bob is 121 Spruce Street. When you run the program, the street address changes to 5 Main Street. Only one row updates because only one row contains the first name Bob. Multiple rows would have been updated if those rows contained Bob as the first name.

You'll probably see an error message stating that no ResultSet was produced. You can ignore this message because this program didn't request any data to be returned by the DBMS since we're updating the table. Therefore, we didn't expect a ResultSet.

Listing 15-1: Updating Data in a Table

```
import java.sql.*;

public class updatetst
{
    private Connection Database;

    public updatetst()
    {
        String url = "jdbc:odbc:customers";
        String userID = "jim";
        String password = "keogh";
        Statement DataRequest;
        ResultSet Results;

        try {
            Class.forName( "sun.jdbc.odbc.JdbcOdbcDriver");
```

(continued)

Listing 15-1 *(continued)*

```
            Database =
          DriverManager.getConnection(url,userID,password);
        }
        catch (ClassNotFoundException error) {
            System.err.println("Unable to load the JDBC/ODBC
          bridge." + error);
            System.exit(1);
        }
        catch (SQLException error) {
            System.err.println("Cannot connect to the
          database." + error);
            System.exit(2);
        }

        try {
            String query = "UPDATE customers " +
                            "SET Street = '5 Main Street' " +
                            "WHERE FirstName = 'Bob'";
            DataRequest = Database.createStatement();
            Results = DataRequest.executeQuery (query );
            DataRequest.close();
        }
        catch ( SQLException error ){
            System.err.println("SQL error." + error);
            System.exit(3);
        }
    }

  public static void main ( String args [] )
  {
    final updatetst link = new updatetst();
    System.exit ( 0 ) ;
  }
}
```

The Updating walk-about

The program begins in the main() method. The method creates an object
of the updatetst class and causes the updatetst constructor to execute.
The updatetst class is defined at the top of the program. The constructor
initializes the url, userID, and password Strings with a reference to the
database, userID, and password that are used to connect the application
to the database.

Next, the constructor loads the JDBC/ODBC bridge (Class.forName()),
which enables your application to communicate with the database. Once the

bridge loads, the constructor calls the getConnection() method to open the connection with the database.

The program uses two catch{} blocks to trap errors that might occur when loading the bridge or connecting to the database. The first catch{} block displays an error message and exits the program if the bridge can't load. The second catch{} block displays an error message and exits the program if a connection cannot be made to the database.

Once the database connection is established, the constructor creates an SQL expression that is assigned to a String. The SQL expression updates the customers table where the FirstName column contains the value Bob. The Street column's value is updated with the value '5 Main Street'.

The program places the SQL expression into an SQL statement and executes it using the executeQuery() method. Afterwards, the SQL statement closes.

The catch{} block traps errors that occur while the SQL statement is executing and displays an SQL error message.

After the constructor is completed, the program returns to the System.exit(0) statement and terminates itself.

Updating Multiple Rows

You can write an application to update multiple rows by inserting the WHERE clause in the SQL statement. The WHERE clause tells the DBMS which rows in the table should be updated. You specify the columns to be updated by placing the name of the columns and the new value within the SET clause in the SQL statement.

There are a number of ways to identify rows to update. The more common methods are

✔ Using the IN test
✔ Using the IS NULL test
✔ Using comparisons
✔ Identifying all rows

The method you decide to use depends on the nature of your application. The examples of these methods in this chapter should help you choose the best method to use in your application.

Using the IN test

The IN test contains two or more values that try to match to the column you specify in the WHERE clause. If any of these values match the value in the column, the row updates with new data. Otherwise, the row doesn't change.

Listing 15-2 tells the DBMS to search the Discount column in the customers table. If the discount is 12 or 15, the DBMS replaces the discount with 25. The DBMS ignores rows where the Discount column isn't 12 or 15.

Replace the second try{} block in Listing 15-1 with the following code segment, compile, and then run the program.

Listing 15-2: Using the IN Test

```
try {
    String query = "UPDATE customers " +
                       "SET Discount = 25 " +
                       "WHERE Discount IN (12,15)";
    DataRequest = Database.createStatement();
    Results = DataRequest.executeQuery (query);
    DataRequest.close();
}
```

Using IS NULL

Someday you may realize you don't have all the data you need to complete a new row. When you do get your missing data, try out the IS NULL test. It's a perfect way to update rows that contain one or more columns that are missing data.

You have written an application that enables a sales rep to enter data about a new customer into the customers table. There will probably be a time when a sales rep doesn't know the fax number of a customer but has the customer's other data, such as name and address. Instead of excluding the customer from the table, he can include the name and address now and later add the customer's fax number with your application.

Your application can test whether a column is empty of data before updating the column by using the IS NULL test. Listing 15-3 illustrates how to do this; it has the application ask the DBMS to determine whether the LastName column is empty. If so, the DBMS replaces the value in the Discount column with 0. (This is because discounts aren't given to customers when there is incomplete customer data.)

Listing 15-3:   Using the IS NULL Test

```
try {
    String query = "UPDATE customers " +
                   "SET Discount = 0 " +
                   "WHERE LastName IS NULL  ";
    DataRequest = Database.createStatement();
    Results = DataRequest.executeQuery (query);
    DataRequest.close();
}
```

Using comparisons

Comparison operators tell the DBMS to compare the value in a column with the value in the WHERE clause of the SQL expression in your program. You can use several kinds of comparison operators for this purpose; each makes a different kind of comparison (see Chapter 13).

Listing 15-4 shows you the greater than comparison operator, which tells the DBMS to determine whether the value in the Discount column is greater than 20. If so, the DBMS replaces the Discount with the value of 20.

You can substitute the greater than comparison operator with the other comparison operators to instruct the DBMS to make other kinds of comparisons.

Listing 15-4:   Using a Comparison Operator

```
try {
    String query = "UPDATE customers " +
                   "SET Discount = 20 " +
                   "WHERE Discount > 20 ";
    DataRequest = Database.createStatement();
    Results = DataRequest.executeQuery (query);
    DataRequest.close();
}
```

Updating all rows

You may run into an occasion when you'll need to have your application update all the rows in a table. For example, you may need to reset the values of all the rows. By specifying the SET clause and excluding the WHERE clause in your application's SQL expression, you update all the rows. Listing 15-5 resets the value in the Discount column of all the rows to 0.

Be careful whenever you exclude the WHERE clause when updating a table because you could inadvertently affect columns that you didn't want updated.

Listing 15-5:   Updating All Rows

```
try {
    String query = "UPDATE customers " +
                   "SET Discount = 0 ";
    DataRequest = Database.createStatement();
    Results = DataRequest.executeQuery (query);
    DataRequest.close();
}
```

Updating Multiple Columns

You can update more than one column for a row by including the names of the columns and the corresponding values in the SET clause. In fact, you have no limit to the number of columns that you can update at one time.

The values associated with columns in the SET clause overwrite the current values in each of the columns as long as the search criteria in the WHERE clause is met. Rows that don't match the search criteria don't update.

Updating multiple columns comes in handy when

✔ You have a minimum amount of data to place in a row when you're inserting a new row into the table.

✔ You're updating several pieces of data simultaneously to reduce the number of times you update the table.

✔ Related data — such as a customer's street, city, and state — changes.

Updating multiple columns is an efficient way to replace data in a row because the DBMS searches once for the row and then updates the columns rather than searches multiple times, one for each column.

Specifying multiple columns

Listing 15-6 shows you how to update more than one column at a time. This example changes the value of the Discount column and the Street column for the rows that have Jones in the LastName column.

After running the program, you'll notice that the Discount for all the Joneses in the customers table is 12, and they reside on Jones Street.

Listing 15-6: **Updating Multiple Columns at One Time**

```
try {
    String query = "UPDATE customers " +
                    "SET Discount = 12, " +
                    "Street = 'Jones Street' " +
                    "WHERE LastName = 'Jones'";
    DataRequest = Database.createStatement();
    Results = DataRequest.executeQuery (query);
    DataRequest.close();
}
```

Updating with a Calculation

You can have your Java database application use an SQL expression to calculate a new value for a column and then replace the current value of the column with the calculated value. This is an efficient way to calculate a new value for a column with minimum Java programming.

Suppose your company wants to raise the prices of their products by 10 percent, and you've been asked to write a program to change the prices of all the products in the Product table. You could do it the hard way by

- ✔ Requesting the price of product from the DBMS.
- ✔ Copying the price from the ResultSet to a Java variable.
- ✔ Calculating the new price.
- ✔ Updating the price in the table.
- ✔ Repeating all these steps until you update the price of each product.

A more efficient method is to have your application execute one SQL statement that tells the DBMS to calculate the new price and update the Price column with the new price.

Calculating on the fly

Listing 15-7 shows you how to direct the DBMS to calculate the DiscountPrice and then update the DiscountPrice column with the calculated value. Before trying this code segment in your program, you need to make a slight modification to the customers table:

1. **Insert two new columns in the table: Price and DiscountPrice.**

   The Price and DiscountPrice columns should be the Currency data type.

2. Enter prices into the Price column.

Here are the values I placed into my Price column:

Bob Jones	$100
Mark Jones	$200
Tom Jones	$300
Tom Jones	$400
Adam Smith	$500
Mary Smith	$600

Once you complete the modifications to the table, substitute the code segment for the second `try{}` block in Listing 15-1 (see "Updating your first table"). Compile and run the program. The DBMS updates the DiscountPrice column in the table.

Listing 15-7:   Making a Calculation

```
try {
    String query = "UPDATE customers " +
                   "SET DiscountPrice = " +
                   "Price * ((100 - Discount) / 100)
";
    DataRequest = Database.createStatement();
    Results = DataRequest.executeQuery (query);
    DataRequest.close();
}
```

Looking closer at the calculation

The calculation in Listing 15-7 seems a bit confusing, so I thought that I'd take a moment to explain it. Basically, the calculation is determining the discount price that will be charged to the customer:

DiscountPrice = Price * ((100 - Discount) / 100)

The Discount column contains the discount value. Let's say that the discount is 10%:

DiscountPrice = Price * ((100 - 10) / 100)

Test your newfound knowledge

1. How do you instruct the DBMS to update a column ?

a. Use the IN clause.

b. Use the SET clause.

c. Use the Santa clause.

d. Use multiple clauses.

2. What happens if you exclude the WHERE clause in your update SQL expression?

a. An error displays.

b. All rows update.

c. Only rows that match the search criteria update.

d. The DBMS becomes lost.

Answers: (1) b. (2) b.

The discount price, therefore, is 90% of the value of the Price column. The code segment subtracts the value of the Discount column from 100. This is done in (100 - Discount) or 100 - 10, which is of course 90:

DiscountPrice = Price * (90 / 100)

The number 90 is a whole number. We need to get it to a decimal value that is equivalent to 90%. We divide 90 by 100, which results in 0.90.

Let's assume that the price is $1,000. We need to multiple 0.90 by the value of the Price column to arrive at the DiscountPrice, which is $900:

DiscountPrice = 1000 * 0.90, so DiscountPrice = 900

Fortunately, the DBMS performs the math for you and replaces the value of the DiscountPrice column with the results of the calculation. All you need to do is properly create the SQL expression and include the expression in your Java database application.

Chapter 16

Get Rid of the Bum: Deleting Data in Tables

In This Chapter

▶ Deleting a row

▶ Deleting multiple rows

▶ Deleting selected rows

*T*he head coach of a professional football team is much like a Java database programmer, although the two seem a distance apart. A week before the football season begins, the head coach ponders his roster and looks to cut the team down to a lean, mean, winning machine.

The coach has hard decisions to make. A Java database programmer has similar decisions to make — which data remains in the database and which data gets the Jersey bounce.

Keeping a database lean of unnecessary data is a major component of every Java database application. Failure to remove data can lead to

- **Large databases and tables:** Databases and tables tend to grow quickly once people start using the database application daily. This leads to an increased amount of resources being used, such as disk space, which can become expensive.

- **Inefficient performance when retrieving or maintaining data:** The more data in the database, the more rows the database management system (DBMS) must process for each query. Response time to receive data from the database increases, especially if that database isn't fine-tuned with indexes (see Chapter 4).

- **Irrelevant data:** After a while, old data retained in a database becomes meaningless to the business operation. Few employees realize the data exists, and even fewer employees find the data informative because it's so old.

This chapter shows you how to keep your database and tables trim of unnecessary data by deleting data from the database.

Finding Data to Delete

Before you begin to reduce the amount of data in your database, you must decide which data to remove. Sometimes this is an easy decision because it's obvious, such as when there are two rows in a table that contain the same data.

Other times, you may find it tricky to decide what to delete from the database. If you have a table of product data — such as a list of products that your company sells — and some of those products have been discontinued, do you delete those products from the table?

Instinct tells us to delete discontinued products because no one can place an order for them. Keep in mind that instincts don't always produce the results that you expect. Take a skunk crossing a dark highway confronted by a ten-ton truck barreling down the road. When faced with danger, the skunk turns his back and sprays — you can imagine the rest of the story.

As for discontinued products, the database probably has a table that contains order data, which is related to data in the Product table. Orders contain product numbers that are joined with product numbers in the Product table, which displays the product description (see Chapter 17 for more about joins).

By deleting the discontinued product, you also permanently lose the product description. A problem arises if a customer has a question about an old order; your application can display the order but not the description for any discontinued products.

Before deleting data from a table, you must

- ✔ Make sure your business isn't currently using the data.
- ✔ Determine whether the data is linked to rows of other tables. This is similar to how the product description in the Product table is linked to rows in the Order table. This is called referential integrity (see Chapter 3).
- ✔ Determine whether you need to retain the data for legal purposes.

No one else who uses your Java database application will likely take these precautions. You should always ask the user of your application whether he or she wants to delete data. And then, you should assess how this deletion will affect your database.

Many users prefer to archive data instead of deleting it. Archiving data removes data from the DBMS and places the data off-line on media, such as a tape or CD, which can be retrieved whenever the user requires access to the archived data.

Finding what you need to delete

Where is the data you want to delete? In the database, of course! I should probably rephrase the question to "Which table in the database contains the data you need to delete?" This isn't as easy to answer.

Data resides in many tables within a database, so whenever someone requests to delete data, he must tell the application the name of the table or tables. A well-designed database reduces the amount of duplicate data to a minimum (see Chapter 2). Very few databases actually remove all duplicate data because this results in an overly normalized database, which impacts performance of the application.

Therefore, you must determine

- ✔ The tables that contain the data you need to delete.
- ✔ The column names of the data. Some tables might contain the same data but use different column names, such as ZipCode and PostalCode.
- ✔ A unique way to identify the data within the table so you target the correct data for deletion.

Always analyze the database structure first before writing code to delete any data from the database. This will ensure that data is thoroughly removed from the database without having a negative impact on the application.

Preventing problems

A relational database is an efficient way to store and retrieve data because it removes nearly all duplicate data from the database (see Chapter 2). While relational databases have many benefits, they do have one major drawback when you remove data from a table. Deleting data might also delete the relationship between two or more tables.

You can prevent breaking up relationships among tables by

- ✔ Reviewing the database schema before writing code to delete data (see Chapter 2).
- ✔ Identifying all the relationships among the tables.

✔ Determining whether the relationship among tables can be broken without affecting the integrity of the database. You do this by carefully analyzing the business needs in relationship to the database schema and your Java database application.

As a general rule, whenever you're in doubt about whether a relationship affects business operations, don't delete the data!

Giving and getting deletion rights

You can imagine the damage that could be done to a business if every user of your Java database application had the right to delete data. Therefore, expect that the database administrator will impose tight restrictions on who can and who cannot delete data.

Talk with your database administrator regarding the policies for deleting data. The user ID used by your application must have the right to delete data; otherwise, your application will receive an "access denied" error message.

Typically, the database administrator will require that you include certain precautions in your Java database applications if your application is given the right to delete data. These precautions include

✔ Being granted delete rights to specific tables within the database. These are usually the tables that are created especially for your application.

✔ Requiring that your application prompt the user to verify that he or she wants data to be deleted before it deletes the data.

✔ Requiring you and possibly the user of your application to receive approval from management before you or the user can delete data.

Restrictions can at times seem to obstruct the efficiency of developing and operating a Java database application. However, restrictions are a level of protection that ensures the data integrity of the application.

Deleting a Single Row of Data

Your Java database application can delete one or more rows in a table by creating an SQL expression that uses the DELETE FROM statement. You follow DELETE FROM with the name of the table that contains the row or rows to be deleted.

You use the WHERE clause to specify a search criteria that the DBMS uses to identify the rows (see the next section). Your application isn't required to include a WHERE clause in the SQL expression. However, leaving out the WHERE clause causes all the rows of the table to be deleted.

You can create an SQL expression that

✔ Deletes one row from a table

✔ Deletes multiple rows from a table

✔ Deletes all rows from a table

Deleting your first row

Before you try your hand at deleting data from a table, create a new table. I suggest creating this customers table:

Column	Data Type	Size
FirstName	Text	50
LastName	Text	50
Street	Text	50
City	Text	50
State	Text	2
ZipCode	Text	12
Discount	Number	

Now insert data into the table. I suggest following my lead:

Name	Address	Discount
Bob Jones	121 Maple Street New York City NY 55555	20
Mark Jones	15 Maple Street Dallas TX 66666	3
Tom Jones	Jones Street Dallas TX 66666	12
Tom Jones	Jones Street Dallas TX 66666	12
Adam Smith	56 Pine Street Trenton NJ 88888	5
Mary Smith	24 Oak Street San Jose CA 77777	10
Adams	2 Pine Street Trenton NJ 88888	25

Listing 16-1 illustrates how to delete a row of data from a table. In this example, I delete all rows from the customers table, where the value of the LastName column is Jones and the value of the FirstName column is Tom.

Try to compile and run this program. You'll see that Tom Jones is deleted.

You'll receive an SQL error when you run the program. The error tells you that the DBMS didn't return a ResultSet. This is fine since the program didn't request a ResultSet from the DBMS.

Listing 16-1:   Deleting a Row of Data

```java
import java.sql.*;

public class deletetst
{
    private Connection Database;

    public deletetst()
    {
        String url = "jdbc:odbc:customers";
        String userID = "jim";
        String password = "keogh";
        Statement DataRequest;
        ResultSet Results;

        try {
            Class.forName( "sun.jdbc.odbc.JdbcOdbcDriver");

            Database =
          DriverManager.getConnection(url,userID,password);
        }
        catch (ClassNotFoundException error) {
            System.err.println("Unable to load the JDBC/ODBC
        bridge." + error);
            System.exit(1);
        }
        catch (SQLException error) {
            System.err.println("Cannot connect to the
        database." + error);
            System.exit(2);
        }

        try {
            String query = "DELETE FROM customers " +
                            "WHERE LastName = 'Jones' and
          FirstName = 'Tom'";
            DataRequest = Database.createStatement();
            Results = DataRequest.executeQuery (query );
            DataRequest.close();
        }
        catch ( SQLException error ){
            System.err.println("SQL error." + error);
            System.exit(3);
        }
```

```
    }

    public static void main ( String args [] )
    {
        final deletetst link = new deletetst();
            System.exit ( 0 ) ;
    }
}
```

The Deleting walk-about

The program begins at the bottom of the list with the main() method, where an object of the deletetst class is created. The program then executes the deletetst constructor, which is defined at the top of the listing.

The constructor assigns the url for the database, userID, and password to Strings. Afterwards, the program loads the JDBC/ODBC bridge (Class. forName()) and opens a connection to the database (getConnection()).

The first catch{} block detects any errors that are caused when the constructor loads the JDBC/ODBC bridge. It displays an error message and terminates the program. Likewise, the second catch{} block detects errors occurring when the program connects to the database. The second catch{} also displays an appropriate error message and terminates the program.

Once the database connection is opened, the program creates the SQL expression. The SQL expression deletes all rows from the customers table where the value of the LastName column is Jones and the value of the FirstName column is Tom.

The program then places the SQL expression in an SQL statement and sends the SQL statement to the DBMS for processing (executeQuery()). The SQL statement then closes.

The third catch{} block traps any errors that occur when the SQL statement executes. The error and an error message display onscreen, and the program terminates.

After the constructor is finished executing, the program returns to the second statement in the main() method, which exits the program.

Deleting Multiple Rows

You can delete more than one row from a table by telling the DBMS which rows you want to delete. And you do this by creating a search criterion. A *search criterion* is an expression that defines a row by a value in the column of the row. The DBMS deletes all rows that have columns matching the search criterion.

Here are the ways you can identify rows to delete:

✔ Use the IN test.

✔ Determine whether a column is empty.

✔ Use a comparison operator.

Test the search criteria before using it in your application to delete rows. Use the search criteria with the SELECT command (see Chapter 13). The rows the DBMS returns when using the SELECT command will be the same rows that your application deletes.

Using the IN test

The IN test tells the DBMS to compare the value of a specified column to one of several values in the SQL expression. If the value of the column matches one of the values in the SQL expression, the DBMS deletes the row.

Listing 16-2 uses the IN test in the WHERE clause to determine whether the value in the Discount column in the customers table is 3 or 5. If it is, the DBMS deletes the row. If not, the DBMS leaves the row unchanged.

Replace the second try{} block in the previous program with this code segment and then recompile the program. The result is that any rows that contain a discount of 3 or 5 are deleted.

Listing 16-2:   Using the IN Test to Delete Rows

```
try {
    String query = "DELETE FROM customers " +
                    "WHERE Discount IN (3,5)";
    DataRequest = Database.createStatement();
    Results = DataRequest.executeQuery (query );
    DataRequest.close();
}
```

Using IS NULL

An empty column value in a row is called NULL. You can use the IS NULL test to delete all rows that have a specific column value empty.

I use the IS NULL test in Listing 16-3 to delete all the rows in the customers table that have the FirstName column empty. Only those rows that don't have a FirstName value are removed from the table.

Listing 16-3: Using IS NULL to Delete Rows

```
try {
    String query = "DELETE FROM customers " +
                        "WHERE FirstName IS NULL  ";
    DataRequest = Database.createStatement();
    Results = DataRequest.executeQuery (query );
    DataRequest.close();
}
```

Using comparisons

A comparison is where you tell the DBMS to compare the value in a column with the value that you specify in the SQL expression. The comparison operator makes the comparison. You have many comparison operators available to you (just check out Chapter 13 if you don't believe me).

I show you how to use them in Chapter 13 to select data from a table. You can use the same comparison operators to identify rows to delete from a table. Listing 16-4 shows you how to delete rows from the customers table.

In this code segment, I tell the DBMS to look at each row in the customers table and identify those rows where the value of the Discount column is greater than 20. If there is a match, the DBMS deletes the row. If there isn't a match, the DBMS skips to the next row in the table.

Listing 16-4: Using a Comparison Operator to Delete Rows

```
try {
    String query = "DELETE FROM customers " +
                        "WHERE Discount > 20 ";
    DataRequest = Database.createStatement();
    Results = DataRequest.executeQuery (query );
    DataRequest.close();
}
```

Deleting all rows

There will come a time when you want your application to remove all the data in a table. Let's say that you've built a Java database application for teachers. One of the tables contains a list of student's grades for each test that the teacher gave in the course.

The teacher erases the table that contains student's grades at the beginning of every semester. Therefore, your application must enable the teacher to delete all the rows in the table.

Deleting all the rows of a table is different than dropping a table. Dropping a table (see Chapter 10) removes the table and all data in the table from the database. You must re-create the table if you want to use the table again. In contrast, deleting all rows removes the data from the table. The table is still intact; you can insert new data into the table without having to first re-create the table.

Listing 16-5 deletes all the rows from the customers table. Notice that the SQL expression in the code segment doesn't contain a WHERE clause. A WHERE clause identifies specific rows to delete. If you don't use the WHERE clause, you aren't specifying any rows in the SQL expression. Therefore, the DBMS deletes all the rows.

Listing 16-5: Deleting All Rows

```
try {
    String query = "DELETE FROM customers ";
    DataRequest = Database.createStatement();
    Results = DataRequest.executeQuery (query);
    DataRequest.close();
}
```

Test your newfound knowledge

1. How do you tell the DBMS that rows containing one of a series of values should be deleted?

a. Use the ESCAPE clause.

b. Use the FROM clause.

c. Use the IN clause.

d. Use MANY clauses.

2. How do you tell the DBMS to delete rows where two columns match values in your SQL expression?

a. Point to the columns that you want to match.

b. Use two SQL expressions.

c. Link two search criteria using the AND operator.

d. Specify column names and separate with a semicolon.

Answers: (1) c. (2) c.

Part IV
Picking and Choosing Data

The 5th Wave By Rich Tennant

"Sometimes I feel behind the times. I asked my 11 year old to build a database for my business, and he said he would, only after he finishes the one he's building for his baseball card collection."

In this part . . .

There is an art to selecting the data from a database that will best satisfy the needs of your Java database application or applet. Your job is to become the artist and write a program that retrieves data in the most efficient way.

This part has tips and techniques that take the guesswork out of selecting data from a database. You can think of chapters in this part as your own art instructor, showing you the right moves to deliver professional results.

After reading this part, you'll know how to utilize the techniques professional Java database programmers use to query a database and let the DBMS crunch data for your program.

Chapter 17

Picking Data from This Table and That Table

My neighbor is a joiner by profession. No, he isn't the guy in town that belongs to every community organization. He is a carpenter whose job it is to make sure that pieces of cabinets, chairs, and other wooden furniture fit together perfectly.

I'm also known as a joiner, but in a more cyber way. Instead of joining together pieces of wood, I join tables of data together to form one virtual table that can be queried for data. My joins are not as appreciated as my neighbor's joins because they are hidden from view.

Yet, joining tables together is just as important to a Java database application as joining wood together is to a fine kitchen. A successful join gives the furniture and the database application a touch of professionalism.

In this chapter, you'll learn how to join tables in your Java database application. You'll learn

✔ The advantages and disadvantages of joins

✔ How to select data used to join tables

✔ How to create the proper join for your application

A join enables you to take full advantage of the features available in a relational database and expand your request for data from one table to multiple tables.

Setting Up the Database for Joins

A *join* is a way to link two or more tables together using a common value that appears in a column of each table. Your application has two tables: One table contains orders and the other table contains customer data.

The primary key of the Orders table is the OrderNumber (see Chapter 4). A unique order number identifies each row. A CustomerNumber is the primary key in the customers table, where a unique Customer Number identifies each row in that table.

If a customer places an order, you would put his Customer Number with the rest of the data about the order in the Orders table. You wouldn't include other data about the customer, such as his name and address, in the Orders table because the data in the database is normalized (see Chapter 3).

You can reference all the data about a customer and his order by joining the desired rows in the customers table and the Orders table using the Customer Number. I'll show you how to do this later in this chapter (see "Joining Two Tables").

Once you join two tables, you can

✔ Access values in the columns from both tables

✔ Update values in the columns of both tables

✔ Calculate values in the columns of both tables

I like to think of joined tables as one big virtual table where I can pick and choose the columns I want my Java database application to use.

Creating a parent-child relationship

Many of the joins that your Java database application will use are based on a parent-child relationship that exists between two tables. The concept of a parent-child relationship is nearly identical to its biological counterpart — a child can't exist without a parent.

In the case of two tables, data contained in one table exists only if corresponding data exists in the other table. The customers table and the Orders table that I describe in the previous section have a parent-child relationship. The customers table is the parent, and the Orders table is the child. A customer places an order; therefore, an order cannot exist without a customer.

For every row in the Orders table, there must be a row in the customers table. However, your Java database application must enforce the parent-child relationship by prohibiting the creation of a row in a child table unless there is a corresponding row in the parent table.

In other words, your application won't permit a sales rep to enter an order into the database unless either the data about the customer already exists in the customers table or your application requires the sales rep to enter the customer data before he places the order.

Other programmers' applications may use the database used by your application. Therefore, the parent-child relationship might be broken unless all programmers enforce the parent-child relationship when they insert data into the database.

Using the same column name

Since a common value in the two tables joins the tables together, you probably want to use the same column name in both tables. For example, you want to use the Customer Number to join the customers table and the Orders table. It would make sense to call the column that contains the Customer Number something like CustomerNumber, Customer Number, or CustNum.

After you decide on a name that describes the value of the column, you should use the same name in both the customers table and the Orders table. In that way, you will easily remember the column that you need to join in your Java database application.

Using different column names

Although you may find it convenient to use the same column name in both tables for the common column, you can use any column name you wish. The database management system (DBMS) actually joins tables based on instructions you provide in the SQL expression of your application.

The DBMS really doesn't care too much about the column name. It uses whatever column names you provide and matches the values in those columns. So, you could name the column that contains the Customer Number in the Orders table XYZ and the call the corresponding column in the customers table Bob.

The DBMS will then compare the values in the XYZ and Bob columns and return the rows that match. Of course, anyone looking at the column names will have no idea what kind of data these columns contain. This could lead to programming errors. You can prevent this type of programming error from occurring by making column names used to join tables the same name.

Creating sample tables

Before you learn about how to join together tables in your Java database application, you should create a few tables that you can practice with. Any group of tables will do as long as you remember to have common columns in each table.

However, I suggest creating the tables that I used for sample programs in this chapter. You'll find these tables easier to use, and you'll be able to compare the results of running your program with the results I show in this chapter.

Here are the tables I use:

✔ Customers table where the CustomerNumber column is the primary key:

Column	Data Type	Size	Required	Indexed
CustNum	Long Integer		Yes	Yes (No Duplicates)
FirstName	Text	50	No	No
LastName	Text	50	No	No
Street	Text	50	No	No
City	Text	50	No	No
ZipCode	Text	12	No	No

✔ ZipCode table where the Zip column is the primary key:

Column	Data Type	Size	Required	Indexed
Zip	Text	10	Yes	Yes (No Duplicates)
State	Text	2	No	No

✔ Stores table where the StoreNumber is the primary key:

Column	Data Type	Size	Required	Indexed
StoreNumber	Number		Yes	Yes (No Duplicates)
Street	Text	50	No	No
City	Text	50	No	No
ZipCode	Text	10	No	No

✔ Products table where the ProductNumber is the primary key:

Column	Data Type	Size	Required	Indexed
ProductNumber	Number		Yes	Yes (No Duplicates)
ProductName	Text	50	No	No

✔ Orders table where the OrderNumber is the primary key:

Column	Data Type	Size	Required	Indexed
OrderNumber	Number		Yes	Yes (No Duplicates)
ProdNumber	Number		No	No
Customer Number	Number		No	No
StoreNumber	Number		No	No
Quantity	Number		No	No

Once you create the tables, you need to enter several rows of data so you can join together the tables. Enter any data you wish into the table. Just make sure that you include common values in other tables.

You'll probably find it convenient to use the same data that I use, so you can compare our results. Enter the data into the corresponding table and you'll be ready to create your first join.

✔ Enter this data into the customers table:

Customer Number	First Name	Last Name	Street	City	ZipCode
591	Anne	Smith	65 Cutter Street	Woodridge	04735
721	Bart	Adams	15 W. Spruce	River Ville	05213
845	Tom	Jones	35 Pine Street	West Town	07660
901	Mary	Smith	5 Maple Street	SunnySide	08513

✔ Enter this data into the ZipCode table:

Zip	State
04735	TX
05213	CA
07660	NJ
08513	NY

✔ Enter this data into the Stores table:

StoreNumber	Street	City	ZipCode
278	222 Riverview	SunnySide	08513
345	5 Main Street	West Town	07660
547	18 Maple Street	River Village	05213
825	350 South Street	Woodridge	04735

✔ Enter this data into the Products table:

ProductNumber	ProductName
1052	CD Player
3255	VCR
5237	DVD Player
7466	50-inch TV

✔ Enter this data into the Orders table:

OrderNumber	ProdNumber	CustomerNumber	StoreNumber	Quantity
122	5237	591	345	1
334	3255	901	278	1
365	3255	901	278	4
534	7466	591	825	3
587	5237	845	345	1
717	1052	721	825	2
874	7466	721	825	1

Knowing the Rules of the Join

When you use a join in the application's SQL expression, you're asking the DBMS to perform several tasks. Sometimes the DBMS performs these tasks quickly and other times it has to work a little harder.

The DBMS follows your directions for joining tables, so the better that you become at writing those directions, the easier it is for the DBMS to comply with your request. Here are a few guidelines to follow when using a join in your application:

✔ Be sure that the columns used to join tables are key values used in a primary or secondary index.

✔ Use as few tables as possible in the SQL expression. The more tables you join together, the more work your DBMS has to do.

✔ Be alert to the number of applications that use the DBMS at the same time. Applications that make complex inquiries for data tend to use more than their fair share of the DBMS's time.

By following these simple guidelines, your application will be able to join together tables needed to retrieve nearly any combination of data that is available from the database.

Diminishing performance with too many tables

The manufacturers of DBMSs design their products to store and retrieve a lot of data in the shortest possible time. However, you're probably scratching your head wondering what is "a lot of data." Unfortunately, there is no easy answer to this question.

The amount of data a DBMS can manage grows very quickly in a typical business. A database stores nearly every piece of data collected by a business — and that can add up to a lot of space!

Whenever you request to join two tables, the DBMS must

✔ Locate each table

✔ Locate the proper index to use to join the columns that you requested

✔ Match columns

✔ Copy into memory data from columns of rows that match your request

✔ Send the copy to your application

These tasks may not appear time consuming, but consider that the DBMS performs them for every row of every table that you want to join. You can improve the performance of the DBMS by determining whether the business need justifies the length of time necessary to retrieve the data.

For example, an application that is used to help management reach a business decision typically needs to access many tables, many of which require a join. The data they need to make their decision is in a variety of tables.

Before writing a decision-support application, you should assess the time and effort necessary to write and run the application, compared with the impact the decision has on the business. The database administrator and managers of the business unit who requests the system can help you assess the impact the application will have on the DBMS and other applications that access the DBMS.

In comparison, a transaction application, such as an application that accepts orders from customers, joins fewer tables than a decision-support application and typically has a minimal impact on the DBMS's performance.

Even if your application doesn't require the DBMS to perform many tasks, other applications may be making heavy demands on the DBMS. Those demands could reduce the response time of your application and mislead you into believing your application has a problem.

The DBMS may impose a limit on the number of tables that you can join with a single SQL statement. The manufacturer of the DBMS sets this limit, which is usually eight tables.

Creating a new table, not combining data

Probably the most confusing concept to understand about joins is that a join results in a new table rather than a combination of columns for two tables. The difference might not be apparent, but here's what is happening.

Let's say you have two tables: a customers table and a ZipCode table. The customers table contains the name and address of customers. The ZipCode table is used in the customers table instead of using the name of the customer's state. The ZipCode table contains the Zip Code and the name of the state.

Whenever an application requires a customer's name and address that includes the name of the state, the two tables join. The Zip Code joins both tables. (I show you how this is done later in this chapter in "Joining Two Tables.")

After the tables join, the DBMS returns only the rows of both tables that have matching Zip Codes. Now three tables exist following the join: the customers table, the ZipCode table, and our new table, which is commonly called the product table.

The product table is a temporary table that exists until either your application receives rows from the joined tables or until you copy data from the product table to a permanent table.

Don't confuse the term *product table,* which refers to joined tables, with a Products table, which contains data about business products.

The product table that results in joining two or more tables is a real table against which you can make other requests for data, which we call a sub-query (see Chapter 20).

Joining Two Tables

The most common type of join that you'll use in your Java database application involves joining two tables. A good example of an application that joins two tables is one that displays a customer's name and a customer's order (see "Creating a parent-child relationship").

Your application can join together two tables by using an SQL expression within your program. The SQL expression must specify

- ✔ **The columns that you want the DBMS to return:** You place the column names in a SELECT statement. You can use the columns from either or both tables in the SELECT statement.

- ✔ **The tables that you want to join:** You place the name of tables you want to use to create the join in the FROM clause. A comma must separate the table names.

- ✔ **An expression that tells the DBMS how to join the two tables:** The WHERE clause contains an expression that uses the names of the columns whose values are used to join the tables and a comparison operator, which indicates how the DBMS should compare the two columns (see Chapter 13 for more about comparison operators).

The equal join: The simplest of them all

The equal join is the most common type of join that you'll use in your application. It tells the DBMS to join two tables and return matching rows to your application. I find that to understand how a join works you must build a program that joins two tables — and Listing 17-1 does just that.

The objective of this program is to display a customer's name, state, and Zip Code. The SQL expression in the program uses SELECT to select FirstName, LastName, State, and ZipCode. These columns will display onscreen.

You don't need to specify in the SELECT statement the name of the table that contains the column name as long as the column names are different in each table. Later in this chapter I show you how to use duplicate column names (see "Creating a column name qualifier").

The FROM clause specifies that the rows will come from the customers table and the ZipCode table (see "Creating sample tables" to set up your tables first). The WHERE clause contains the criteria for the DBMS to use when joining the tables (WHERE Zip = ZipCode).

Zip is the name of the column that contains Zip Codes in the ZipCode table. ZipCode is the name of the column in the customers table that contains Zip Codes. The equal operator directs the DBMS to join rows of the customers and the ZipCode tables where the Zip Codes in the Zip and ZipCode columns match.

The DBMS returns the columns requested in the SELECT statement for rows that match the criteria in the WHERE clause. Those rows that don't match aren't returned to the application. Figure 17-1 shows the results when you run this program.

Listing 17-1:   Creating an Equal Join

```
import java.sql.*;
import javax.swing.*;
import java.awt.event.*;
import java.awt.*;
import java.util.*;
import java.lang.*;

    public class jointst extends JFrame
    {
        private JTable DataTable;
        private Connection Database;

        public jointst()
        {
            String url = "jdbc:odbc:customers";
            String userID = "jim";
            String password = "keogh";
            Statement DataRequest;
            ResultSet Results;

            try {
                Class.forName( "sun.jdbc.odbc.JdbcOdbcDriver");

                Database =
              DriverManager.getConnection(url,userID,password);
            }
            catch (ClassNotFoundException error) {
```

```
            System.err.println("Unable to load the JDBC/ODBC
        bridge." + error);
            System.exit(1);
    }
    catch (SQLException error) {
        System.err.println("Cannot connect to the
        database." + error);
            System.exit(2);
    }

    try {
        String query = " SELECT
        FirstName,LastName,State,ZipCode " +
                        "FROM Customers, ZipCode " +
                        "WHERE Zip = ZipCode";
        DataRequest = Database.createStatement();
        Results = DataRequest.executeQuery (query);
        DisplayResults (Results);
        DataRequest.close();
    }
    catch ( SQLException error ){
        System.err.println("SQL error." + error);
        System.exit(3);
    }

    setSize (500, 200);
    show();
}

private void DisplayResults (ResultSet
        DisplayResults)throws SQLException
{
    boolean Records = DisplayResults.next();

    if (!Records ) {
        JOptionPane.showMessageDialog( this, "End of
        data.");
    setTitle( "Process Completed");
    return;
    }
    setTitle ("Customer Names");
    Vector ColumnNames = new Vector();
    Vector rows = new Vector();

    try {
        ResultSetMetaData MetaData =
        DisplayResults.getMetaData();

        for ( int x = 1; x <= MetaData.getColumnCount();
        ++x)
            ColumnNames.addElement (MetaData.getColumnName (
        x ) );
```

(continued)

Listing 17-1 *(continued)*

```
        do {
           rows.addElement (DownRow( DisplayResults,
         MetaData ) );
        } while ( DisplayResults.next() );


        DataTable = new JTable (rows, ColumnNames ) ;
        JScrollPane scroller = new JScrollPane (DataTable )
          ;
        getContentPane(). add ( scroller,
          BorderLayout.CENTER );
        validate();
      }
    catch (SQLException error ) {
        System.err.println("Data display error."  + error);
        System.exit(4);
      }
   }

  private Vector DownRow ( ResultSet DisplayResults,
        ResultSetMetaData MetaData )
        throws SQLException
  {
    Vector currentRow = new Vector();
    for ( int x = 1; x <= MetaData.getColumnCount(); ++x )
        switch ( MetaData.getColumnType ( x ) ) {
        case Types.VARCHAR :
          currentRow.addElement( DisplayResults.getString
        ( x ) ) ;
          break;
        case Types.INTEGER :
          currentRow.addElement( new Long(
        DisplayResults.getLong( x )) ) ;
          break;
        }
    return currentRow;
  }

  public static void main ( String args [] )
  {
    final jointst link = new jointst();

    link.addWindowListener (
            new WindowAdapter() {
        public void windowClosing(WindowEvent WinEvent )
        {

          System.exit ( 0 ) ;
        }
```

```
        }

    );
    }
}
```

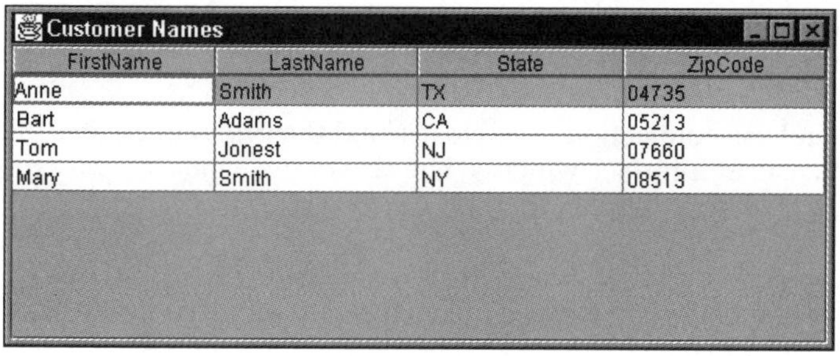

Figure 17-1:
Join
together the
customers
table and
the ZipCode
table.

FirstName	LastName	State	ZipCode
Anne	Smith	TX	04735
Bart	Adams	CA	05213
Tom	Jonest	NJ	07660
Mary	Smith	NY	08513

Customer Names

The program begins with the first statement in the main() method. This
statement creates an object of the jointst class, which is defined at the top
of the listing. When the object is created, the program automatically executes
the jointst constructor.

The constructor assigns data needed to access the database to Strings.
These are the url of the database (jdbc:odbc:customers), userID (jim),
and password (keogh).

The first try{} block in the constructor loads the JDBC/ODBC bridge (see
Chapter 7), connects, and opens the database using the getConnection()
method, which is passed the data needed to log onto the database.

One of the first two catch{} blocks trap any errors. The first catch{} block
traps errors that occur when the JDBC/ODBC bridge loads. The second
catch{} block traps errors occurring when the program connects to the
database. An error message displays onscreen, and the program terminates
when it finds an error.

Once a connection is made to the database, the constructor creates an SQL
expression in the second try{} block. The SQL expression uses the SELECT
statement to identify the column names that the DBMS must return to the
program.

The FROM clause specifies the customers and ZipCode tables that contain the
columns and the WHERE clause tells the DBMS how to join the customers and
ZipCode tables. The program returns rows where the value of the Zip column
and the value of the ZipCode column match.

After the program creates the SQL expression, the constructor creates (createStatement()) and executes (executeQuery()) the SQL expression, which returns a reference to the ResultSet of rows received from the DBMS. This reference is passed to the DisplayResults() method, which is defined later in the program.

The third catch{} block traps any errors that occur during the execution of the SQL statement. This block displays an error message onscreen and exits the program.

The database connection then closes, and the program creates and shows a graphical user interface window. The size of the window is measured in pixels and set by the setSize() method.

The DisplayResults() method shows each row that the DBMS returned onscreen. It begins by moving the virtual cursor to the first row of the ResultSet by calling the next() method.

The next() method returns a true value if the virtual cursor isn't pointing to the end of the ResultSet. If it is, next() returns a false value. A false value causes the program to enter the if statement, which displays a dialog box that states that the virtual cursor is at the end of the data. The program then returns to the jointst constructor and closes the connection to the database (DataRequest.close()).

A true value causes the program to skip over the if statement and proceed to create two Vectors. One Vector holds column names of the ResultSet, and the other Vector holds values of those columns. The try{} block copies metadata values from the ResultSet to the Vector that holds column names.

Next, the program enters a do...while loop that calls the DownRow() method and loads the data for each row in the Vector. The DownRow() method is defined later in the program and is used to move the virtual cursor to the next row in the ResultSet.

When the program finishes copying the column names and values of all the columns in the ResultSet in the Vectors, the Vectors load into a Java table (JTable (rows, ColumnNames)) and the Java tables display onscreen (JScrollPane (DataTable) and add (scroller, BorderLayout.CENTER)). The program calls the validate() method to make sure that there aren't any graphical user interface errors. The catch{} block traps errors and displays them onscreen.

Each time the program calls the DownRow() method, it creates a temporary Vector to hold data collected from the current ResultSet row. The getColumnCount() method determines the number of columns in the ResultSet, which is used by the program as the maximum value for the for loop.

The `DownRow()` method retrieves the data type of the column (`get.ColumnType()`) and a switch statement to use the proper method to copy data from the column into the Vector. The Vector then returns to the `DisplayResults()` method, where the contents of the Vector are copied to another Vector that contains the data. The data later displays onscreen.

The `jointst` constructor finishes when all the ResultSet data displays onscreen. At that time, the program returns to the second statement in the `main()` method. The second statement creates a WindowListener (`addWindowListener()`). A WindowListener monitors messages sent to the program by the operating system and passes those messages to the WindowAdapter (`WindowAdapter()`).

For example, clicking the Close button on a window is an event detected by the operating system such as Windows. The operating system then sends a message to the Java program telling it that someone wants to close the program.

The WindowListener receives the message from the operating system and then passes the message along to the WindowAdapter, which calls the `windowClosing()` method to end the program.

Parent-child join: Mammas and papas

A *parent-child join* is created when the data in one table of a join is dependent on the existence of the other table. This is the case between the Products table and the Orders table — the Products table is the parent and the Orders table is the child.

Here's how this works in a typical Java order-entry application. The application displays an empty order form onscreen and prompts a person to enter a new order. The person can order only those products that are in the Products table. Therefore, a product that isn't included in the Products table cannot be ordered and won't appear in the Orders table.

Listing 17-2 shows you how to create a parent-child join. Figure 17-2 shows you the results when you substitute the code segment for the second `try{}` block in Listing 17-1, compile, and run the program.

The DBMS joins together the Orders table and the Products table using the ProdNumber column of the Orders table and the ProductNumber column of the Products table. The DBMS then returns the OrderNumber column from the Orders table and the ProductName column from the Products table for all rows that have the same product number.

Listing 17-2: Using a Parent-Child Join

```
try {
    String query = " SELECT OrderNumber, ProductName
" +
                        " FROM Orders, Products " +
                        " WHERE ProdNumber =
ProductNumber";
      DataRequest = Database.createStatement();
      Results = DataRequest.executeQuery (query);
      DisplayResults (Results);
      DataRequest.close();
}
```

Figure 17-2:
The product
number is
used to join
the Orders
table with
the
Products
table.

OrderNumber	ProductName
122	DVD Player
334	VCR
365	VCR
534	50-inch TV
587	DVD Player
717	CD Player
874	50-inch TV

Customer Names

Multiple comparison joins

A Java database application can specify more than one way to choose rows
from multiple tables by combining comparison criteria in the WHERE clause.
Listing 17-3 tells the DBMS to join the Orders table and the Products table
using the product number and then return any rows of orders that have a
quantity greater than two.

Listing 17-3: Using Several Comparison Joins

```
try {
    String query = " SELECT OrderNumber,
ProductName, Quantity " +
                        " FROM Orders, Products " +
                        " WHERE ProdNumber =
ProductNumber " +
                        " AND Quantity > 2";
      DataRequest = Database.createStatement();
      Results = DataRequest.executeQuery (query);
      DisplayResults (Results);
      DataRequest.close();
}
```

Figure 17-3 shows the end result. The OrderNumber and Quantity columns are from the Orders table, and the ProductName column is from the Products table.

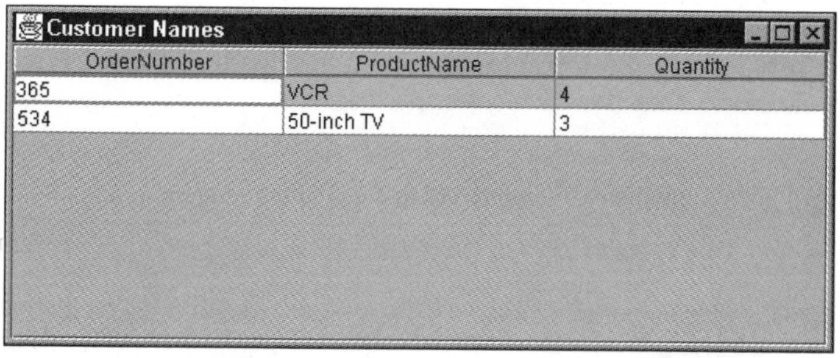

Figure 17-3:
Show
orders that
have a
quantity
greater than
two items.

OrderNumber	ProductName	Quantity
365	VCR	4
534	50-inch TV	3

Joining Three or More Tables

Professional databases contain many tables in an effort to eliminate or at least reduce the amount of duplicated data stored in the database (see Chapter 3). So you may run across situations where your Java database application needs to join together more than two tables.

Let's say that your application needs to generate an invoice for an order. An invoice contains a customer name, customer address, product description, quantity of products ordered, and price.

A customers table stores the customer's name and most of the customer's address. The state where the customer resides is found in the ZipCode table. You would find product descriptions in the Products table. And finally, the Orders table would hold quantity, price, and other data about the order.

The application must join together the customers table, ZipCode table, Products table, and the Orders table before it can generate a customer's invoice.

I'll show you how to join three tables. However, you would use the same method to join more than three tables — just specify the names of the tables in the SQL expression.

When joining multiple tables, you must specify the criteria for two joins. The first join criteria tells the DBMS how to join together two of the tables and the other join criteria tells the DBMS how to join the other two tables.

Listing 17-4 shows you how this is done. I ask the DBMS to join together the customers table, the Orders table, and the Products table. The first join uses the CustNumber column in the customers table with the CustomerNumber column in the Orders table. The second join is between the ProdNumber column in the Orders table and the ProductNumber column in the Products table. The DBMS returns only those rows that match both joins.

In this example, I ask the DBMS to return the customer's first name and last name from the customers table, the order number and quantity from the Orders table, and the product name from the Products table. Figure 17-4 shows the rows that the DBMS returns.

Listing 17-4: **Joining Three or More Tables**

```
try {
    String query = " SELECT FirstName,
        LastName,OrderNumber, ProductName, Quantity " +
            " FROM customers, Orders, Products " +
            " WHERE ProdNumber = ProductNumber " +
            " AND CustNumber = CustomerNumber";
    DataRequest = Database.createStatement();
    Results = DataRequest.executeQuery (query);
    DisplayResults (Results);
    DataRequest.close();
}
```

Figure 17-4: Select values from three tables.

FirstName	LastName	OrderNumber	ProductName	Quantity
Anne	Smith	122	DVD Player	1
Mary	Smith	334	VCR	1
Mary	Smith	365	VCR	4
Anne	Smith	534	50-inch TV	3
Tom	Jonest	587	DVD Player	1
Bart	Adams	717	CD Player	2
Bart	Adams	874	50-inch TV	1

Customer Names

Name-calling: The Short and Long of It

The more tables that you join, the higher the likelihood that you'll encounter at least two tables that have the same column name. You need to specify the column that you want in your application's SQL expression by prefacing the column name with the name of the table that contains the column. This is called a *column name qualifier*.

As you can imagine, the SELECT statement and the WHERE clause can quickly become very long since each column you mention needs to include the table name and the column name. You can keep these statements shorter by giving each table name a nickname called an *alias*.

I show you how to specify the table name and create an alias for tables in this section. However, before doing so, you need to make a small modification to the customers table to use the code segments in this section: Change the name of the CustNumber column to CustomerNumber.

Creating a column name qualifier

You would use a column name qualifier in an SQL expression whenever more than one table contains the same column name. The column name qualifier is the table's name or the table name's alias (see "Creating a table alias").

Listing 17-5 joins together three tables: Two tables are the customers table and the third table is Orders, where you use the CustomerNumber column to create the join. The listing specifies which CustomerNumber to use by placing the table name before the column name.

In the `SELECT` statement, `customers.CustomerNumber` tells the DBMS that the value of the `CustomerNumber` from the customers table must return to the application.

A period must separate the column name qualifier (`customers`) and the name of the column (`CustomerNumber`).

Listing 17-5:   Using a Column Name Qualifier

```
try {
    String query = "SELECT customers.CustomerNumber , " +
                    " FirstName, LastName,
        OrderNumber, " +
                        " ProductName, Quantity " +
                " FROM customers, Orders, Products " +
                " WHERE ProdNumber = ProductNumber " +
                " AND customers.CustomerNumber =
        Orders.CustomerNumber";
    DataRequest = Database.createStatement();
    Results = DataRequest.executeQuery (query);
    DisplayResults (Results);
    DataRequest.close();
}
```

Creating a table alias

A *table alias* is a nickname for a table; you would use it in place of the table name as a column name qualifier. You can use any single letter or letters as your table alias. However, you'll find that using an alias implies that the table name will make your code easier for you to read.

Listing 17-6 illustrates how you can create a table alias. The WHERE clause defines the table alias by inserting it between the name of the table and the comma that separates tables in the WHERE clause.

I use the first letter of each table as the table alias since I can easily remember that the letter is a substitute for the entire table name. I'd probably use a different alias if two of the tables began with the same letter. In that case, I might use the first three letters of each table name as the table alias, such as cus, ord, and pro.

After running this program you should see the same results as is shown in Figure 17-4.

Listing 17-6:   Using a Table Alias

```
    try {
        String query = "SELECT c.CustomerNumber , " +
                         " c.FirstName, c.LastName,
        o.OrderNumber, " +
                         " p.ProductName, o.Quantity " +
                      " FROM customers c, Orders o,
        Products  p" +
                      " WHERE o.ProdNumber =
        p.ProductNumber " +
                      " AND c.CustomerNumber =
        o.CustomerNumber";
        DataRequest = Database.createStatement();
        Results = DataRequest.executeQuery (query);
        DisplayResults (Results);
        DataRequest.close();
    }
```

Enjoying the Ins and Outs of Joins

Whenever a Java database application needs related data that is contained in more than one table, the application tells the DBMS to join together tables. The kinds of rows that the DBMS returns to the application depend on the type of join that the application requests the DBMS to perform.

The application requests two common types of joins:

- ✔ **Inner join:** The DBMS returns only matched rows to the application.
- ✔ **Outer join:** The DBMS returns matched rows and some unmatched rows to the application.

The objective of the application determines the type of join it requires. For example, an application that wants rows of customers who have placed an order uses an inner join. This is because the application needs only matched rows between the customers table and the Orders table.

In contrast, an application that wants rows of customers who have placed orders and customers who have not placed orders requires an outer join. This is because the application wants matched rows between the customers table and Orders table, and rows in the customers table that are unmatched with the Orders table.

Creating an inner join

You already know how to create an inner join if you've been reading this chapter and trying the programs in it. An inner join returns rows where the values of two columns are the same, which all the programs in this chapter do.

Listing 17-7 shows you two inner joins: the ProdNumber value joins the Products table and the Orders table, and the CustomerNumber value joins the customers table and the Orders table. Refer to Figure 17-4 for the results of running this program.

Listing 17-7:   Creating an Inner Join

```
try {
    String query = " SELECT FirstName,
        LastName,OrderNumber, ProductName, Quantity " +
                    " FROM Customers,Orders, Products " +
                    " WHERE ProdNumber = ProductNumber " +
                    " AND Customers.CustomerNumber =
        Orders.CustomerNumber";
    DataRequest = Database.createStatement();
    Results = DataRequest.executeQuery (query);
    DisplayResults (Results);
    DataRequest.close();
    }
```

Creating an outer join

An outer join returns matched and unmatched rows to your Java database application. The three types of outer joins are

- ✔ **Left outer join:** Returns matched and unmatched rows from the first table in the join, and only matched rows from the second table in the join.

- ✔ **Right outer join:** Returns only matched rows from the first table in the join, and matched and unmatched rows from the second table in the join.

- ✔ **Full outer join:** Returns matched and unmatched rows from the first and second tables in the join.

I show you how to create each of these outer joins; however, before doing so, you need to delete the order for customer 845, which is Tom Jones, from the Orders table.

Creating a left outer join

You create a left outer join in your Java database application by using an *= in the SQL expression, as shown in Listing 17-8. The *= tells the DBMS to return all rows from the customers table and only those rows in the Orders table that match the CustomerNumber in the customers table.

I like to think of the asterisk as a wild card that means "any row." Figure 17-5 shows the results after you run this program.

Listing 17-8: Creating a Left Outer Join

```
try {
    String query = " SELECT FirstName,
LastName,OrderNumber" +
                     " FROM Customers c, Orders o" +
                     " WHERE c.CustomerNumber *=
o.CustomerNumber";
    DataRequest = Database.createStatement();
    Results = DataRequest.executeQuery (query);
    DisplayResults (Results);
    DataRequest.close();
}
```

Some DBMSs, such as Microsoft Access, may not understand that you want a left outer join when you use the *=. Instead of receiving the rows that you are expecting, your application receives an SQL error message. Check with your database administrator for the proper syntax if the database you are using doesn't recognize *=. Listing 17-9 shows the syntax to use in your application if you are using Microsoft Access as the DBMS.

Listing 17-9: Creating a Left Outer Join in Microsoft Access

```
try {
    String query = " SELECT FirstName,
LastName,OrderNumber " +
                     " FROM Customers LEFT JOIN
Orders " +
                     " ON Customers.CustomerNumber =
Orders.CustomerNumber";
    DataRequest = Database.createStatement();
    Results = DataRequest.executeQuery (query);
    DisplayResults (Results);
    DataRequest.close();
}
```

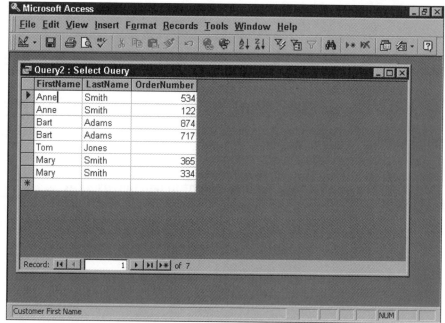

File Edit View Insert Format Records Tools Window Help

Query2 : Select Query

FirstName	LastName	OrderNumber
Anne	Smith	534
Anne	Smith	122
Bart	Adams	874
Bart	Adams	717
Tom	Jones	
Mary	Smith	365
Mary	Smith	334

Record: 1 of 7

Customer First Name

NUM

Figure 17-5:
The results
of creating a
left outer
join.

Creating a right outer join

A right outer join returns matched rows of the first table in a join and all the rows in the second table in the join. Before trying the following code segments, insert a new row in the Orders table and use 999 as the Customer Number for this order. Here are the values for the other columns in the Orders table:

OrderNumber	ProdNumber	CustomerNumber	StoreNumber	Quantity
555	1052	999	278	14

You create a right join by using =* in the SQL expression, as is shown in Listing 17-10. This tells the DBMS to return rows from the customers table that match the CustomerNumber value in the Orders table and return all the rows in the Orders table. Figure 17-6 shows the results.

ON THE WEB

Listing 17-10:   Creating a Right Outer Join

```
        try {
            String query = " SELECT FirstName,
        LastName,OrderNumber" +
                    " FROM Customers c, Orders o" +
                    " WHERE c.CustomerNumber =*
        o.CustomerNumber";
            DataRequest = Database.createStatement();
```

(continued)

Listing 17-10 *(continued)*

```
        Results = DataRequest.executeQuery (query);
        DisplayResults (Results);
        DataRequest.close();
    }
```

Microsoft Access and other DBMSs may not recognize =* as a right outer join. Consult your database administrator for the proper syntax to use if you receive an error message when using =* for a right join. Listing 17-11 illustrates how to create a right join in Microsoft Access.

Listing 17-11:   Creating a Right Join in Microsoft Access

```
    try {
        String query = "SELECT FirstName,
    LastName,OrderNumber " +
                    "  FROM Customers RIGHT JOIN
    Orders " +
                    "  ON Customers.CustomerNumber =
    Orders.CustomerNumber";
        DataRequest = Database.createStatement();
        Results = DataRequest.executeQuery (query);
        DisplayResults (Results);
        DataRequest.close();
    }
```

Creating a full outer join

A full outer join returns matched and unmatched rows from both tables. You use *=*, as shown in Listing 17-12, to create a full outer join. This tells the DBMS to return all the rows from the customers table and the Orders table that match. It also returns all rows from the customers table and Orders table that don't match.

Listing 17-12:   Creating a Full Outer Join

```
    try {
        String query = "SELECT FirstName,
    LastName,OrderNumber " +
                    " FROM Customers c, Orders o" +
                    " WHERE c.CustomerNumber *=*
    o.CustomerNumber";
        DataRequest = Database.createStatement();
        Results = DataRequest.executeQuery (query);
        DisplayResults (Results);
        DataRequest.close();
    }
```

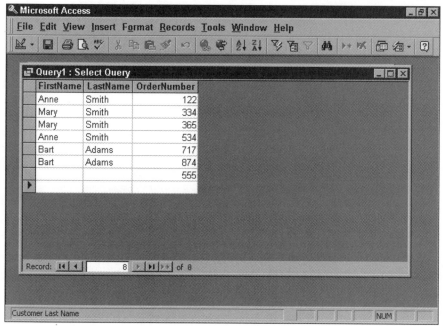

Figure 17-6:
An outer
join is
created
using
Customer
Number.

Chapter 18

Getting Together: Grouping and Ordering Data

. . . .

. . . .

*Y*ou'll find that the database management system (DBMS) crunches data better than you or I can, but it does have at least one behavior that is a little disconcerting. It isn't particular in the way it returns columns of data to a Java database application.

You don't have to accept the haphazard way in which the DBMS organizes its results. You can tell it to organize the ResultSet in practically any order that you need. This chapter shows you how. In this chapter, you learn how you can

✔ Group rows by the value of a column

✔ Group rows by the value of multiple columns

✔ Group a subset of rows

✔ Sort rows by the value of a column

✔ Sort rows by the value of multiple columns

✔ Sort rows by a calculated column in the ResultSet

You'll find that having the DBMS organize the ResultSet is much more efficient than writing grouping and sorting routines to organize the data yourself. Why do all that tricky programming when the DBMS will do the work for you?

Only Group-ies Need Apply

The DBMS can organize the data it returns into groups of related rows. Let's say that you want to see customer orders. You could simply tell the DBMS to return all the order data contained in the Orders table.

Typically the DBMS returns rows in the order the rows were processed, which is the same order that the rows were entered into the table. This means that rows containing several orders for the same customer are likely to be disbursed throughout the table, based on when the customer placed each order.

You'll probably find the lack of order confusing because your application probably needs to display orders grouped by customer. That is, display a customer's name followed by all that customer's orders.

The DBMS can group rows of the ResultSet for you if you include a GROUP statement in your Java database application's SQL expression. The GROUP statement specifies the column name that is to be used to group rows.

Grouping single columns

You'll need to create a table and enter rows of data into the table before you can practice grouping rows of data. I suggest creating this table and calling it sales:

Column	Data Type	Size
Store	Text	50
Sales	Number	
Estimate	Number	
SalesRep	Text	50

Now insert some data into your new sales table:

Store	Sales	Estimate	SalesRep
123	300	200	4
223	450	500	3
123	322	200	4
345	56	30	8
345	125	100	5
223	76	50	2
345	200	156	5

Listing 18-1 is a simple program that illustrates how to group rows by the value in one column. In this example, I tell the DBMS to return the store number and the total sales for each store from the sales table. The SUM( ) function calculates the total value in the Sales column.

The GROUP BY statement tells the DBMS to group rows in the ResultSet by values in the Store columns, which is by store number.

Listing 18-1:   Grouping Rows by the Value in One Column

```
import java.sql.*;
public class grouptst
    {
        private Connection Database;

        public grouptst ()
        {
            String url = "jdbc:odbc:customers";
            String userID = "jim";
            String password = "keogh";
            Statement DataRequest;
            ResultSet Results;

            try {
                Class.forName( "sun.jdbc.odbc.JdbcOdbcDriver");

                Database =
                DriverManager.getConnection(url,userID,password);
            }
            catch (ClassNotFoundException error) {
                System.err.println("Unable to load the JDBC/ODBC
                bridge." + error);
                System.exit(1);
            }
            catch (SQLException error) {
                System.err.println("Cannot connect to the
                database." + error);
                System.exit(2);
            }

            try {
                String query = " SELECT Store, SUM(Sales) " +
                                " FROM sales " +
                                " GROUP BY Store";
                DataRequest = Database.createStatement();
                Results = DataRequest.executeQuery (query);
                System.out.println("Store      Sales");
                System.out.println("-----      -----");
                DisplayResults (Results);
                DataRequest.close();
            }
```

(continued)

Listing 18-1 *(continued)*

```
        catch ( SQLException error ){
            System.err.println("SQL error." + error);
            System.exit(3);
        }
        shutDown();
    }

private void DisplayResults (ResultSet
        DisplayResults)throws SQLException
{

    boolean Records = DisplayResults.next();

    if (!Records ) {
      System.out.println( "End of data.");
      return;
    }

    try {
        do {
            DownRow( DisplayResults) ;
        } while ( DisplayResults.next() );

    }
    catch (SQLException error ) {
        System.err.println("Data display error." + error);
        System.exit(4);
    }
}

private  void DownRow ( ResultSet DisplayResults )
        throws SQLException
{
    String Store;
    long Sum;
    Store = DisplayResults.getString ( 1 ) ;
    Sum = DisplayResults.getLong ( 2 ) ;
    System.out.println(Store + "            " + Sum);
}

public void shutDown()
{
    try {
        Database.close();
    }
    catch (SQLException error) {
        System.err.println( "Cannot break connection." +
          error ) ;
    }
}
public static void main ( String args [] )
{
```

```
        final grouptst link = new grouptst ();
                System.exit ( 0 ) ;
    }
}
```

The result of the listing should look like this:

Store	Sales
123	622
223	526
345	381

Let's begin our walk-about at the bottom of the listing in the main() method because that's the first method of the program that executes. The first statement in the main() method creates an object of the class grouptst, which automatically executes the grouptst constructor.

The constructor is defined at the top of the listing in the definition of the grouptst class. The constructor creates three String objects and assigns data about url, userID, and password to the appropriate String objects. The constructor also creates a Statement object, used for the SQL statement, and the ResultSet object, used to reference data that the DBMS returns.

Next, the constructor loads the JDBC/ODBC bridge and connects to the database. If either of these events fails, the catch{} block traps the error. The first catch{} block traps errors when the JDBC/ODBC bridge loads, displays those errors onscreen, and exits the program. The second catch{} block traps errors that happen when a connection is made to the database. It also displays an error message and terminates the program.

If there are no errors, the program continues by creating the SQL expression in the second try{} block. The SQL expression tells the DBMS to return values in the Store column from the sales table, return the total sales for each store, and then group rows by store.

The program creates an SQL statement that is given an SQL expression to execute. The Results object of the ResultSet class references the data returned by the DBMS.

Next, the program displays a header. A *header* is descriptive text that identifies the values in each column of the returned data when the returned data displays. The program also displays the data by calling the DisplayResults() method, which the program defines next. After data is displayed, the program closes the SQL statement.

The catch{} block traps any SQL errors, displays an error message, and terminates the program. If there aren't any errors, the program calls the shutDown() method, which the program defines later. The shutDown() method breaks the connection with the database.

The DisplayResults() method begins by moving the virtual cursor to the next row (next()) in the ResultSet. This should point the virtual cursor to the first row of the ResultSet. However, the next() method returns a false value if no rows return, which causes the if statement to display the "End of data" message on the screen before returning to the constructor.

If there are no errors, the program enters a do...while loop that calls the DownRow() method, defined next in the program. It then moves the virtual cursor down a row in the ResultSet. The do...while loop continues as long as the next row has data. Otherwise, the next() method returns a false value, causing the program to break out of the do...while loop.

The catch{} block traps any errors, displays an error message on the screen, and exits the program.

The DownRow() method uses the getString() and getLong() methods to copy data from the ResultSet to variables. The program then displays the variables onscreen. Each time after a row of data is copied, the DownRow() returns to the DisplayResults() method, which returns to the constructor when there are no more rows in the ResultSet.

The constructor then returns to the second statement in the main() method, where the program terminates.

Grouping multiple columns

You can organize the rows the DBMS returns to your application into sub-groupings within the main group. You can use many subgroupings by specifying the column names for the group. The first column name in the GROUP BY statement is the main group and the column names that follow represent subgroupings.

Suppose that you want to tally sales by store and within each store you want to tally sales by the sales representative.

Grouping sales by the store is the main grouping and grouping sales within each store by the sales rep is a subgrouping. You specify the level of grouping by placing the appropriate column names in the GROUP BY statement.

Listing 18-2 illustrates this technique. I tell the DBMS to return values from the Store and SalesRep columns, and return the total sales from the sales table. Within the GROUP BY statement, I place the Store column name followed by the SalesRep column name.

Listing 18-2: Grouping Multiple Columns

```
try {
    String query = " SELECT Store,SalesRep,
SUM(Sales) " +
                   " FROM sales " +
                   " GROUP BY Store, SalesRep";
    DataRequest = Database.createStatement();
    Results = DataRequest.executeQuery (query);
    System.out.println("Store   SalesRep   Sales");
    System.out.println("-----   --------   -----");
    DisplayResults (Results);
    DataRequest.close();
}
```

Your results should look like this:

Store	SalesRep	Sales
123	4	622
223	2	76
223	3	450
345	5	325
345	8	56

The previous code segment returns three columns of data. Therefore, you need to replace the DownRow() method in the original program (see Listing 18-1) with the following DownRow() method.

Listing 18-3: Replacing the DownRow() Method

```
private  void DownRow ( ResultSet DisplayResults )
       throws SQLException
{
   String Store;
   String SalesRep;
   long Sum;
   Store = DisplayResults.getString ( 1 ) ;
   SalesRep = DisplayResults.getString ( 2 ) ;
   Sum = DisplayResults.getLong ( 3 ) ;
   System.out.println(Store + "        " + SalesRep + "
       " + Sum);
}
```

NULLs and groups: A dangerous combination

A row that has an empty column can be hazardous to your grouping's result. A column without a value is said to have a NULL value. The DBMS typically ignores a NULL value — for example, when the DBMS is using built-in functions to calculate values in a column.

However, the DBMS doesn't ignore NULL values when it groups rows using a column that contains a NULL value. The DBMS groups rows

with NULL values in the column used for grouping together in the ResultSet.

For example, if you are grouping rows by store number, but somehow a couple of store numbers have been inadvertently erased from several rows in the table, the DBMS will group those rows without store numbers together.

Knowing the group restrictions

Placing data into groups gives more meaning to your data than if you just have your data displayed randomly. Everyone who will use your database will appreciate being able to see related data together in one spot onscreen or in a report.

By having the DBMS group data before returning it to your application, you actually reduce programming. You don't need to write Java statements to group data from the DBMS. However, the DBMS imposes restrictions on how you can group your data. Your job is to work within these restrictions so your Java database application can take advantage of the grouping capabilities of the DBMS.

Here are grouping restrictions that you obey:

- A column name used for grouping rows must have a value in every row
- A grouping must use a single value
- A column function whose result is a single value that summarizes the row can be used for grouping rows
- A column that contains a constant value can be used for grouping rows
- An expression that combines a column name, column function, and/or a constant value can be used for grouping rows

Conditional Searches

Your Java database application can group the ResultSet on a subset of the entire table by using the HAVING clause. The HAVING clause contains an expression used by the DBMS to identify rows that should be included in the grouping. A conditional search uses search criteria (called a condition) to determine whether the DBMS returns a row in a table to your program.

An expression can include any comparison operator (see Chapter 13) and either a column name of a column in the table or a built-in function. The DBMS excludes rows that don't pass the expression test from the ResultSet.

The HAVING clause resembles the WHERE clause in that both clauses use an expression to select rows (see Chapter 13). However, they are different. The HAVING clause applies to a group of rows, and the WHERE clause applies to individual rows.

Using the HAVING clause

Listing 18-4 shows you how to use the HAVING clause in your application. In this example, I tell the DBMS to return the store and the total sales data from the sales table. The DBMS then groups the ResultSet by store. The DBMS will return the total sale by store to my program. Furthermore, I want only returned rows whose total sales are greater than 400.

Here's what happens:

- ✔ The DBMS groups rows by the value in the Store column of the sales table. You can think of this as placing all the rows containing the same store one after the other in the ResultSet.

- ✔ The DBMS totals the Sales column for each store and places the total in the row of the ResultSet that corresponds to the row that contains the store.

- ✔ The DBMS removes all rows from the ResultSet where the total is greater than 400.

- ✔ The DBMS returns the ResultSet to my application.

In contrast, the WHERE clause removes rows from the ResultSet before rows are grouped.

Listing 18-4: Using the HAVING Clause

```
        try {
            String query = "SELECT Store, SUM(Sales) " +
                            " FROM sales " +
                            " GROUP BY Store" +
                            " HAVING SUM(Sales) > 400";
            DataRequest = Database.createStatement();
```

(continued)

Listing 18-4 *(continued)*

```
            Results = DataRequest.executeQuery (query);
            System.out.println("Store      Sales");
            System.out.println("-----      -----");
            DisplayResults (Results);
            DataRequest.close();
        }
```

The result of this code should look like this:

Store	*Sales*
123	622
526	

Replace the DownRow( ) method with the following DownRow( ) method. This enables you to display the Store and Sales columns onscreen.

Listing 18-5:   Displaying Store and Sales Columns Onscreen

```
private  void DownRow ( ResultSet DisplayResults )
        throws SQLException
{
    String Store;
    long Sum;
    Store = DisplayResults.getString ( 1 ) ;
    Sum = DisplayResults.getLong ( 2 ) ;
    System.out.println(Store + "          " + Sum);
}
```

Following the search restrictions

You must abide by a few restrictions when using the HAVING clause in your application's SQL expression. Keeping the conditional expression within these restrictions ensures that the DBMS will return data that you requested.

Here are the restrictions that you must follow:

- The conditional expression must result in a single value.

- The conditional expression must result in a value that appears in every column named in the expression.

- The conditional expression can be a DBMS built-in function.

Sorting Results

You can control the order in which data appears in the ResultSet by using the ORDER BY clause. I like to think of the ORDER BY clause as the sort command for the DBMS. The ORDER BY clause requires you to specify the column name that will be used to sort the ResultSet.

By not using the ORDER BY clause, you are leaving the DBMS to decide on the order of rows in the return set. There is no guarantee on the order unless you use the ORDER BY clause in your application's SQL expression.

Many DBMSs return rows in the order in which the row appears in the table, which is typical data-entry order. You'll probably prefer to sort data in a more advantageous order than data-entry order.

Here are the ways you can sort data in a table:

✔ By a single column, called a major sort key

✔ By multiple columns, called a major and minor sort key

✔ By descending order

✔ By ascending order

✔ By a combination of descending order and ascending order

✔ By an equation using columns in the table

Your first sort

Listing 18-6 shows you how to reorder the ResultSet by the values in the Store column. Here's what is happening: I tell the DBMS to return values in the Store column and values in the Sales column from the sales table.

The ORDER BY clause sorts the ResultSet by the values in the Store column.

Listing 18-6:   Sorting Values

```
try {
    String query = "SELECT Store, Sales " +
                   " FROM sales " +
                   " ORDER BY Store";
    DataRequest = Database.createStatement();
    Results = DataRequest.executeQuery (query);
    System.out.println("Store       Sales");
    System.out.println("-----       -----");
    DisplayResults (Results);
    DataRequest.close();
}
```

These values appear in ascending order by default, as you see here (see "Descending sort" later in the chapter to learn how to reverse the direction of the sort):

Store	Sales
123	322
123	300
223	76
223	450
345	200
345	125
345	56

You'll need to replace the DownRow() method in Listing 18-1 with the following version of the DownRow() method. I'm using different variables to show you how to reorder data than I used when grouping data.

Listing 18-7:   Replace DownRow() to Display Two Columns

```
private  void DownRow ( ResultSet DisplayResults )
        throws SQLException
{
    String Store;
    long Sales;
    Store = DisplayResults.getString ( 1 ) ;
    Sales = DisplayResults.getLong ( 2 ) ;
    System.out.println(Store + "           " + Sales);
}
```

Sort keys

A *sort key* describes the columns used to reorder rows in the data the DBMS returns. If you are sorting the ResultSet by values in the Store column, for example, the Store column is the sort key to the sort.

The two types of sort keys are

- **Major sort key:** A major sort key is the first column used to sort the ResultSet.

- **Minor sort key:** Minor sort keys are subsequent columns used to sort the ResultSet.

The terms major and minor sort keys can be confusing; however, Listing 18-8 will solidify this concept in your mind. Here I tell the DBMS to return the Store and Sales columns from the sales table.

I've also stated that I want rows sorted using the Store column as the major sort key and the Sales column as the minor sort key. Store numbers appear in ascending order, and within each store, sales display in ascending order.

You can use as many sort keys as there are columns or calculations that you use in the SELECT statement.

Listing 18-8:   Sorting with Major and Minor Keys

```
try {
    String query = "SELECT  Store, Sales " +
                   " FROM sales " +
                   " ORDER BY Store, Sales";
    DataRequest = Database.createStatement();
    Results = DataRequest.executeQuery (query);
    System.out.println("Store      Sales");
    System.out.println("-----      -----");
    DisplayResults (Results);
    DataRequest.close();
}
```

The result of this sort looks like this:

Store	Sales
123	300
123	322
223	76
223	450
345	56
345	125
345	200

Descending sort

The DBMS orders rows in ascending order whenever you use the ORDER BY clause in your application's SQL expression. However, you can change the direction of the sort by using the DESC modifier, which is shorthand for descending order.

Listing 18-9 selects the Store and the Sales columns from the sales table, and then places the ResultSet in descending order based on the value of the Store column.

Listing 18-9: Using a Descending Sort

```
try {
    String query = "SELECT  Store, Sales " +
                   " FROM sales " +
                   " ORDER BY Store DESC";
    DataRequest = Database.createStatement();
    Results = DataRequest.executeQuery (query);
    System.out.println("Store     Sales");
    System.out.println("-----     -----");
    DisplayResults (Results);
    DataRequest.close();
}
```

The results of the sort look like this:

Store	Sales
345	200
345	125
345	56
223	450
223	76
123	322
123	300

Ascending sort

You can explicitly specify that you want an ascending sort of the ResultSet by using the ASC modifier, which is shown in Listing 18-10. You'll notice that the results of running this program are the same as if you didn't include a direction modifier (ASC or DESC) in the SQL expression.

Sometimes I include the ASC modifier in an SQL expression as a reminder to myself — and to any of my colleagues who need to read the code of my Java database application — that the ResultSet is in ascending order.

Listing 18-10: **Using an Ascending Sort**

```
try {
    String query = "SELECT  Store, Sales " +
                   " FROM sales " +
                   " ORDER BY Store ASC";
    DataRequest = Database.createStatement();
    Results = DataRequest.executeQuery (query);
    System.out.println("Store      Sales");
    System.out.println("-----      -----");
    DisplayResults (Results);
    DataRequest.close();
}
```

Combined ascending and descending sort

Each row that the DBMS returns can be sorted in either ascending or descending order by specifying the ascending or descending modifier after the column name in the ORDER BY clause.

Take a look at Listing 18-11. Again, I tell the DBMS to return values in the Store column and Sales column from the sales table, however, this time I have the values in the Store column placed in descending order and the values in the Sales column placed in ascending order.

Listing 18-11: **Using Both Ascending and Descending Sorts**

```
try {
    String query = "SELECT  Store, Sales " +
                   " FROM sales " +
                   " ORDER BY Store DESC, Sales
   ASC";
    DataRequest = Database.createStatement();
    Results = DataRequest.executeQuery (query);
    System.out.println("Store      Sales");
    System.out.println("-----      -----");
    DisplayResults (Results);
    DataRequest.close();
}
```

The result of this program looks like this:

Store	Sales
345	56
345	125
345	200
223	76
223	450
123	300
123	322

Sorting a column in the ResultSet

You can sort the results of a calculation that appears in the SELECT statement by referencing the calculation's column number in the ORDER BY clause. Here's how this works. Column names and calculations appear in a sequence in the SELECT statement. In Listing 18-12, the Store column is first, followed by the calculation (Sales-Estimate).

The DBMS assigns each column name and calculation to a column in the ResultSet based on the sequence noted in the SELECT statement. So, for example, Store is column 1 and the calculation (Sales-Estimate) is column 2 of the ResultSet.

You can have the DBMS sort the ResultSet using a calculation as the sort key by specifying the number of the column in the ResultSet that contains the result of the calculation. In the following example, I insert the value 2 in the ORDER BY clause to tell the DBMS that I want the ResultSet sorted by the value of the second column in the ResultSet, which is the result of the calculation in the SELECT statement (Sales-Estimate).

Listing 18-12:   Sorting a Column in a ResultSet

```
try {
    String query = "SELECT Store, (Sales-Estimate) " +
                        " FROM sales " +
                        " ORDER BY 2 ";
    DataRequest = Database.createStatement();
    Results = DataRequest.executeQuery (query);
    System.out.println("Store      Difference");
    System.out.println("-----      -----");
    DisplayResults (Results);
    DataRequest.close();
}
```

The result of the listing looks like this:

Store	Difference
223	–50
245	25
223	26
345	26
345	44
123	100
123	122

Test your newfound knowledge

1. What is a sort key?

a. Columns or calculations used to sort the ResultSet

b. A sorta key used to start an airplane

c. Columns or calculations used to sort the WHERE clause

d. Columns or calculations used to sort the SQL expression

2. What does the GROUP BY clause do?

a. Sorts values in the ResultSet

b. Organizes the ResultSet into related groups

c. Places the short letters in front of the taller letters

d. Organizes the ResultSet in descending order

Answers: (1) a. (2) b.

Chapter 19

The Art of Subqueries

In This Chapter

▶ Using a comparison subquery

▶ Creating an IN subquery

▶ Building an EXISTS subquery

▶ Trying ANY subqueries

*Y*ou probably remember from your school days that the prefix "sub" meant "below." So I'll assume that you already figured out that a *subquery* is a query that is below another query.

You're probably wondering, "How can a query be below another query?" The concept of subquery is a bit confusing to understand at first. However, I hope to clear up any doubts you may have in this chapter. You'll learn that a subquery is

✔ A two-part question

✔ Used to structure SQL expression into logical components

✔ A technique for dealing with complex requests for data

Using a subquery reduces the number of queries that you need to write in a typical Java database application. This is because an SQL expression that contains a subquery actually contains multiple queries that are executed simultaneously.

Subqueries: The Silent Service

Think of an SQL expression that contains a subquery as a two-part question that you would find on a final exam. The first part of the question is the subquery, and the second part is the query. The subquery executes first, and the result of the subquery helps answer the query.

Here's an example: You have two tables. One table contains orders and the other contains important customers. You want your Java database application to total the sales amount of orders placed by your important customers. Here's what the database management software (DBMS) needs to do to provide the data to your application:

- ✔ Determine whether the customer who placed an order is a "key" customer.
- ✔ Total the sales amount for customers who are key customers.

The first part of the process creates a virtual list of customers who placed orders and who are key customers. This is a subquery. The second part of the process tallies the sales amount for those customers who appear on the virtual list.

A *virtual list* is a list of items, such as customers, that exists temporarily in the computer while the DBMS answers the second part of the question. The virtual list disappears once the DBMS returns data to your application.

Facts about a subquery

A subquery is nearly identical to a query because it contains a SELECT statement and a FROM clause. In addition, a subquery uses the WHERE clause (see Chapter 13) or the HAVING clause (see Chapter 19).

However, a subquery is different than a query in several ways:

- ✔ **Only one column is selected:** The job of a subquery is to create a single-column virtual list that is used by the query to select the data to be returned to the Java database application.
- ✔ **Never sorted:** Your application doesn't receive the result of a subquery, so there isn't any purpose for sorting the data. The query doesn't require sorted data.
- ✔ **Never seen:** The DBMS uses the result of a subquery internally. Your application never receives the result of a subquery.

Set up the table before company comes

Before getting down and dirty with a subquery, you need to create a few good tables and populate the tables with data that you can use with programs in this chapter.

First, create a table and call it sales:

Column	Data Type	Size
Store	Text	50
Estimate	Number	
SalesRep	Text	50

Now, add some data into your sales table:

Store	Estimate	SalesRep
345	200	4
278	500	3
825	200	2

You're ready to create your other table, the Orders table:

Column	Data Type	Size	Required	Indexed
OrderNumber	Number		Yes	Yes (No Duplicates)
ProductNumber	Number		No	No
CustomerNumber	Number		No	No
StoreNumber	Number		No	No
Amount	Number		No	No

Now you can add data into the Orders table:

OrderNumber	ProdNumber	CustomerNumber	StoreNumber	Amount
122	5237	591	345	200
334	3255	901	278	321
365	3255	901	278	433
534	7466	591	825	523
555	1052	999	278	23
717	1052	721	825	75
874	7466	721	825	354

Once you've created these tables and inserted data into the tables, you'll be at the starting line to begin learning how to use a subquery.

Components of a subquery

A subquery is a query that is associated with the WHERE clause or HAVING clause of a query. It's used with an operator to compare the results of the subquery with a column or calculated value of the query.

The following code segment shows a typical query and subquery. You would place the subquery within parenthesis as part of the WHERE clause.

```
SELECT Store
     FROM sales
     WHERE Estimate =
          (SELECT SUM(Amount)
               FROM Orders
               WHERE StoreNum = Store)
```

Let's take apart the query and subquery so you'll have a clear picture of what's going on in the code. The following code segment is the subquery without the query. You probably recognize most of the components of the subquery if you've read other chapters of this book. The SELECT statement uses the SUM() built-in function to tally the Amount column of the Orders table.

This produces a virtual list of tallies. You're probably more than a little suspicious about the WHERE clause. It states that the Amount column should be tallied only when the value of the StoreNum column of the Orders table matches the value in the Store column. However, the Orders table doesn't have a Store column. The Store column is in the sales table. In essence, the sales table and the Orders columns that contain store numbers join the two tables.

```
(SELECT SUM(Amount)
     FROM Orders
     WHERE StoreNum = Store)
```

Now let's take a look at the query in the next code segment. The SELECT statement returns values in the Store column, which is the number of the store from the sales table. The WHERE clause places a condition on the returned rows. The condition is that the Estimate value in the sales table is equal to the result of the subquery. The result of the subquery is a sum of the Amount column of each store.

```
SELECT Store
     FROM sales
     WHERE Estimate =
```

The DBMS returns only store numbers if the Estimate value of the store is equal to the sum of the Amount column for the store in the Orders table.

Your first subquery

Let's begin by creating a Java database application that displays stores that have total sales amounts that are equal to the estimate sales amounts. This is a two-part question. The first part is for the application to total the sales amounts for each store. The second part is to compare the total sales amount to the estimate and return rows that match.

Listing 19-1 contains an SQL expression with the query and subquery from the "Components of a subquery" section.

Listing 19-1:   Using a Subquery

```java
import java.sql.*;

   public class squtst
   {
       private Connection Database;

       public squtst()
       {
           String url = "jdbc:odbc:customers";
           String userID = "jim";
           String password = "keogh";
           Statement DataRequest;
           ResultSet Results;

           try {
               Class.forName( "sun.jdbc.odbc.JdbcOdbcDriver");

               Database =
             DriverManager.getConnection(url,userID,password);
           }
           catch (ClassNotFoundException error) {
               System.err.println("Unable to load the JDBC/ODBC
               bridge." + error);
               System.exit(1);
           }
           catch (SQLException error) {
               System.err.println("Cannot connect to the
             database." + error);
               System.exit(2);
           }

           try {
               String query = " SELECT Store " +
                             " FROM sales "+
                             " WHERE Estimate = " +
                             " (SELECT SUM(Amount) " +
                             " FROM Orders " +
```

(continued)

Listing 19-1 *(continued)*

```
                          " WHERE StoreNum = Store) ";
          DataRequest = Database.createStatement();
          Results = DataRequest.executeQuery (query);
          System.out.println("Store");
          System.out.println("-----");
          DisplayResults (Results);
          DataRequest.close();
      }
      catch ( SQLException error ){
          System.err.println("SQL error." + error);
          System.exit(3);
      }
      shutDown();
   }

private void DisplayResults (ResultSet
        DisplayResults)throws SQLException
{

   boolean Records = DisplayResults.next();

   if (!Records ) {
     System.out.println( "End of data.");
   return;
   }

   try {
       do {
          DownRow( DisplayResults) ;
       } while ( DisplayResults.next() );

   }
   catch (SQLException error ) {
       System.err.println("Data display error." + error);
       System.exit(4);
   }
}
private  void DownRow ( ResultSet DisplayResults )
       throws SQLException
{
   String Store;
   Store = DisplayResults.getString ( 1 ) ;
   System.out.println(Store);
}

public void shutDown()
{
   try {
       Database.close();
   }
   catch (SQLException error) {
```

```
            System.err.println( "Cannot break connection." +
                error ) ;
        }
    }
    public static void main ( String args [] )
    {
        final squtst link = new squtst();
            System.exit ( 0 ) ;
    }
}
```

The result of running this program looks like this:

Store

345

Let's start our review of the listing at the beginning of the program, which is really at the bottom of the listing in the main() method. The main() method creates an object called link of the squtst class.

Once the program creates the object, it automatically executes the constructor of the squtst class. You'll find the constructor defined at the top of the listing. The constructor creates three String objects that are assigned the url for the database and login information. It then creates a Statement object, which executes the SQL statement later, and a ResultSet object to reference results coming from the DBMS.

Next, the program loads the JDBC/ODBC bridge and connects to the database (getConnection()). One of the two catch{} blocks traps errors that occur during either task. The first catch{} block traps errors that happen when the program loads the JDBC/ODBC bridge. The second catch{} block traps errors when connecting to the database. Both catch{} blocks display an error message on the screen and exit the program.

If the catch{} blocks detect no errors, the program creates the SQL expression that contains the subquery. (I explain this expression in "Components of a subquery.")

Next, the program creates an SQL statement (createStatement()) and executes the SQL statement (executeQuery()). Test information (System.out.println()) then displays onscreen, followed by a call to the DisplayResults() method. Afterwards, the program closes the SQL statement.

The catch{} block traps any errors that occur while the SQL statement executes, displays an error message, and exits the program.

Barring any errors, the `DisplayResults()` method executes. The `DisplayResults()` method moves the virtual cursor to the next row in the ResultSet. The `next()` method returns either a true or false value, depending upon whether the virtual cursor is at the "`End of data`".

The `if` statement displays the "`End of data`" message and returns to the constructor if the virtual cursor is at the end of the data in the ResultSet. Otherwise, the program enters the `do...while` loop and calls the `DownRow()` method, which displays a row of the ResultSet onscreen. The program then moves to the next row of the ResultSet and returns to the top of the `do...while` loop as long as the virtual cursor is not at the end of the ResultSet. The program returns to the constructor if the end of the ResultSet is reached.

The `catch{}` block traps any errors that occur in the `DisplayResults()` method, displays an error message, and then exits the program.

The `DownRow()` method retrieves the value of ResultSet's first column and assigns the value to the `Store` object of the `String` class, which then displays onscreen. The program returns to the `do...while` loop in the `DisplayResults()` method.

After the constructor finishes executing, the program returns to the `main()` method again, where the program exits.

Subqueries and comparison operators

You can use comparison operators with a subquery to determine the rows of data that the DBMS will return. Check out Chapter 13 for a complete discussion and examples of comparison operators.

Listing 19-2 shows you how to use the less than comparison operator in a subquery. In this example, I tell the DBMS to return rows from the sales table that contain store numbers where the value of the Estimate column is less than the total sales per store.

Here's what the DBMS will do when you place Listing 19-2 into the previous program, compile, and execute the program:

- ✔ It tallies values in the Amount column of the Orders table for each store.

- ✔ It compares each store's tally with the store's estimate in the sales table.

- ✔ It returns to the application the value in the Store column of the sales table, where the value of the Estimate column of the sales table is less than the sum of the store's Amount column from the Orders table.

You use other comparison operators the same way I use the less than operator in this example. The results will be different, of course, but you probably knew that already.

Listing 19-2: Using Comparison Operators

```
try {
    String query = " SELECT Store " +
                   " FROM sales "+
                   " WHERE Estimate < " +
                   " (SELECT SUM(Amount) " +
                   " FROM Orders " +
                   " WHERE StoreNum = Store) ";
    DataRequest = Database.createStatement();
    Results = DataRequest.executeQuery (query);
    System.out.println("Store");
    System.out.println("-----");
    DisplayResults (Results);
    DataRequest.close();
}
```

The result of the listing looks like this:

Store

278

825

Subqueries and the HAVING clause

You use the HAVING clause to select rows based on values in the ResultSet of a query. This is different than using the WHERE clause; the WHERE clause selects rows of the table, which I explain in Chapter 13.

You can use the HAVING clause with a subquery and use the GROUP BY clause to order the data that's returned to your application. Listing 19-3 shows how to do this in your application. Before running this code segment, you need to insert some new rows into the sales table:

Store	Estimate	SalesRep
345	150	5
278	300	6
825	230	7

Now you're ready to enter the code. Before you do, here's an explanation of how this listing works:

- ✔ It tallies the Amount column in the Orders table for each store.
- ✔ It tallies the Estimate column in the sales table for each store.
- ✔ It compares the total Estimate with the total Amount for each store.
- ✔ It selects values in the Store column of the sales table if the total Estimate for the store is less than the total Amount of the store.
- ✔ It sorts the result in ascending order by store number.
- ✔ It returns the ResultSet to the application.

Listing 19-3:   Using the HAVING Clause

```
try {
    String query = " SELECT Store " +
                   " FROM sales  "+
                   " GROUP BY store " +
                   " HAVING SUM(Estimate) < " +
                   " (SELECT SUM(Amount) " +
                   " FROM Orders " +
                   " WHERE StoreNum = Store) ";
    DataRequest = Database.createStatement();
    Results = DataRequest.executeQuery (query);
    System.out.println("Store");
    System.out.println("-----");
    DisplayResults (Results);
    DataRequest.close();
}
```

The results of running this code should look like this:

Store

825

Conditional Tests

A conditional test is the comparison of an expression in either the WHERE clause or HAVING clause of the query and the result of the subquery. You can have the DBMS perform several kinds of conditional tests. The type you select for your database application depends on your application's needs.

The four kinds of conditional tests are

✓ **Comparison test:** A comparison test uses comparison operators to determine the rows that should be returned to the application. I show you how to use a comparison test in Listing 19-2 and the other code examples in this chapter.

✓ **Existence test:** An existence test determines whether a value in the query is contained in the result of the subquery (see "Existence test" next).

✓ **Set membership test:** A set membership test determines whether a value of a query is in the results of a subquery.

✓ **Qualified comparison test:** A qualified comparison test determines whether a value of a query is either in a single row of the results of a subquery or in all of the rows of a subquery.

Existence test

You can use the existence test to have the DBMS determine whether a value in one table is also in the results of a subquery. Listing 19-4 illustrates the use of the existence test in a Java database application.

This example tells the DBMS to return the value of the Store column in the sales table only if the store number is in the ResultSet of the subquery. Run this code segment as part of Listing 19-1 (see "Your first subquery").

Listing 19-4: Using the Existence Test

```
try {
    String query = " SELECT DISTINCT Store " +
                   " FROM sales   "+
                   " WHERE EXISTS " +
                   " (SELECT StoreNum " +
                   " FROM Orders " +
                   " WHERE StoreNum = Store) ";
    DataRequest = Database.createStatement();
    Results = DataRequest.executeQuery (query);
    System.out.println("Store");
    System.out.println("-----");
    DisplayResults (Results);
    DataRequest.close();
}
```

Here is the result from the existence test:

Store

278

354

825

Set membership test

You can use the set membership test to determine whether the result of a sub-query contains the value of a query. Listing 19-5 illustrates how this works. The subquery returns store numbers from the Orders table, where the value of the Estimate column of the sales table is less than the value of the Amount column in the Orders table.

The query uses the set membership test IN modifier (see Chapter 13) to determine whether store numbers in the sales table are in the store numbers returned by the subquery. If so, the query displays the value of the SalesRep column of the sales table.

Listing 19-5:   Using the Set Membership Test

```
    try {
        String query = " SELECT SalesRep " +
                       " FROM sales  "+
                       " WHERE Store IN " +
                       " (SELECT StoreNum " +
                       " FROM Orders " +
                       " WHERE Estimate < Amount) ";
        DataRequest = Database.createStatement();
        Results = DataRequest.executeQuery (query);
        System.out.println("Store");
        System.out.println("-----");
        DisplayResults (Results);·
        DataRequest.close();
    }
```

Here are the results of running the code segment:

Store

2

5

6

7

The ANY qualified comparison test

The ANY qualified comparison test determines whether any rows returned by the subquery contain the value of the query. In Listing 19-6 I tell the DBMS to join the Orders table and the sales table using the store number as the join value.

Next, I tell the DBMS in the subquery to return the value of the Amount column of the Orders table. The query then compares each of the returned rows of the subquery with each row of the query.

If the value of the Estimate column of the sales table is greater than any of the returned rows from the subquery for a particular store, the query returns the store number. Since the query could return duplicate stores, I use the DISTINCT modifier to remove the duplicate store numbers from the query's ResultSet.

Listing 19-6: Using the ANY Qualified Comparison Test

```
try {
    String query = " SELECT DISTINCT Store " +
                   " FROM sales   "+
                   " WHERE Estimate  > ANY   " +
                   " (SELECT Amount" +
                   " FROM Orders " +
                   " WHERE store = StoreNum) ";
    DataRequest = Database.createStatement();
    Results = DataRequest.executeQuery (query);
    System.out.println("Store");
    System.out.println("-----");
    DisplayResults (Results);
    DataRequest.close();
}
```

Here is the result of running this code segment:

Store

278

825

The ANY qualified comparison test can be deceivingly easy to understand. However, you may discover that you receive unexpected results. The ANY test follows rules that explain the results you'll receive under various situations. Here are the ANY rules:

- ✔ The subquery must return a value. Otherwise, the ANY test is false and the query doesn't return any values.

- ✔ If the query doesn't return a value and the subquery does return a value, the value of the query doesn't exist in the subquery ResultSet.

- ✔ The query returns a NULL if one or more values in the subquery result are NULL. The ANY test is basically saying that it's unsure whether the value of the query is or is not in the result of the subquery since a value in the subquery result is unknown (NULL).

The ALL qualified comparison test

The ALL qualified comparison test determines whether the value of the query compares to all the values returned by the subquery.

Here's how this works: In Listing 19-7, I tell the DBMS to join the sales table with the Orders table, using store numbers. The subquery returns the value of the Amount column from the Orders table before the DBMS performs the ALL test. The DBMS then compares the value of the Amount column of the subquery ResultSet with value of the Estimate column in the sales table.

If each Estimate value of rows in the sales table is greater than the value of the Amount column in the ResultSet of the query for the same store, the DBMS returns the store number from the sales table. However, the query doesn't return columns if the Amount for a store is lower than the corresponding Estimate value for the same store.

Listing 19-7:   Using the ALL Qualified Comparison Test

```
    try {
        String query = " SELECT DISTINCT Store " +
                       " FROM sales   "+
                       " WHERE Estimate  > ALL   " +
                       " (SELECT Amount" +
                       " FROM Orders " +
                       " WHERE store = StoreNum) ";
        DataRequest = Database.createStatement();
        Results = DataRequest.executeQuery (query);
        System.out.println("Store");
        System.out.println("-----");
        DisplayResults (Results);
        DataRequest.close();
    }
```

The result of running this code is that Store number 278 is returned.

The ALL qualified comparison test follows rules that explain the results you receive when you use this test in your Java database application. Here are the rules:

- ✔ The query returns empty rows if any row in the subquery fails to match the value in the query.

- ✔ The query returns values in rows if any row in the subquery matches the value in the query.

- ✔ The query returns a NULL if at least one row in the subquery contains a NULL. This is because the test cannot determine whether there is a match. NULL implies that it's unknown.

Part V
The Part of Tens

The 5th Wave — By Rich Tennant

"Look, I've searched the database for 'reanimated babe cadavers' three times and nothing came up."

In this part . . .

1 get to tell you about all sorts of things that just didn't come up in the regular chapters, including things that were too involved to get into. Here you can find out about granting and revoking access to tables created by your applications (and I know you've been waiting for the chance). And to top everything off, you even get a potpourri of topics that I couldn't fit elsewhere.

Chapter 20

Ten Most Common Mistakes

In This Chapter

▶ Misspelling table and column names

▶ Missing spaces in the SQL expression

▶ Giving the source file and class different names

▶ Using double quotations instead of single quotations

▶ Extracting the wrong data type from the ResultSet

▶ Incorrectly referencing columns in the ResultSet

▶ Carelessly designing the database

▶ Forgetting to extract values from the ResultSet

▶ Excluding the semicolon in the SQL expression

▶ Forgetting to concatenate the SQL expression

*E*xpect to make errors when you write your Java database application. It's rare that any application compiles and runs perfectly without a few bumps along the way. And chances are pretty good that you'll make the same common errors as other Java database programmers.

Read this chapter before you begin hitting your head against the wall in frustration. This chapter lists the ten most common errors made when creating a Java database application — and it also shows you how to correct those errors.

Misspelling Table and Column Names

Did the table name end with the letter *s*? You'll find yourself asking this question whenever the name of a table instinctively could be either. For example, throughout this book I use a table called customers to store customer data. Whenever I wrote code, I had to remember if I named the table *customer* or *customers*.

I also ran into a similar problem with column names because I was unsure of the name I had given to a few columns in a table. Fortunately, the database management system (DBMS) catches this kind of error and reports it back to your application as an SQL error.

You can avoid this problem by writing down the table names and column names on a piece of paper, and then refer to the paper each time you reference a table or column in your application.

Missing Spaces in the SQL Expression

SQL expressions in your Java database application can become difficult to read because the statement stretches across a single line in your program. In Chapter 13, I show you how you can break up the SQL expression into several lines by using the plus sign to concatenate multiple lines of the SQL expression.

However, you might get strange SQL error messages from the DBMS if you forget to place a space between the last character and the quotation on each line of the SQL expression, as is shown in the first line of the following code segment.

```
String query = "SELECT FirstName, LastName" +
               "FROM customers " +
               "WHERE LastName = 'Jones' ";
```

Here's how the compiler sees the previous code segment:

```
SELECT FirstName, LastNameFROM customers WHERE LastName =
       'Jones'
```

Notice there isn't a space between LastName and FROM. This is an SQL error. The previous code segment looks fine at first glance. However, if you look carefully you'll notice that LastName" should have a space between LastName and the quotation mark. This is the cause of the error.

The Source File Name Is Different than the Class Name

The name of the file that contains your Java database application, which is called the *source file,* must have the same name as the class defined in the file. If these names are different, the compiler will complain by displaying a compiler error.

The following code segment contains the first few lines of code that define the `selecttst` class (see Chapter 13 for the complete listing). The file name that contains this code must also be named `selecttst`.

```
public class selecttst extends JFrame
{
    private JTable DataTable;
    private Connection Database;

    public selecttst()
    {
```

Using Double Quotations Instead of Single Quotations

Sometimes you can become confused when to use single quotations and double quotations in an SQL expression. All alphanumeric values must appear in single quotations, as I illustrate in the next code segment. An alphanumeric value is any character or number combination that is treated as a character, such as the numbers in a street address.

```
String query = "SELECT FirstName, LastName" +
               "FROM customers " +
               "WHERE LastName = 'Jones' ";
```

Single or double quotations don't enclose numeric values, such as the quantity of products purchased. Double quotations enclose the SQL expression within your Java database application.

Extracting the Wrong Data Type from the ResultSet

A data type that describes the kind of data stored in the column defines each column in a table (see Chapter 10). You must use a method of the same data type to extract data from columns of the ResultSet; otherwise, you receive compiler errors.

Let's say in the next code segment that column 3 in the ResultSet contains the amount of sales associated with the sales representative named in column 1 and column 2. `Sales` is likely to be a Numeric data type. However,

I use the getString() method to extract the value of the Sales column and assign sales to a variable. This causes a compiler error. Instead of using the getString() method, I should be using the getLong() method.

```
FirstName = DisplayResults.getString ( 1 ) ;
LastName = DisplayResults.getString ( 2 ) ;
Sales = DisplayResults.getString ( 3 ) ;
Profit = DisplayResults.getLong ( 4 ) ;
```

You'll find yourself making this error if you copy the previous line, and then modify the copy of the line according to the values that you want to extract from the column. For example, I copy

```
LastName = DisplayResults.getString ( 2 ) ;
```

Then I change the column number to 3 and the variable name to Sales. I should have changed the getString() method to getLong(), but I overlooked this change.

Incorrectly Referencing Columns in the ResultSet

You must know the order of columns in a ResultSet before you can extract data from those columns. The DBMS returns columns in the ResultSet in the order the columns were named in the SELECT statement of the SQL expression that retrieves columns of data.

Numbers identify the columns in the ResultSet. The first column name in the SELECT statement is referenced as column 1, the second column name is referenced as column 2, and so on.

Let's say that the first two columns of the SELECT statement are FirstName and LastName. However, I reversed the column numbers in the first two statements in the next code segment. This results in the value of the LastName column (column 2) being assigned to the FirstName variable. Likewise, the value of the FirstName column (column 1) is assigned to the LastName variable. Both of these are errors.

```
FirstName = DisplayResults.getString ( 2 ) ;
LastName = DisplayResults.getString ( 1 ) ;
Street = DisplayResults.getString ( 3 ) ;
City = DisplayResults.getString ( 4 ) ;
State = DisplayResults.getString ( 5 ) ;
```

Designing the Database Carelessly

It's an unfortunate reality that programmers tend to minimize the importance of carefully designing a database. Many programmers tend to intuitively design a database and related tables without much forethought.

Such a lack of planning typically results in a redesign of the database after the application becomes operational. You can avoid this error by spending the first few weeks of your Java database project designing your database (see Part I).

Forgetting to Extract Values from the ResultSet

Yes, even the best programmers can overlook the obvious. This can easily happen if you reuse and modify previously written code. For example, you probably noticed that many of the programs I show throughout the book are similar, yet each is slightly different from the other.

Instead of writing those programs from scratch, I copied the original program into an editor, changed lines of the program, and inserted new statements to illustrate another aspect of Java database programming.

However, occasionally I'd forget to include a statement to extract a column from the ResultSet. This meant that the program compiled correctly and ran without any SQL errors from the DBMS, but I couldn't see all the data displayed on the screen. The problem was I forgot to write statements into the program to extract and display the missing columns of data.

You can avoid similar errors in your programming by carefully reading your code before compiling and running the program.

Excluding the Semicolon in the SQL Expression

Some Java database programmers can easily become confused when writing an SQL expression because an expression consists of statements to instruct the DBMS to return data. And the SQL expression is embedded into a Java string to form an assignment statement, as is illustrated in the next code statement.

This means the Java statement containing the SQL expression actually contains two instructions: one for the Java compiler (the assignment statement) and the other for the DBMS (the SQL expression within the assignment statement).

It's easy to forget that statements in the SQL expression don't end in a semicolon, and the Java statement does end in a semicolon. A mistake occurs when you leave off the semicolon in the Java statement. The compiler complains with a compiler error.

```
String query = "Select DISTINCT * " +
               "FROM customers " +
               "WHERE Sales IN (10000, 20000,
         30000)";
```

Forgetting to Concatenate the SQL Expression

The best way to make the SQL expression readable is to break up the SQL expression into multiple lines in your program and use the plus sign to concatenate those lines into one Java statement. However, it's common for programmers to forget to include the plus sign at the end of each concatenated line.

The next code segment illustrates this problem. Originally this SQL expression appeared on one line in my program. I divided the line into two lines by placing the cursor where I wanted the line broken and then pressing the Enter key. This placed the characters right of the cursor on a new line.

But as you can see in the following code segment I forgot to place the plus sign at the end of the first line. This causes a compiler error because the compiler is expecting to see a semicolon at the end of the first line.

You can avoid this problem by carefully proofreading each line of the SQL expression in your program.

```
String query = "DELETE FROM customers "
               "WHERE LastName = 'Jones' and
         FirstName = 'Tom'";
```

Chapter 21

Ten Places to Find More Information

*B*ecause you're a beginner in the area of Java database programming, there's much more for you to discover. Even professional programmers have to hit the books, take courses, and go to conferences to keep up with the latest changes in technology — and you can expect to do the same. This chapter presents a few suggestions for ways you can find out more about Java database programming.

Go Back to School at Your Local College

One of the better places to pick up some tricks and tips of the Java database programming trade is close to home, at your local college.

Sometimes you need more help in locating this type of information than a book can provide. You need someone to look over your shoulder until you get on the right track — and that person (an instructor) is usually at your local college.

Many four-year universities and community colleges offer courses in Java database programming. Give your local college a call to find out when the next course is being offered. You don't have to go for the whole college degree. These institutions love to have students who just want to brush up on their skills. (They hope that you will get hooked and come back for more.)

Attend a Conference

A good source for the latest information about Java and Java database programming is computer conferences. Computer professionals, vendors, and nerd wannabes gather at these meetings to exchange ideas. Java database programming is such a hot topic these days that many conferences — even those that don't have Java in their name — discuss it.

Popular conferences are widely advertised in trade publications such as *PC Week* and *InfoWorld.* Keep your eyes peeled for these ads, which usually list scheduled speakers and topics. Some presentations cover topics that might be of interest to you (and others may be way over your head!).

Plan to pay for this experience. Conferences are usually held in major cities, so you may have to pay for airfare, accommodations, and a fee to get into the conference. You may also have to pay for each presentation you attend.

Visit Sun Microsystems on the Web

The Sun Microsystems Web site (www.sun.com) covers various aspects of Java and Java programming, so be sure to stop by their site once a week to read the latest. You'll also find the Web site helpful whenever you get stuck on a Java problem, because they offer links to many sites that offer Java programmer assistance.

Find a Newsgroup on the Internet

Usenet news is the part of the Internet you can tap into for sources of information from around the world. Each of the newsgroups that comprise this service focuses on a particular topic. If you're still unsure of this Internet stuff, consider books such as *Internet For Dummies,* by John Levine and Carol Baroudi (Hungry Minds, Inc.).

Thousands of newsgroups are available. You can use your Internet browser to skim through the available newsgroups and then choose the ones you want to subscribe to (for free!).

To find newsgroups, use keywords with your browser's built-in search feature to quickly skim the list for newsgroups. If you type the keyword **Java** or **Java database**, for example, a large list of newsgroups appears onscreen.

After you enter a newsgroup, you'll see a list of subjects that briefly describe the related messages people have posted. (The messages can contain anything from meaningful information to just plain garbage.) Skim the subject list to see whether any of them seem interesting. When you find one, open the message and see what that person has to say.

You can post (send) your own message to a newsgroup using your Internet browser. You can comment on other messages, post questions, or answer questions that other people have posted.

It may take a while until your newsgroup messages get posted. Be patient. And keep watching the subject listings for the newsgroup to see whether anyone responds to your posting.

A word of caution: Just because something gets posted doesn't necessarily mean that it's true. Even someone with good intentions can post incorrect information.

Review Online Documentation

When you have questions about Java database programming or any other aspect of Java programming, you want your questions answered quickly and accurately. Where can you find a response, though, when you're sitting in front of your computer at 2 a.m.?

Ask your computer! One of the best features of the Java Development Kit from Sun Microsystems is the online help. It provides a discussion of topics, including how to implement all the options. What more can you ask for (except for someone else to do the programming)?

Read Other Books about Java

You should expand your knowledge of Java. This book covers the Java database programming aspect of your Java education. To find out more about the Java, pick up a copy of _Java For Dummies,_ 3rd Edition, by Aaron Walsh (Hungry Minds, Inc.).

Subscribe to Computing Magazines

Don't limit yourself to newsstands — bookstores and major computer stores also offer a wide selection of computer magazines. Keep your eyes peeled for articles and columns about Java and Java database programming. Those magazines are the ones you should subscribe to.

Also check out trade magazines, such as *PC Week* and *InfoWorld*. They talk about the latest developments in the computer industry and the world of technology, and are a must-read for serious programmers.

Join or Create a Java Database User Group

You're probably not the only person in your town or city who's interested in computer programming. Computer user groups are great places to exchange ideas. Ask around to find your local computer club. Start with the computer teachers in your local school district and the manager of your local computer store. They should have an idea whether a club exists. If you can't find a local club, visit Yahoo! and enter the search words **Java user groups**. You're bound to find a user group that's right for you.

Ask for Technical Help at Your Local College Computer Lab

If you end up in a bind, stop by the computer lab at your local college or university. All sorts of nerds hang out there, and they are usually more than happy to give you an opinion about how to solve your problem. Try to build a friendship with a few of these folks. Before long, you'll become part of the family.

Computer labs are usually open to members of the general student body. Teaching assistants or advanced computer science majors who are looking to make a few extra dollars oversee the labs. It also helps to take a course or two to become an official student.

Send E-mail to Authors of Articles about Java Database Programming

One way to quiz the experts is to send an e-mail message to them. Most authors of computer articles and books now include their e-mail address as part of their byline. If you have a question about an article or book topic, ask your question in an e-mail message.

Authors are usually pleased to hear from their readers and do their best to answer questions. Keep in mind, however, that they don't want to become your tutor or your pen pal. Because authors might be busy with other projects, your request may be a low priority.

Chapter 22

Ten Things That Didn't Fit into This Book

*N*ow that you are at the end of this book (even if you haven't read it yet and just skipped back here to see the possibilities), you are probably wondering whether this book includes everything you need to know about Java database programming.

I'm sorry to say, but the answer is no. This is just the beginning. This chapter has some tidbits that you may find useful and interesting as you continue your quest to build that killer Java database program (the one that will make you more money than Bill Gates).

Nested Subqueries

A subquery is a query within a query. That is, the main query queries the results of a subquery. Chapter 19 shows you how to use two-level subqueries. The first level is the main query, and the second level is the subquery.

However, you can use more than two levels in a subquery. These are called *nested subqueries*. If you have a three-level subquery, the DBMS would begin with the third level. The second-level subquery would query the result of the third-level subquery, and the main query would query the result of the second-level subquery.

Although the SQL standard doesn't limit the number of nested subqueries that you can have in your Java database application, many DBMSs set a limit. This is because the more levels used in your query, the longer the DBMS takes to return data to your application.

The GRANT Statement

You become the owner of the table or view whenever your application creates a table or view in the database. One of the rights of ownership is the capability of granting other users and applications of the database access to your tables and views.

You use the GRANT statement when setting privileges for a user or application to grant access. Typically, you grant privilege to use SELECT, INSERT, DELETE, and UPDATE in the table or view. You can grant one, multiple, or all privileges.

The following code segment grants UPDATE privileges to the user ID SalesRep1 to the customers table. The GRANT statement contains the name of the privilege (SELECT, INSERT, DELETE, UPDATE, ALL PRIVILEGES). The ON clause identifies the name of the table or view. And the TO clause identifies the user ID that is receiving the privilege.

```
GRANT UPDATE
ON customers
TO SalesRep1
```

The REVOKE Statement

Your application can remove previously granted privileges to tables and views that you created by using the REVOKE statement. The REVOKE statement is similar in construction to the GRANT statement in that you specify the privileges in the statement.

The following code segment illustrates how to construct a REVOKE statement. In this example, I'm revoking the privilege of the SalesRep1 ID to select and

update data that is stored in the customers table. Once the REVOKE statement
executes, the user ID no longer has the privilege to either select data from
the customers table or update date data in the customers table.

```
REVOKE  SELECT, UPDATE
ON customers
TO SalesRep1
```

Column Privileges

Your application can grant privileges to a subset of columns in a table or view
by specifying column names using the GRANT statement. This is called *granting column privileges*. You would do this whenever a user requires access to
some, but not all, of the data in a table or view.

Here is a segment of code that shows how to grant column privileges. In this
example, I'm granting the SalesRep1 user ID the privilege to select only data
in the FirstName and LastName columns of the customers table.

```
GRANT SELECT (FirstName, LastName)
ON customers
TO SalesRep1
```

Passing Privileges

Only the application that creates a table or view can assign privileges to
access the table or view. However, any user ID can be given the right to grant
privileges to a table or view that the user ID doesn't own.

To do this, the owner of the table or view must use the WITH GRANT OPTION
when granting the user ID privilege to access the table or view. I illustrate
how this is done in the next code segment. You'll notice that I grant the
SalesRep1 permission to select and update data from the customers table.

I also grant SalesRep1 the right to grant the same permissions to another
user ID. I use the WITH GRANT OPTION in the GRANT statement. I'm doing this
so that the SalesRep1 can grant his or her permissions to a sales assistant.

```
GRANT SELECT, UPDATE
ON customers
TO SalesRep1
WITH GRANT OPTION
```

System Catalog

Every database management system (DBMS) uses special tables called a *system catalog* to keep track of databases, tables, views, and other database objects that users of the DBMS create. So when your Java database application builds a table, the DBMS makes note of the table and all its columns in the system catalog.

The system catalog also contains information about the user IDs, passwords, user ID privileges, and the user IDs of those who own databases, tables, and views. Your application may be able to access information from the system catalog if the database administrator grants permission. This information can be helpful if you want to review the privileges of user IDs to your tables and views.

Table Alterations

You can modify an existing table by using the ALTER TABLE statement within your Java database application as long as the user ID used by your application created the table. The ALTER TABLE statement removes or adds columns to an existing table as well as adds or drops primary keys and foreign keys.

The first code segment shown below uses the DROP clause to remove the Ranking column from the customers table. The second code segment illustrates how to place a new column in the table by using the ADD clause. In this example, I add the Ranking column to the customers table. The Ranking column has a CHAR data type of ten characters.

```
ALTER TABLE customers
DROP Ranking
```

```
ALTER TABLE customers
ADD Ranking CHAR(10)
```

Primary Key Creation

A primary key is the value of one or more columns that uniquely identifies rows in a table. Your application can create a primary key for your table by using the PRIMARY KEY clause when the application creates a table. (See Chapter 11 for more about primary keys.)

The code segment below creates a table called customers that contains two columns. These are the CustNum column that contains customer numbers, and the CustName column that contains the customer names. The CREATE TABLE statement defines both columns (see Chapter 10).

You use the PRIMARY KEY clause to tell the DBMS to use values in the CustNum column to create a primary key for the customers table. This increases the efficiency of searching for rows within the customers table.

```
CREATE TABLE customers
    (CustNum, INTEGER NOT NULL,
    CustName INTEGER NOT NULL
    PRIMARY KEY (CustNum) )
```

Foreign Key Creation

A foreign key is a key value from another table used to link together two tables (see Chapter 11). For example, you have two tables in a database. One table is the customers table; it contains the names and addresses of customers. The other table is the Orders table, and it contains customers' orders.

The Orders table contains a customer number for each order. The customer number also appears in the customers table and joins together both tables (see Chapter 17). The customer number is a foreign key in the Orders table because the customer number is the primary key of the customers table.

The following code segment shows you how to create a foreign key when creating the Orders table. A foreign key makes it efficient for the DBMS to join together two tables.

```
CREATE TABLE Orders
    (OrderNum, INTEGER NOT NULL,
    CustNum INTEGER NOT NULL
    FOREIGN KEY (CustNum) )
```

Trigger

A *trigger* is an event that occurs when an action takes place in a table. If, for example, each time your application places order in the Orders table, your application needs to increment the number of orders for the sales rep in the SalesRep table.

Your application could create a trigger in the Orders table that automatically tells the DBMS to update the SalesRep table whenever a new order is placed in the Orders table. Placing the order in the Orders table is the event, and updating the SalesRep table is the action that is caused by the event.

The next code segment illustrates how to create a trigger. I call the trigger CreditSale. The ON clause identifies the table of the event, which is the Orders table. The FOR clause identifies the event that triggers the CreditSale trigger, which is the INSERT event.

The AS clause defines the action that takes place when the event occurs. In this example, the action is to update the Sales column of the SalesRep table by incrementing the current value by one. The WHERE clause identifies the row in the SalesRep table that is to be updated, which is the row where the RepNum (sales rep's number) is equal to the OrderRepNum. OrderRepNum is the sales representative's number in the order.

```
CREATE TRIGGER CreditSale
ON Orders
FOR INSERT
AS UPDATE SalesRep
    SET (Sales = Sales + 1)
FROM SalesRep
WHERE RepNum = OrderRepNum
```

Index

Notes

Notes

Notes

Notes

Notes

Notes

Notes

Notes

Notes